Frederic William Farrar

The fall of man and other sermons

Frederic William Farrar

The fall of man and other sermons

ISBN/EAN: 9783742860361

Manufactured in Europe, USA, Canada, Australia, Japa

Cover: Foto ©Lupo / pixelio.de

Manufactured and distributed by brebook publishing software (www.brebook.com)

Frederic William Farrar

The fall of man and other sermons

THE FALL OF MAN

AND OTHER SERMONS,

*PREACHED BEFORE THE UNIVERSITY OF CAMBRIDGE,
AND ON VARIOUS PUBLIC OCCASIONS,*

BY

FREDERIC W. FARRAR, M.A., F.R.S.,

FORMERLY FELLOW OF TRINITY COLLEGE, CAMBRIDGE,
HONORARY FELLOW OF KING'S COLLEGE, LONDON,
ONE OF THE MASTERS AT HARROW SCHOOL.

London and Cambridge:
MACMILLAN AND CO.
1868.

TO THE

REV. CHARLES JOHN VAUGHAN, D.D.

VICAR OF DONCASTER,

AND LATE HEAD MASTER OF HARROW SCHOOL,

I DEDICATE THESE SERMONS,

WITH DEEP GRATITUDE FOR MANY KINDNESSES,

AND WITH SINCERE AFFECTION

AND RESPECT.

1.

PREFACE.

IT is with great diffidence that I allow these Sermons to see the light. It had long been my intention not to publish any volume of Sermons, and I have often stated that intention to friends who spoke to me on the subject. When, however, the Vice-Chancellor did me the honour to request that I would publish the three Sermons preached before the University of Cambridge, it became necessary to add others to them, and I have done so, not because I thought that the Sermons were worthy of preservation,—for no one can be more painfully aware of their imperfections than I am myself,—but because some, who had a right to judge for themselves, wished to know the topics on which I ordinarily preached, and the manner in which I handled them.

I have therefore published them exactly as they were delivered, and not given them the advantage of that complete revision, and even reconstruction, by which many of them would have been improved. I have not even thought it desirable to remove an occasional recurrence of the same form of expression in Sermons preached at different places, and before widely different audiences. It is hardly necessary to observe that they are not in any way intended for a complete *systematic* exposition of theological truths.

I have acknowledged all that I have consciously derived from other writers; but doubtless there are many thoughts and some expressions for which I am either indebted unconsciously, or to which I have alluded in a manner that did not admit of formal recognition.

I need only add, in justice to that distinguished Churchman who has allowed me to offer him this Volume as a proof of my personal friendship and gratitude, that he has neither heard nor read the majority of these Sermons, and that very probably they may contain passages with the spirit of which he would be unable to sympathize.

CONTENTS.

I.

THE FALL OF MAN.

(Preached before the University of Cambridge, March 1, 1868.)

GENESIS III. 13.

And the Lord God said unto the woman, What is this that thou hast done? 1   [PAGE]

II.

THE LAW OF DEATH; AND THE MEANS OF DELIVERANCE.

(Preached before the University of Cambridge, March 8, 1868.)

GENESIS II. 17.

In the day that thou eatest thereof thou shalt surely die . 27

III.

THE PATH OF CHRIST.

(Preached before the University of Cambridge, March 15, 1868.)

MATTHEW VIII. 22.

Follow me, and let the dead bury their dead . . . 55

IV.

RESURRECTION FROM THE DEAD.

(Preached before Harrow School, June 28, 1863.)

ROMANS VIII. 21.

The creature itself also shall be delivered from the bondage of corruption 80

V.

ASCENSION WITH CHRIST.

(Preached before Harrow School, on Ascension Day, 1865.)

ACTS I. 9.

And a cloud received him out of their sight . . . 97

VI.

THE IMMORTALITY AND THE MEANNESS OF MAN.

(Preached at Nottingham, during the Meeting of the British Association, August, 1866.)

PSALM VIII. 4.

What is man, that thou art mindful of him? and the son of man, that thou visitest him? 111

VII.

RIGHTEOUSNESS THE STRENGTH OF NATIONS.

(Preached before the National Rifle Association, in the Volunteer Camp at Wimbledon, July 15, 1866.)

1 CORINTHIANS XVI. 13.

                                               PAGE

Quit you like men, be strong 131

VIII.

THE HISTORY AND HOPES OF A PUBLIC SCHOOL.

(Preached before Harrow School, on Founder's Day, October 6, 1859.)

ISAIAH LIV. 11—13.

Behold, I will lay thy stones with fair colours, and lay thy foundations with sapphires. And I will make thy windows of agates, and thy gates of carbuncles, and all thy borders of pleasant stones. And all thy children shall be taught of the Lord; and great shall be the peace of thy children 152

IX.

CHURCH SERVICES.

(Preached in the Parish Church of Doncaster, at the Choral Festival, 1867.)

PSALM CXXII. 1. (Prayer-book Version.)

I was glad when they said unto me, We will go into the house of the Lord 175

X.

GOD'S BANQUET AND THE WORLD'S.

(Preached before Harrow School, January 15, 1863.)

LUKE XV. 16.

And he would fain have filled his belly with the husks that the swine did eat: and no man gave unto him . . 198

XI.

THE ANIMAL AND THE SPIRITUAL.

(Preached before Harrow School on the First Sunday of the Summer Term, 1864.)

GENESIS XXV. 27.

And the boys grew, and Esau was a cunning hunter, a man of the field; and Jacob was a plain man, dwelling in tents 218

XII.

ANGELS ON THE PATH OF LIFE.

(Preached on the Anniversary at Marlborough College [St Michael and All Angels], September 29, 1864.)

GENESIS XXXII. 26.

And he said, I will not let thee go, except thou bless me . 236

XIII.

THEIR WORKS DO FOLLOW THEM.

(Preached at All Saints', Huntingdon, December 28, 1862.)

REVELATION XIV. 13.

And their works do follow them 256

XIV.

THE WAR IN WHICH THERE IS NO DISCHARGE.

(Preached before the 18th Middlesex Volunteers, in Harrow Church, May 7, 1865.)

ECCLESIASTES VIII. 8.

And there is no discharge in that war 273

XV.

YEARS THAT THE LOCUST HATH EATEN.

(Preached at All Saints', Huntingdon, January 6, 1866.)

JOEL II. 25.

And I will restore to you the years that the locust hath eaten 292

XVI.

SEEING THE FACE OF GOD.

(Preached before Harrow School, September 30, 1866.)

REVELATION XXII. 4.

And they shall see his face; and his name shall be in their foreheads 311

XVII.

THE TEMPLE OF GOD.

(Preached before King's College School, at the Reopening of King's College Chapel, June 23, 1864.)

I CORINTHIANS III. 16.

Know ye not that ye are the temple of God, and that the Spirit of God dwelleth in you? 330

XVIII.

THE BLESSED TRINITY.

(Preached before Harrow School, on Trinity Sunday, May 26, 1861.)

REVELATION IV. 8.

Holy, holy, holy, Lord God Almighty . . . 346

XIX.

DELIVERANCE THROUGH CHRIST.

(Preached before Harrow School, 1864.)

1 SAMUEL XII. 20.

Fear not: ye have done all this wickedness: yet turn not aside from following the Lord, but serve the Lord with all your heart 364

XX.

HOPE IN CHRIST.

(Preached after the First Communion of the Boys confirmed at Harrow on March 19, 1868.)

ISAIAH LX. 1.

Arise, shine; for thy light is come, and the glory of the Lord is risen upon thee 382

I.

THE FALL OF MAN.

(Preached before the University of Cambridge, March 1, 1868.)

GEN. iii. 10—"And the Lord God said unto the woman, What is this that thou hast done?"

THE season at which we are assembled, my brethren, scarcely leaves us any latitude as to the choice of our meditations. The Church which for half of her year turns our thoughts to the great doctrines of her faith, and for the other half to their direct bearing upon the practice of our lives, has especially set apart this solemn season to lessons of temptation, of punishment, of warning, of repentance. Her Lenten fast is ushered in with the dread voices of commination and the wail of penitential Psalms; in to-day's Gospel she brings before us the temptation in the wilderness of our Lord and Master; and throughout the earlier Sundays of this period, and that which immediately precedes it, alike in Epistles, Gospels, and Lessons, she points our awe-struck contemplations to some of the darkest possibilities which can befal an apostate soul. There are many who would willingly keep these stern lessons out of sight; the appalling simplicity of such Scripture narratives at once horrifies and angers them. They would not indeed go so far as to bid the prophets "prophesy not unto us right things, speak unto us smooth things, prophesy deceits;" but, as though by way of compromise, they eagerly bid us wrap our moral teaching in those vague conventional euphemisms from which their conscience can escape. They are indignant that even Scripture should draw the curtain from the dark chambers in which the unregenerate heart abounds, and should turn full into them that blinding, painful, intolerable glare. And, were it in our hands, we should probably listen to such appeals, and if we could not obliterate altogether, should at least bury in eternal oblivion some of the saddest records preserved in the sacred page. Our Church has acted otherwise. She has judged that the mysteries of human iniquity are too awful, too wide-spread, too ruinous to be ignored. Knowing that the day cometh when every heart shall lie bare before that Eye to whose gaze the very heavens are not clean, she has striven to purify the darkness by rending the films of self-deceit, and by making the soul start under ,the healing agony of shame. Looking round her on a world that lieth in wickedness,—conscious of the continuous tragedies which have been enacted on the narrow stage of sacred history, and of that history, in one sense no less sacred, which we call profane,—not ignorant of the deceitfulness which underlies the smooth conventionalities of nominally Christian lives,—she has bidden him who "thinketh he standeth, to take heed lest he fall;" and she has taught us to judge ourselves not by the superficial standards of ordinary society, but by the things written in that book of record which lies ever open before the throne of God. If you would know whether she has done aright, examine your own hearts; and for the answer trust, not to the delicate susceptibilities of intellectual refinement, but to the voice of an awakened, aye, even of a terrified conscience, when, with threatening aspect and out-stretched arm, it points at us with the steady and dreadful accusation, "Thou art the man!"

And because I assume that all among us, even those who have striven best and longest, and not in vain, to win the answer of a good conscience towards God and towards man, would yet see enough in their own lives to beat upon their breasts with the cry of the publican, "Lord, have mercy upon me, a sinner;" therefore I follow the guidance of our Church in speaking to you to-day of sin and temptation. Such thoughts may be little pleasing, but I cannot believe them superfluous. With Scripture, with history, with experience, with the records of countless biographies before me, I cannot doubt that sin has been, and is, the over-shadowing influence—the transient, if not the long-continued gloom—of most men's lives; and that while there are many among my hearers who are resting (it may be after long and weary battle) in the peace and light of God, others again are in the twilight, others in the evening, and some, alas! it may be, in the black and dark night. Rather do I fear, and I may well fear, lest my words be altogether too weak to reach your hearts. And therefore I pray you, my brethren, rivet not up those hearts in that triple panoply of resistance through which no arrow of conviction can wing its way, but rather, seeing that we stand all of us before God this day, believe that for each one of you there may be some message of prophecy, even though it be spoken by feeble and unworthy lips. For us all alike now is the accepted time; for *one* here on this moment may hang eternity, and that one may be you; for he who stands here is, for this hour, God's appointed messenger, and He may send His seraphim unseen with the hallowed fire of His altar, to touch into inspiration the stammering lips of whom He will.

And be not surprised, my brethren, if in speaking to you of the growth of sin I purposely draw my text from its oldest record, though round these first pages of Scripture have raged most loudly the angry voices of controversy. It is one of our trials that the Bible, with its tender and hallowed bearing upon all that is sweet and noble in our lives—with its words so stately and full of wonder, and full of music, like the voice of an archangel—should have been made in these days the wrangling-ground for sectarian differences; but if with our whole hearts we are striving to live according to its spirit, we need fear but little that we shall trip in a right pronunciation of the shibboleths of its letter. Surely it is deplorable that, because of mere questions which after all are but questions of doubtful authorship, of historical accuracy, of verbal criticism, having for the most part little or no bearing on the spiritual or moral life, party should be denouncing party, and Christian excommunicating Christian, and so many hands tearing in anger the seamless robe of Christ. It is, alas, the due punishment for our lack of charity, our Pharisaism, our unwisdom, that while we have been so eager about such controversies, the love of many should have waxed cold. Yet they who thus cease altogether to reverence God's written word, lose one of the most elevating, one of the most comforting influences of human life. Oh, if such an irreparable loss, my younger brethren, have happened to any one of you, let me entreat you no longer to mistake the shadow for the substance; not to confuse mere questions of exegetical or scientific learning with the deep, awful, imperishable lessons which the Bible, and the Bible only, can bring home to your souls. In whatever way those questions may be decided, the infinite inner sacredness of God's word remains inviolate for ever. There may be shifting clouds about it, but through them break gleams of the eternal radiance; there may be mingled voices, but clear and loud among them all are heard the utterances of eternal wisdom. Other books may make you learned or eloquent

or subtle; this book alone can make you wise
unto salvation. Other books may fascinate the
intellect; by this alone can you cleanse the
heart. In other literatures may trickle here and
there some shallow runnel from the "unempti-
able fountain of wisdom,"—and even these, alas!
turbid too often with human passions, fretted
with human obstacles, and choked at last in
morass or sand,—but in this book, majestic
and fathomless, flows the river of the water of
life itself, proceeding out of the throne of God
and of the Lamb. Your time here is largely
spent in searching out the gold which, mingled
with much alloy, may be found scattered in the
treasuries of Pagan wisdom; but here alone—
in more infinite abundance, of more incompar-
able worth—are the pearls of great price, the
wisdom more precious than rubies, the "Light
from beyond the sun." And be sure that the
hour will come not rarely to you in the destinies of life—the hour of sickness, of bereavement, of bitter disappointment, of deathful
agony—when all other knowledge and all other
insight shall be as useless dross; but every text
stored up in the memory, each pure lesson, each
bright example from the sacred page, shall be
to your stricken and fainting souls "better than

gold, yea, than much fine gold; sweeter also than honey and the honeycomb."

How deep, for instance, are the lessons involved in the story of the Fall, and how little are they affected by any of the innumerable criticisms to which it has given rise. Men have long been questioning whether it be a divine philosopheme or a literal fact; whether man arose in one or, like the fauna and the flora which surround him, in many centres; whether the material elements of which our bodies are composed sprang at a single creative fiat into fullgrown and perfect manhood, or in virtue of one omnific law had been swept by the magic eddy of nature's unseen agencies through generations of lower organisms; whether Adam and Eve, and the happy garden, and the tempting serpent, and the waving sword of the Cherubim, and the trees of knowledge and of life, be transparent allegory[1] or historic narrative. Enter,

---

[1] This opinion has been held without blame by "divines of the most unimpeachable orthodoxy and most averse to the allegorizing of Scripture history in general. And indeed no unprejudiced man can pretend to doubt, that if in any other work of Eastern origin he met with trees of life and knowledge, or talking snakes,...he would want no other proofs that it was an allegory that he was reading, and intended to be understood

my brethren, if you will into such inquiries, secure and undismayed, if you but carry in your hands the golden clues of humility and prayer; nothing doubting that by such a spirit you shall know of the truth, and the truth shall make you free. Only remember that such inquiries do not touch for a moment the deep importance of the sacred narrative, or its direct personal bearing on our religious life. The lessons to be here learnt are moral, not ethnological; spiritual, not scientific. For even if the facts be not literal, they remain divinely and unalterably true. To prove that they are so needs neither learning nor research: it needs but the solemn light of each man's personal experience; it needs but that spirit of man which is "the candle of the Lord." The story reveals to us how sin came into the world, and death by sin, and we find each one of us, that it is even thus, and thus only, and thus always, that sin enters into each individual heart. The history is no dead letter, but a living symbol, a sacred symbol which neither scepticism can disparage, nor experience can modify, nor philosophy enlarge: it contains the very essence

as such." Coleridge, *Aids to Reflection*, p. 104; Bp. Horsley, *Serm*. XVI.

and principle of the whole matter, and he who would have a thorough insight into the origin of sin may learn more, though he be a child, from these few and simple verses, lighted up by such a commentary as his own experience may furnish, than from all else that the united wisdom of mankind has ever discovered on the subject with which they deal.

For what, in briefest outline, are the points which give to the narrative its main significance? We see our parents placed at first in the happiness of a sinless Eden in which the whisper of temptation is as yet unknown; but very soon sin, taking occasion by the single commandment to which they were subjected, deceived them, and by it slew them. First came the faint suggestion, as of some outer voice, "Yea, hath God said?"—the suggestion of a restless uneasy doubt, and with it the undefined impulse to rebel, to shake off authority, to exert the power of self-will. At first indeed this formless temptation is met by the barrier of a direct command, and in the spirit of a holy dread, "God hath said ye shall not eat of it;" but then in the exaggerated addition "neither shall ye touch it, lest ye die," we see perhaps a very subtle indication that there was from the first a lurking desire, an undeveloped tendency to disobey. And in any case the next step is fraught with danger; for the woman, in all her softness, in all her weakness, shutting her eyes to the awful issues involved in the workings of her self-will, dallies with the tempter, lingers with guilty irresolution on the scene of the temptation. She dwells jealously on the one thing prohibited, rather than joyously on the many things permitted, until almost unconsciously to herself the tempting voice has passed from the timid suggestion of a doubt, to the impudent promise of a gain, to the bold assertion of a lie. "Ye shall not surely die," "your eyes shall be opened," "ye shall be as gods." And then ambition, curiosity, concupiscence are all awake. The good that she knows begins to pall upon her, the evil that she knows not to shine in alluring colours. Ever, as she gazes passionately upon it, the tree seems good for food, and pleasant to the eyes, a tree to be desired to make one wise. More and more she turns herself from the voice and thought of God to the fragrancy and imagined sweetness of that forbidden fruit. And from such a beginning there can be but one result. They who would pluck flowers from the very edge of the precipice must be prepared to fall. Them who long to sin God suffers to sin. The lingering thought passes into the vivid imagination, the vivid imagination into the burning wish, the burning wish into the half-formed purpose, the half-formed purpose into the hasty act[1]. Swiftly, as in a moment, the crisis is upon her, sharp and sudden, as such crises always are, the crucial instant of temptation when life and death hang in trembling equipoise in the balance of our destiny. Oh, each soul has need of all its resolution then, and of all the Holy Spirit's aid, but too often we meet that moment, as Eve met it, shaken, weakened, half-despairing by long familiarity with sin. In an evil hour she stretches her rash hand, and a deed is done irrevocable for omnipotence, irrevocable till time shall be no more. And then the floodgates are open; the tiny ripple of an illicit thought, ever swelling, deepening, broadening, has burst into an irresistible river, waters to swim in, a river that could not be passed over. The guilty wish of one woman has swollen into the irremediable corruption of a world. One after another, like crash on crash

[1] "Primo occurrit menti simplex cogitatio; deinde fortis imaginatio: postea delectatio et motus pravus et assensio." Thomas à Kempis.

of thunder, the sentences of judgment roll over their heads, till the windows of heaven are opened, and the fountains of the great deep are broken up, and the world must be rebaptized in the overwhelming waves. In one Sunday Lesson we read the story of the Fall, in the next the story of the Deluge;

> "'Twas but a little drop of sin
> We saw this morning enter in,
> And lo! at eventide a world is drowned!"

Is there nothing here for our instruction? Has there been nothing like this in your own past lives? Is not the same process repeated at each fresh development of the mystery of iniquity? Look back through the mists of memory, and remembering the sins of your past years, tell me if you might not have been forewarned then—if you may not be forewarned even now—by the method and progress of Eve's temptation? You too have had your Eden of happy ignorance, and of an innocence yet unassailed. You too, in a sunlit childhood, have

> "heard, borne on the wind, the articulate voice
> Of God, and angels to your sight appeared
> Crowning the glorious hills of Paradise;"

but almost with the dawn of an intellectual

life, began the struggle of good with evil, and in that strife the innocence of childhood, which is as the dew of God, was brushed away from the soul. Self-will sprang up. You found the physical nature strong, the moral weak. The voice of doubt whispered, "Yea, hath God said;" the voice of impatient rebellion and conscious passion shouted, "Ye shall be as gods." But so dear to God is the human soul that it cannot at first go astray without a shudder and a pang. He has mercifully planted a thick hedge around our first transgressions, and relying it may be upon that, confident it may be in some instinctive sense of horror and of peril, in some frightened momentary cry for deliverance, in some remembered threatening of God's word, in some sweet and holy lesson learnt at a mother's knee, above all in some divine yearning intuition of a Saviour's love, you did not at once forsake the covenant of your God, but as though thoughts at least were harmless, you indulged your *thoughts* in a dangerous familiarity with wrong. But he whose thoughts are filled with earthly imaginations has no room left for thoughts of God. His fall is certain. Sin becomes to him more fair, more full of alluring sorcery. He who, not led as the Saviour was by the Spirit of God, but turned aside by the guilty glamour of a self-deceiving heart, leaves the ways of pleasantness and the paths of peace, to wander in the desert of spiritual danger, must be prepared in that desert to be with the wild beasts, to meet temptation at every turn, to be tortured more and more with a "burning Tantalian thirst," to be dazzled more and more to his own destruction by the delusive shine of the desert phantom[1], which, as it ever flies before him, will but vanish at last before his disenchanted eye amid the waste and glare of the scorching sands. Seldom in any case, and *never* save by the special grace of God, do guilty thoughts end in guilty thoughts. They are but the serpent's egg, from which breaks forth the cockatrice. On us, as on Eve, at some unguarded moment, the temptation springs "terrible and with a tiger's leaps," and then we fall; we fall, and we pity ourselves because we fall in a moment; but that fall is the fall, not of the moment, but of all the previous life; it was but "the sign-manual

---

[1] It might be a matter of wonder if so common and striking an Arabian phenomenon as the mirage were not alluded to in the metaphors of Scripture. There can, however, be little doubt that this is the real meaning of the word שָׁרָב, Is. xxxv. 7 (A.V. 'the parched ground.' LXX. ἡ ἄνυδρος), and xlix. 10 (A.V. 'the heat,' LXX. ὁ καύσων).

of deed" which sooner or later the powers of evil demand from him who in heart has been long their own. And, when this sacrament of evil is over, then follows the common history. The sin which was at first cowardly, becomes next shameless, and lastly secure. The "only this once" ends in "there is no harm in it." "*Abeunt studia in mores.*" The scarlet blossom ripens into the poisonous and ashy fruit. Delusion ends in denial; denial in insensibility; insensibility unawakened deepens into everlasting death. Oh, if there be one here whose feet have gone astray into evil paths, let him be warned in time. That road hath but one ending; the hurrying feet of many a generation have trodden it; yet there is not one of them but would confess with hollow voice, as from the grave and gate of death, that it is the entrance into "those regions, whither, whosoever passeth finally, shall lie down and groan with an eternal sorrow."

1. The general lessons which result, at once, my brethren, from such a retrospect are clear and full of solemn warning. And the first is the necessity—alas! the often forgotten, the often wholly-despised necessity—for constant watchfulness. From the very constitution of our nature, from the inherited tendencies of many

sinful generations, from the occasion which sin takes by the law for our perdition, from the intensity and multiformity of the temptations which may beset us, the very best of us is in constant danger; but none more so than you who are yet in youth. None—not even the oldest warrior—can ever in this world lay aside one piece of his panoply; for our warfare is a warfare in which there is no discharge. But, if even the strongest Christian—if even he whose courage has been tested in many a mighty struggle, and whose hope has been confirmed by many a mighty victory over the powers of evil—if even *he* feels that his hand may never leave the cross-hilt of his sword, nor his weary arm drop the shield which has been given him— can you, in the very beginning of the battle, you whose enemies are stronger, more passionate, more inflamed with the fury of conquest—can you, while the fiery darts of the wicked one are falling thick around you, strip off your armour, and with unlit lamp and ungirded loin give yourselves up to sloth or sleep? Yes; it may seem so to you for a time. If you be at ease in your youth, if you be living in pride, fulness of bread and abundance of idleness, the foes of your spiritual being may have abandoned the semblance of battle, only because they are secure in the confidence of victory. But oh, if you would escape them, WATCH. Remember that terrible metaphor which the Lord addressed to Cain when first the fierce, sullen, brooding spirit of revenge seized possession of his heart: "If thou doest well, shalt thou not be accepted? and if thou doest not well, sin lieth at the door." At the door of *your* hearts, no less than at that of the first murderer, sin is crouching like some wild beast of prey; but "subject unto thee shall be his desire, and thou shalt rule over him". Thou art the master of that πολυκέφαλον θηρίον[1], that blind wild beast of all that is evil within thee, and thou canst place thy foot upon his neck. But if not, if thou feedest him to thine own ruin, then suddenly will he spring upon thee with flame in his eye, and wrath and thunder in his roar, and then God help thee! Thou mayest be saved indeed from his devouring fury, but it shall be in the wild awful image of the peasant prophet, "as the shepherd taketh out of the mouth of the lion two legs or a piece of an ear[2]."

2. Then as a second warning, I would bid you beware of underrating the exceeding sinful-

---

[1] Plato, *Rep.* ix. 12.   [2] Amos iii. 12.

ness of sin. Echo not the scornful and faithless question "Yea, hath God said?" There are not wanting in society alarming symptoms that grave sins are lightly thought of, are tolerated, are condoned; and that which is abomination to the Lord, that which is the inward curse and devastation of men's lives, that which crucified to the bitter cross the Son of God himself, is forsooth and, I fear, increasingly a subject for slighting allusions or idle jests. Unhallowed actions are the natural sequence of spurious notions; and men shrink not from sin and worldliness, when its sinfulness is questioned, and its penalties are disallowed.

Daily is this Gospel of Iniquity more insolently preached, and its proselytes are more shamelessly assured. Nay, if we do not take a firm stand, not only will this tide of corruption flood the back-streams of our meaner literature, but men will not be ashamed to advocate the cause of lawlessness, will not blush while they "foam out their own shame," and strive "to paint the gates of hell with Paradise;" nay, even will have no sense of guilt or of degradation while they drag the sacred name and the laurel garland of the Poet into unutterable mire. But be sure that that nation is on the high-road to

ruin where men are what St Paul calls ἀπηλγη-
κότες, i.e. where they have once felt but feel no
longer[1]; where the fumes of the poison which
they have tasted fill them with headiness and
pride, and before God, and men, and the glittering faces of the angel-witnesses, they are
leprous, and seek no solitude, they are naked,
and not ashamed. Tell me not that to speak
thus shews a want of *savoir faire*—tell me not
that such a view of sin is unphilosophical, or
that it is not in accordance with the view taken
by sensible men of the world, or that men of
genius have spoken otherwise. I speak not as a
man of the world,—not as would-be philosophers
have spoken, or as men of genius have sung ere
the day came which made them repent in dust
and ashes; but I speak as that God has spoken
whose minister I am, I speak as His Prophets
and Apostles and Martyrs have spoken; nay, I
speak even as has been spoken by not a few of
the best and wisest of the very heathen, whose
words might well call up a blush, were blushes
possible, upon many a professing Christian's
cheek. And I say, Woe to the man, be he
headstrong youth or would-be philosopher, be

---

[1] Eph. iv. 19. (ἀπηλγηκότας, ἀντὶ τοῦ παυσομένους ἀλγεῖν. Schol. ad Thuc. II. 42).

he an applauded genius, or a successful man of the world—woe unto the man who dares to exalt his petty impotence against the divine majesty of the Moral Law. Be not deceived; to violate it is a peril, to deny it is a blasphemy, which brings its own crushing Nemesis behind. The fires of Sinai still burn over the history of men and nations, and its dread thunders still roll across the centuries. "Opinions alter," it has been said, "manners change, creeds rise and fall, but the moral law is written upon the tablets of eternity. For every false word, or unrighteous deed, for cruelty and oppression, for lust and vanity, the price has to be paid at last....Justice and Truth alone endure and live; Injustice and Falsehood may be long-lived, but doomsday comes to them in the end."

3. Then once more I would say to you, "If you would learn rightly the lesson of the Fall, beware of the theory that sin indeed may be sinful, but that no strict notice will be taken, no stern account exacted for the sins of your youth; beware of the wicked and perilous theory that you can sow (as they call it) your 'wild oats' now. What! do you think that *inclination* to break God's laws will be accepted as a valid excuse for doing so? that there is no harm in

bidding your Maker await your pleasure; in refusing to God the present which you have, and offering to Him only the future which you have not? no harm in squandering as the portion of your youth those fine gifts and inestimable opportunities which were meant to furnish the capital of your manhood? What! has God granted a plenary indulgence to the days of your youth? has he told you that you may pour its brightest years as a libation to the powers of evil, and fling its brightest jewels to be trampled underfoot of swine? Never surely did the world in its worst folly invent a theory so false, so dangerous, so utterly fatuous as this. Every fact of history, every lesson of experience, every law of nature, every doctrine of Scripture, brand it as a lie. It is to poison the fountain, and to hope that the river will be pure. It is to make the Holy of Holies a place of riot and infamy, and yet to assume that the desecrated chamber will breathe none less sweetly with hallowed incense, nor reflect less brightly the Shechinah of God. It is to break down the hedge of God's vineyard, and to suffer the wild boars to rend and trample it, yet to expect the purple clusters of the vintage unimpaired. It cannot be, my brethren; he that sows the wild oats must reap them too. Yes, men *have* been delivered from the snare of Satan, who have thus been led captive by him at his will. They have lived to know that "strong passions mean weak reason," and that they have weakened still more their reason, and full-fed their passions into fiercer strength. They have been plucked as brands from the burning; saved indeed, but saved out of agony, saved so as by fire, saved with the scathing, ineffaceable mark of many a wound upon their souls. Ask them, and they will tell you that they have "possessed the sins of their youth"—possessed them in weary lives, in wasted intellects, in weakened powers—possessed them in the sadness of remorseful memory, in the bluntness of moral sensibility, in the stings of physical decay. And they will tell you further, that to have stood thus on the very threshold of manhood with the bitter consciousness of a blighted past,—to have, as it were, stumbled over that threshold under the burden of a debt which may be owing for a little while, while strength lasts, but which shall be paid hereafter to the uttermost farthing—to have felt that their only return to "the unific rectitude of a manly life" lay through erasing the names they had entered in such dark characters upon the roll of death, was about the saddest, about the bitterest thought that a man could face. They indeed have been saved; but how many have not been saved? "You see," said the old philosopher, "the votive garments of those who have been rescued from shipwreck; where are the memorials of those more countless ones who have perished under the stormy waves?"

O then, in conclusion, my brethren, reverence yourselves in reverencing the high and merciful commands of God. Even if Christianity were not, if man had nothing to guide him but the dim gleam of tradition, or the smouldering torch of an unilluminated reason,—even then there should be in him "such an honest haughtiness of nature," so ingenuous and noble a sense of shame, as should make him scorn to sell his high birthright of honourable instincts for the mess of miserable pottage which sin alone can offer; as should enable him, as indeed has often been the case, to sit

> "*Self-governed*, in the fiery prime
> Of youth, obedient at the feet of law."

But you, my brethren, are not heathen, but Christians. You are the brethren of Christ, the sons of God; the dignity of His image and likeness is upon you; the sign of His cross upon your brows. Your bodies are His holy temple, your hearts the altar on which He has kindled the fire of His love. You hear His word, you receive His sacraments. You are called by His high calling to be holy and pure. The glory of your adoption, the inestimable price paid for your redemption, the ennobling mystery of sanctification, have made you more sacred than a dedicated thing. There is nothing high, there is nothing noble, there is nothing godlike to which you are not clearly summoned, for which you are not naturally fit. And shall *you* descend voluntarily into the defilement and pollution of sin? Nay, reverence[1] yourselves, for you are greater than you know. Oh surely when you think of the high and holy men, the household and city of God on earth; or when, yet passing upwards, you mingle in thought with the spirits and souls of the righteous, in those

"Solemn choirs and sweet societies
That sing, and singing in their glory move;—"

or when, soaring yet higher on the wings of solemn and consecrated thought, you fix your

[1] Many readers will recognize in these words an echo of the noble language on this subject which is to be found in more than one mighty page of Milton's prose works.

contemplations on the Father who created you, on the Spirit who sheds His light abroad in your hearts, on the great High Priest who stands to intercede for you by the throne of the Majesty on high;—surely in the light of such thoughts, the philosophy which jests at sin, and the worldly wisdom which bids you descend from the sunlight of holy communion to fill your belly with the husks that the swine do eat,—surely, I say, in the light of such contemplations, the rank theories of the worldling and the sensualist become hideous and revolting then. So may they ever seem, not for the condemnation of others, but for the ennoblement of ourselves. So may they ever seem to us, till our lives are worthy of the holy name whereby we are called. Wholly worthy in this life they cannot be; but by God's grace they shall be hereafter, when in that city, into which can enter no evil, no abominable thing, He who hath loved us, and purchased us to Himself with His own blood, clothe our sinful souls in the white robe of His own righteousness, and confess our names before His Father, and before the angels.

II.

THE LAW OF DEATH; AND THE MEANS OF DELIVERANCE.

(Preached before the University of Cambridge, March 8, 1868.)

GENESIS ii. 17.—"In the day that thou eatest thereof thou shalt surely die."

IT was the first voice of warning uttered by God to man, the earliest prohibition rendered awful by the denunciation of the earliest and extremest penalty. Yet almost as soon as the voice which uttered it had died away into silence the command was broken, and the penalty enforced. It is the same solemn and humiliating lesson which reappears in the history of Moses. The tablets of stone, inscribed by God's own finger, were shattered even before their laws were promulgated; and while around the riven hills yet wreathed the enfolding fire, and thick darkness which hid the Presence, the people "sat down to eat and to drink, and rose up to play." It is ever so, alas! in the history of man. All the imaginations of the thoughts of his heart are only evil continually, and by the works of the law shall no flesh be justified in God's sight.

And the one main cause of this fatal history is Disbelief. God strives to sway our hearts by the two most powerful of motives—Love and Fear. But as sin and self-will allure us, we first doubt, then disbelieve, then deliberately and determinately forget, until that forgetfulness has become a penal blindness. If it be well to startle that forgetfulness—if the thoughts once realized, of death, judgment, and eternity, be always potent to arrest the most headlong course, let us humbly pause to-day for a few moments on our path of life, and consider whether we are walking in wickedness, and, if so, to what goal that path is leading us. Last Sunday, in the record of Adam's fall, we strove to learn from the *growth* of sin some lessons for our instruction; to-day with the same guidance let us strive to learn something from its *consequences*. Here too, if I mistake not, we shall find an infinite truthfulness in that simple story of the forbidden fruit; a story the form of which the critic and the man of science may explain as they will, but which to our faith as Christians has a divine inmutable lesson, of which we can neither improve the significance, nor exhaust the depth. But to learn that lesson we must learn humility. It is a gloomy lesson, it is a monotonous lesson, it is a displeasing lesson, it is a lesson absolutely revolting to our intellectual and spiritual pride. My brethren, were I seeking to please or to flatter, were I mindful of you or of man's judgment[1], assuredly I should not choose it; but I ask only, is it needful, and is it true? and, I see, in answer, that it *is* needful, because the present disbelief of it is pregnant with disaster; and it is true, for not only from the first page of the Bible to the last, but also from the highest realm of Nature to the lowest, in the necessities of physical life, in the developments of history, in the workings of the soul, we see that sin and punishment are *riveted together*[2] *by an indissoluble link.* The fact that they are so, is as much God's revelation as the record that they have been, and the prophecy that they shall be so ; and the fact is too often wilfully ignored, because the

---

[1] 1 Cor. iv. 3. Ἐμοὶ δὲ εἰς ἐλάχιστόν ἐστιν ἵνα ἀνακριθῶ, ὑφ' ὑμῶν ἢ ὑπὸ ἀνθρωπίνης ἡμέρας.

[2] Plato, *Phæd.* IX. Ὥσπερ ἐκ μιᾶς κορυφῆς συνημμένω δύ' ὄντε. Isocr. *Or. ad Demonic.* p. 20. Εὐθὺς αἱ λῦπαι ταῖς ἡδοναῖς παρατετήγασιν.

warning is conventionally avoided. But unless the voice of God be too plain for us, and the certainties of moral government too distasteful for our notice, it seems to me that the warning is as little superfluous as the fact. Both are needed: the rolling thunder often startles the careless wayfarer, over whose head the forked lightning has flasht unseen.

Let us then with meek heart and due reverence on this 2nd Sunday of Lent take up the story from the point at which we left it. The forbidden fruit is eaten, the knowledge of evil is obtained. Flushed and vainglorious as the imagination of the poet has pictured her, (for, utterly wonderful as it may seem, an insolent self-complacence is often the first result of sin), Eve may have fancied for a moment that the tempter's lie was true; and feeling this intoxication of self-will, this blithe disobedience, this disordered fancy, this vehement revolt, and knowing not that *they* were Death, she did eat, and—passing with fatal celerity from the tempted into the tempter—" gave also unto her husband with her, and he did eat." And barely was that brief and feverish fruition past, when, lo, " the eyes of them both were opened, and they knew that they were naked." That verse is like the first stroke of the knell which tolls the message of a departed soul, and while it still shivers upon the startled air, chilling the hearts of all that hear it, it is followed, verse after verse, with ever-increasing intensity, like stroke on stroke, pealing ever with a dull and terrible monotony that the wages of sin is death. For next they hear "the voice of the Lord God walking[1] in the garden," and hide among the trees; so came fear after shame, and then follow self-excuse and mean recrimination, as their hearts are searched; and then the curse falls,—for the man labour and sorrow and sweat of brow, and the thorns and thistles of the soil; and for the woman, subjection and anguish in travail; and for *both*, the loss of their happy Eden, and of the fruit of the tree of life; and for *both*, the sentence of physical decay. And this was death—the spiritual death, which, if unarrested, ends in eternal death—the glory of the soul quenched by the knowledge of evil, the light of it burning dimmer and yet more dim amid the vapours of the charnel-house, as it descends deeper and deeper into the living tomb of years where there is neither God nor hope.

---

[1] *i.e.* "the sounding *footstep* of God." Cf. 1 Kings xiv. 6. Kalisch, *ad loc.*

Now into their future history, Scripture, which was written, not for our idle curiosity but for our eternal profit, enters not[1], and but twice again in all the Bible[2] does the name of Eve occur. Whether, as has happened to other sinners, they sank deeper and deeper into sin, or whether they embraced the hope of mercy which was offered to them in the earliest prophecy, and were healed by faith in that seed of the woman which should break the serpent's head, we cannot tell. But ere it leaves them, Scripture adds *one* scene from their after life, as though expressly to clear up the poor hallucination that by "death" God had intended only, or even mainly, the death of the body. Yet as one single item in the sum-total of their loss, we are told under what circumstances they first encountered in their own race that terrible phenomenon. Over them indeed

"Triumphant Death his dart
Shook,—but delayed to strike;"

---

[1] It is instructive to compare Scripture in this respect with Rabbinical and Mohametan legends, which abound in strange details about Adam and Eve. Any one curious in such matters may find them to his heart's content in Hottinger, *Hist. Orient.*, p. 187. D'Herbelot, *Bibl. Orient.*, s. vv. Buddæus, *Phil. Hebr.*, pp. 383—388. Heidegger, *Hist. Patr.*, p. 148, &c. &c.

[2] Viz. 2 Cor. xi. 3; 1 Tim. ii. 13.

yet they must have long conjectured something of what this phantom was. Ages before the first man, the primeval monsters had torn each other in their slime. For long æons the world had been a theatre "of conflict and carnage, of wounds and mutilation," and naturalists tell us that " no armoury can compete for variety, for beauty, for polish, for sharpness, for strength, for barbed effectiveness with the lethal weapons of the fossil world[1]." Doubtless therefore they were familiar—familiar with an intensity of dread—with the phenomena of decay. They had seen it in plants and animals; they had watched it in the fading beauty of the flower and the blasted foliage of the tree; they had seen how loathly at the touch of dissolution became the dazzling hide of the wild beast, or the glowing plumage of the bird, but never yet had they seen that spectacle which some of us have seen, that spectacle which of all others can palsy the stoutest heart with the sense of unutterable helplessness—the spectacle of those whom we loved most dearly, who were most necessary to the peace and happiness of our mortal life, passing irrevocably from us into an unknown void—that awful spectacle of the fair

[1] Professor Owen. Lecture on "The Power of God."

human face growing white and cold in the deformities of death, and the soft and loving eye fading gradually in its sightless stare. And how did they see it now? Like a mighty conflagration their sin had rolled on, and now the voice of a brother's blood was crying from the ground. Was that lifeless clay the son whom they had loved? Yes, and they were standing amazed, helpless, terror-stricken, beside the distenanted abode of a human soul. The wail of heart-rending anguish, the burst of a father's grief, the hot streaming of a mother's tears upon the brow, were as little to it as to the cold sod on which it lay; of its beauty and tenderness nothing left, save what must be buried out of sight in "the intolerable indignity" of dust to dust. Nor was this all. For this natural death—ghastly, terrifying, humiliating as it was—was but a fearful analogy of that other and worse death. For whither had the murderer fled? A fugitive and a vagabond, with God's mark stamped in the shrinking lineaments of guilt and fear upon his brow, Cain had departed from the presence of the Lord. Such then is the dread picture wherewith opens the revelation of God to man. The first pair driven from Eden, the firstborn child an alienated outcast, the second a murdered victim, the gentle worshipper dead, the murderer dead with a death yet more awful—oh, terrible fruit, is this what comes of thee? Yes! in the day that thou eatest thereof dying thou shalt die[1].

It was fulfilled *then;* it has been fulfilled ceaselessly thereafter. We live, my brethren, in a world, in a universe of death. Nature herself, as though stricken with a curse, seems to groan and travail with the anguish of her child. She too has her blight and desolation, her plague and famine, her phenomena of wrath and terror, her hues of earthquake and eclipse; she too has her terrified stillness before the hurricane, and lights up her volcanic hills with awful testimonies of her central flames[2]. And over her surface, thicker than the autumnal leaves, lie the mortal relics of our race. Where are the great nations who built the Pyramids of Egypt, and the temples of Babylon? "Where is the king of Hamath, and the king of Arpad, the kings of the cities of Sepharvaim, Hena, and Iva?" Their very memorial is perished with them. "The soil we tread on," it has been said, "is a great city of the dead, with ever-extending pavements of gravestones, and ever-lengthening streets of

[1] מוֹת תָּמוּת. [2] Cf. 2 Pet. iii. 7.

tombs and sepulchres, the burial-place of all that ever lived in the past, dead individuals, dead species, dead genera, dead creations, a universe of death." And we, no less than they, are but grass for the mower's scythe. We too have advanced far on our way towards that great silence into which we have seen so many pass. The phenomenon is common to us, but no familiarity can rob it of its dreadfulness; for the dead who are the more in number have kept their awful secret unrevealed; and the child who died yesterday knows more than can be guessed at by the 1000 millions of living men. Yet this death is but the least, and the least dreaded part of that other, that second, that spiritual death which God meant in that earliest warning, "In the day that thou eatest thereof, dying thou shalt die."

1. In considering the nature of this spiritual death, I would call your attention to three things. And *first* let us learn its certainty; let us learn to be early undeceived by the tempter's falsehood, 'Ye shall not surely die.' Oh how how often has that first lie beguiled the sons of Adam! how often to this day does the sinner whisper it to his own erring heart! Yet never once—never once in any single human experience—has it proved true. If a man will serve

his sin, let him at least reckon upon this, that in one way or other it will be ill with him; his sin will find him out; his path will be hard; there will be to him no peace. It is marvellous in how many ways the retribution works, sometimes by divers diseases and sundry kinds of death; sometimes by utter unspeakable weariness of life; sometimes by a bitter series of unbroken disappointments; sometimes by the interferences of human law and the humiliation of open shame; sometimes by terrible surprises of strong temptation which shock the soul into despair. And sometimes on the other hand by none of these things, so that on the contrary the sinners have been wealthy and prosperous and to all appearance pre-eminently blessed, and yet at the very summit of their hopes have been tortured by the sense of an aimless existence, and the thirst and hunger of an unsatisfied soul. And such a man is never safe; his fate may come upon him very suddenly, ere the game of his guilt is well played out, as when the ashes of Achan mingled with those of the stolen garment which he had never worn, or as when on the morning after his crime Ahab was met by the prophet at the vineyard gate; as when Uzzah fell dead beside the violated ark, or the brow of Gehazi burned with leprosy, or Judas flung down the unspent price of blood in horror upon the temple floor: or again it may not come upon him till after long, long years, as when Esau's selling of his birthright ended forty years after in that fruitless repentance, and that exceeding great and bitter cry. The night of concealment may be long, but Dawn comes like the Erinnys[1] to reveal and avenge its crimes. Even the ancients saw it; in their proverbs, the Furies walk with leaden feet, but strike with iron hands; the mills of the gods grind late, but they grind to powder[2]. In the stories of Glaucus the son of Epicydes[3], and of the cranes of Ibycus[4], and the gold of Toulouse[5], and of him who trampled on the nest of young swallows because he heard them calling him "parricide[6]," we have but illustrations of the same teaching as that which warned us that there is "nothing covered that shall not be revealed, neither hid that shall not be known." Such truths even the heathen

---

[1] Erinnys is Saranyû the Dawn. Max Müller, *Lectures, Second Series*, p. 517. Comp. *Mytholog.* p. 40.

[2] 'Οψὲ θεῶν ἀλέουσι μύλαι ἀλέουσι δὲ λεπτά. Cf. ὑστερόπουϛ 'Ερινύϛ. Æsch. *Ag.* 58. ὑστερόπουϛ Νέμεσιϛ. *Anth. P.* 12. 229.

[3] Herod. VI. 85.   [4] Antip. Sidon. *Epigr.* lxxviii.

[5] Cic. *de N. D.* III. 30.   Just. 32. 3.

[6] Plut. *De Sera Num. Vind.*, Opp. VIII. 190.

teach us. Think not then, my brethren, think not that throughout a godless life you can eat and drink and sin, and yet escape. If our first parents did not, neither will you. God has no favourites, he is no respecter of persons; the youngest, strongest, gladdest among you, the most promising and the most popular, if he have forgotten God, if he be giving himself up to the world the flesh or the devil, will find no exemption from the inexorable consequence. Oh the quiver of God is full of arrows, sharp and manifold; and for you, if you be living in sin, no less certainly than if you saw it with your eyes, the arrow is drawn to the very head upon the bow of God,—nay, even now it may be singing through the parted air,—whose wound shall eat into your soul like fire.

2. For, *secondly*, not only is this punishment *inevitable*, but it is *natural;* not miraculous but ordinary, not sudden but gradual, not accidental but necessary, not exceptional but invariable. However striking may be those strange instances of sudden and unexpected retribution which men regard as due to immediate interventions, it is a yet more solemn warning to know that this retribution is the impersonal evolution of an established law. The criminal

may escape external consequences; he cannot escape natural results. You sin, and no miracle is wrought; the darkness is not peopled with avenging faces, nor do the walls around you begin to burn with messages of flame, yet then nevertheless, as an inevitable sequence, the law begins to work, and "God's light shines on patiently and impartially, justifying or condemning simply by shewing all things in the slow history of their ripening." "In the day that thou eatest thereof thou shalt surely die." Some of the ancients doubted, because the thunderbolts seemed to strike impartially the innocent and the guilty[1]; but God does not avenge Himself by thunderbolts, He but leaves the sinner to the necessary outcome of his sin; aye even the repentant sinner. For long after a man has done with his sin, his sin has by no means done with him; his deeds live apart from him, and claim their fellowship with him long after he has grown ashamed of them; and he inherits them for they are his. Look at the harvest rippling and bowing under the summer breeze with all its innumerable ears; innumera-

---

[1] Ar. *Nub.* 399:
Εἴπερ βάλλει τοὺς ἐπιόρκους πῶς οὐχὶ Σίμων᾽ ἐνέπρησε;...
'Αλλὰ τὸν αὑτοῦ γε νεὼν βάλλει, κ.τ.λ.

ble as they seem yet there is not one of them that did not spring from some seed which the sower sowed. Even so it is with the harvest of shame, of loneliness, of ruin, of agony which springs up in the lives of many men. "Nature," says one, "acts with fearful uniformity,—stern as fate, absolute as tyranny, merciless as death,—too vast to praise, too inexorable to propitiate,—she has no ear for prayer, no heart for sympathy, no arm to save." And he who thus wrote believed not in God; but that which he called Nature is but the sum-total of God's laws,—laws which will work in the moral world as certainly as gravitation in the physical—laws established in mercy for our warning and our deliverance,—laws which on every cloud of the stormy heavens, and every grave of the wrinkled earth, and on every gleam of that fiery Urim which is the awakened conscience of mankind, write with plainness unmistakeable that the wages of sin is death.

3. And *thirdly*, from these first chapters of the Bible we see that retribution is not only certain—that it is not only due to the onward flowing of a great law "in the rhythmical succession of causes and effects,"—but also that it takes the form which of all others the sinner

would most passionately deprecate,—for it is *homogeneous* with the sins on whose practice it ensues. Eve had desired the knowledge of evil, and she had it to her own confusion. The pure sweet rose of innocence is changed into the burning confusing, branding blush of shame. Before, they were naked and were not ashamed; now there eyes were opened and they knew that they were naked. They had doubted God's love, and now they dare not even gaze upon His face. His anger, as it always does, had "followed the method of their sins." It is ever thus that He "writes the cause of the judgment upon the forehead of the judgment itself," and makes the very sins which insult His majesty, the instruments to avenge His will. We often observe this frightful resemblance of sin and suffering even in God's direct judgments; as when the cruel king is mutilated under whose table mutilated kings had gathered crumbs,—as when they who professed themselves wise became fools,—as when the haughtiest of conquerors is degraded into the most pitiable of delusions,— as when on the house of him who had become a murderer and adulterer descended the twin furies of adultery and blood. And it is so in physical and moral consequences;—in "the troubles of the envious and the fears of the cowardly, the heaviness of the slothful and the shame of the unclean." And oh, when God thus punishes the sinner with his own sin, He is most angry then. When he is less angry He may smite with tribulation or disease, but when He is most angry He lets alone, He suffers the wicked to eat of his own way, and to be filled with the fruit of his own devices. The coward would flee upon horses, therefore shall he flee. The guilty cities shall burn in the madness of sinful flames. The unjust shall be unjust still, and the filthy filthy still. To the gluttonous Israelites when the heavy wrath of God came upon them it was said, "Therefore the Lord will give you flesh and ye shall eat. Ye shall not eat one day, nor two days, nor five days, neither ten days, nor twenty days; but even a whole month of days, until it come out at your nostrils and be loathsome unto you." A modern historian[1] has told us of a Queen who wrote a letter to her paramour about the murder of her own husband : and with these thoughts in her head, he adds, "she lay down upon her bed to sleep doubtless, sleep with the

---

[1] Froude.

soft tranquillity of an innocent child. Remorse may disturb the slumber of a man who is dabbling with his first experiences of crime; and when the pleasure has been tasted and is gone, and nothing is left of the crime but the ruin it has wrought, then too the furies take their seats upon the midnight pillow. But *the meridian of evil* is for the most part left unvext, and when a man has chosen his road he is let alone to follow it to the end."

Such then are the workings of sin in our mortal members, and this is the condition which Scripture calmly and deliberately and with no sense of metaphor calls *death*. For indeed it *is* death. When the glory of an unsullied heart is gone,— when in lieu of it has come that sense of self-disgust which is the bitterest of woes,—when the fiery barrier of a corrupted will waves between us and the heaven of our lost innocence,—when like some "desolate wreck upon the lonely shore" we lie at the mercy of every storm of misfortune, and every surge of sin,— when to us, in our guilty fear, the heavens seem to be full of anger, and "earth to be made of glass,"—when that which we do we loathe, and of all that we feel to be sweetest and noblest our souls despair,—when we are suffering in every region of our being the ignoble martyrdom of sin, "the scathing of the flame without its purification," and the burden of the cross without its peace,—above all, when conscious of our vileness we hear as it were the sound of God's awful footsteps walking among the garden trees, and He who is our Friend, our Father, the author of our life, the Redeemer of our souls, Has turned away his face from us, and has become to us a thick darkness or a consuming fire,—then *we* may call it a death-in-life or a life-in-death, but the stern plain Scripture calls it death. For when goodness is dead, and hope is dead, and the fire of God's love is dead on the altar of his heart, a man may have a *name* to live, but he is dead. To be carnally minded is death; to have lost sight of God in the world's wilderness is death. Nay, to shew you this yet more plainly, yet more unmistakeably, Solomon takes the young man by the hand as he sits at the lighted banquet amid the ghastly gaieties in the home of sin, and pointing to the faces around him, though they be in the flush of youth and strength, though the winecup be in their hands, and the garlands on their brows, and the hoarse laughter ringing on their lips,—he bids him see that the dead are there, and that those guests are in the depths of hell.

And oh, if some of the dead be here—and if they be they will be the very proudest, the most contemptuous, the most self-satisfied—if they be seated among you with their dead and scornful and misbelieving hearts unstirred, to them I will say this only, that thus "to be least afraid when most in peril," to have strong delusion sent them so that they believe a lie, to have grey hairs upon them yet to know it not, to have "so much of the heart eaten away that there is not enough heart left to know that the rest is gone"—oh this is indeed to be beneath God's heaviest frown. Seasons like this, with their heart-searchings and spiritual admonitions, were appointed, my brethren, to save us from sinking into that deathful sleep. But if any one here be so sunk, he is past man's awakening; God only, and only God by the sharpest, most burning, most intolerable pangs, can awake his soul. It is the only thing he can hope for, for all God's love has been in vain: and oh what a state is this, when the only thing left a man to hope for is that God's mercy may come to him in the fell guise of earthly ruin. And will that convert him? will it save him, even in extremes, from the death that cannot die? Alas, does it not often harden men into impenitence and despair? "God hath promised pardon," says St Augustine, "to him that repenteth, but He hath nowhere promised repentance to him that sinneth." Oh, surely we all need, and that from our very inmost hearts, the cry of the psalmist, " Lighten Thou mine eyes, *that I sleep not in death.*"

Do you trust, my brethren, to time to save you? "Time is no agent[1]," and cannot save. Do you trust to a deathbed repentance? Alas, my brethren, have you ever stood by deathbeds? For you too the end may be near which we have seen in others, when in pain and anguish, the mind dazzled and confused, the soul dark and troubled, the heart distracted with earthly cares, the tongue stammering and failing, the thoughts wandering aimlessly in the wilderness of a sinful past, our last hour is drawing nigh. Think you that penitence is common, think you that it is always valid, think you that it is even possible in such a state as this? And if not, "then comes what comes hereafter." And I know not how or why, but respecting that hereafter men seem to make

[1] Bishop Coplestone.

themselves strangely at their ease. Alas, my brethren, I know not whence comes this confidence.

I should hold it indeed to be mere folly to dogmatise about a state between which and us is drawn the impenetrable vail of death; I should hold it wrong to assert as positive that which, it seems to me, Scripture does not assert as positive, that at death the fate of every man alike is decided finally, hopelessly, and for ever; I should tremble to limit so far the merits of Christ's infinite sacrifice as to force on any conscience with bold anathemas the uncertain doctrine that its efficacy cannot by any possibility extend beyond the grave; but while on the one hand Scripture may not have excluded the tenability of such a hope, mingled with fear and trembling, on the other hand it discountenances utterly the calm, presumptuous indifference with which thousands of sinful men regard their end. In these days it is quietly assumed that sin can have no consequences in the world to come, and a man is coolly set down as deficient in intelligence if he believe that there is any danger in the death of even a sinful, impenitent, and hardened soul. And yet I see in life a certain stern law of continuity; I see that the God of the future is the God of the present too; I see that it is from the soul that sins arise, and that sinfulness of the spirit cannot be destroyed by the dissolution of the dust which was but its instrument. And when I read in the Bible of the undying worm, and the outer darkness, and the quenchless flame, I ask who spoke those words? Were they uttered on Sinai that their echoes might roll in thunder upon the desert winds? Did Hebrew prophets threaten them in the torrent of their scathing denunciation and unutterable scorn? Nay, it is a fact which I dare not ignore, that He spoke them who died for us; He who told us of His Father's care for the falling sparrow, and the raven's callow brood; He who willeth not that any should perish, but that all should come to repentance. Oh voice of most just judgment, more terrible because it fell from the lips of eternal love. Where then is there room for confidence? Do we believe Christ? Are we more just than our Redeemer? Do we love human souls more tenderly than He loved them? It is indeed an agony to think that for some human souls, aye for some who have rejoiced under the blue sky, and played in the green fields,—for some who were once children in the sanctity of their lovely innocence, and who once lifted their little white hands as they lisped to their heavenly Father an infant's prayer,—it should have been better that they had never been born. Yet Christ said it. And indeed why should the moral dispensation of the present be founded on the law of retribution, and yet the same law be set down by modern theosophies as an absurd superstition in the dispensation of the future? Is there then no hell *here*, that we can be so very certain that there will be none hereafter? Nay, seeing here that indignation and wrath, tribulation and anguish, fall upon every soul of man that doeth evil; seeing that the Scriptures, from beginning to end, and whole books of them, blaze like the wall of Belshazzar's palace with messages of doom; seeing that God hath declared His wrath against sin as clearly as though He had engraven it upon the sun, or written it in stars upon the midnight sky;—this presumptuous ease about the after life, this growing indifference to the thought of future punishment, this philosophy which is so treacherous and so timid, seems to me, and I say it deliberately, at once an aberration of the intellect, and an infatuation of the will. Oh, better surely that a sinner should tremble with agony, as the last leaves of the aspen shudder in the late autumnal wind, than that he should thus falsely presume that he knows more of God than God Himself hath taught him, and seeing, as has been said, "that wrath is written in Scripture against his way of life, should hope that it is not wrath but mercy, and so rush upon the bosses of the Almighty's buckler as the wild horse rusheth into the battle."

Awake then thou that sleepest, and arise from the dead, and Christ shall give thee light! Tell me not, my brethren, that all this is but an appeal to the lower motives of fear, and that you are too wise, too learned, too philosophical, too enlightened, to be moved by *fear*. God has said, "Be ye not highminded, but fear." These warnings are God's warnings, and to despise them is to despise Him who gave them. But after all, my brethren, these stern voices of God are the daughters of His love; He has established throughout His universe this law of inevitable death because He loves us, because He is very good to us, because a human soul is an unspeakably awful thing, and He regards its loss with a pity too infinite for our stained and finite nature to understand. And therefore He would save it, if it *will* be saved, aye even by fire. It is never He that condemns, or ruins, or curses it; it is self-ruined and self-condemned. It is not He who hardens Himself against us, but we who harden ourselves against Him; it is "not He who withdraweth His mercy, but we who lose our capacity for mercy." And therefore that we may not be cut off from Him who is our only life, in whom alone our souls find, or can find, their fruition and satisfaction, He teaches us that *sin is death*, as nature teaches us that fire burns or water drowns. The laws we have been considering are but meant to warn us that the lust of the flesh, and the lust of the eyes, and the pride of life, are cruel and pitiless taskmasters; that in following them we are hurrying to our proper ruin; that sin, of its very nature, is self-deception, a missing of the mark[1], a selling of the soul for nought, a bartering for our own destruction of all that can ennoble, and beautify, and bless. Such warnings are, the voice of the loving father telling his disobedient prodigal that the squandered portion and the riotous living end in a dark exile and a life among the swine. And ever in lieu of this

---

[1] 'Αμαρτία from ἁμαρτάνω, "I miss the mark." The same notion of sin as essentially *a failure* may be traced in the words אֱוִיל and נְבָלָה. See Müller on *The Christian Doctrine of Sin*. (Engl. Tr. I. pp. 92, 172).

death He offers us His gift of eternal life. Every sin we willingly commit drags us further from it; every year of life which ebbs away from us in unrepented wickedness makes it harder and harder to obtain. But while yet we live, while yet we hear the words of invitation, while yet we receive the ordinances of grace, the door is not yet shut, and we may pass to it by the narrow way. We have been dwelling upon death,—here is the method of deliverance; we have been gazing on the clouds,—here, far brighter than that of the early covenant, is the rainbow which encircles them. To Eve was given the dim promise that her seed should bruise the serpent's head; for us Christ has trampled sin and Satan under his feet. The star of her distant hope has brightened for us into the Sun of Righteousness. But only by faith and prayer, only, if we have been rebels against God, by the old hard path of repentance, of confession, of self-abasement, only by that necessary mortification of all that is evil within us, of which Lent is the too neglected symbol, can we pass from our darkness into His light. And for all who have been sinners this repentance is the very work of life, a work to which all other work is insignificant indeed. But it is a work which never failed, and of which the end is eternal life. There is no life but that; it is to have found a physician for the soul's great sickness, a robe for its inward nakedness; it is to be rescued by a perfect and permanent deliverance from the law of death; it is to hunger no more, and thirst no more, drinking from the living fountains, feeding on the heavenly bread; it is the light of God's countenance, the hallowing influence of His Spirit, the eternal blessing of His peace. It is the only happiness possible, and it is open to us all. Without it our lives on earth, nay, perhaps our very immortality, will be a melancholy failure, an unutterable curse. But that this might not be so, Christ died for us, and in dying bruised the serpent's head. Whatever we once were, whatever we now are, we may still be accepted in the Beloved; we may seek even now in humble penitence the fountain opened for sin and for uncleanness; we may arise and go unto our Father, against whom we sin so often and so grievously, in deep contrition, until to us, as to the happiest of His redeemed children, He have granted the sweet assurance that we are washed, that we are sanctified, that we are justified in the name of the Lord Jesus, and by the Spirit of our God.

III.

THE PATH OF CHRIST.

(Preached before the University of Cambridge, March 15, 1868.)

MATT. viii. 22.—"Follow me, and let the dead bury their dead."

IT was the answer of our Lord to one of His disciples, possibly, as an old tradition tells us[1], to the Apostle Philip, who before following Him wished to go and bury his father. The extreme urgency of the command is plain, nor is its meaning mistakeable. 'Thou art living in a world of natural and of spiritual death; thou art called to a kingdom of life. Let the spiritually dead bury their physically dead. Follow thou me.'

Who in our Lord's day were the spiritually dead? In the lower strata of society were the dangerous classes, sinners and harlots, dishonest

---

[1] Κἂν συγχρήσωνται τῇ τοῦ Κυρίου φωνῇ λέγοντος τῷ Φιλίππῳ ἄφες τοὺς νεκροὺς θάψαι τοὺς ἑαυτῶν νεκρούς. Clem. Alex. *Strom.* III. c. 4. § 25.

servants and discontented labourers, soldiers violent and brutal, publicans degraded and extortionate. And among these Christ laboured, and was received with passionate love, with awe-struck gratitude, with penitence and tears; but more indifferent, and more blind, and naked, and dead were those upper classes of society, who fancied themselves so increased with goods, so needful of nothing, and over the stagnancy of whose surface-respectabilities was stretched the glittering film of hypocrisy and pride. There were easy full-fed Sadducees, who believed in neither angel nor spirit; temporising Herodians, careful only for quiet and success; orthodox scribes, indignantly eager about the letter of the law, profoundly ignorant of its spirit; Priests and Levites, self-complacent and dignified, who with supercilious indifference could leave the wounded in their lonely agony; treacherous and selfish Pharisees, arraying all their splendid authority on the side of a corrupt tradition, and ready to put in force every engine of popular ignorance and established power to crush the truth and those who loved it. From forth this congregation of the dead our Lord summoned His disciple, and the voice of His summons is sounding still. Our age, like that of our Saviour, is formally and professedly religious, yet no less now than then he who would follow Christ must come forth, and leave the dead to bury their dead. Christianity was a religion eminently heroical and high; yet how little of high or heroical do we see in surrounding society; how little, alas, in our own hearts. "Come from the four winds, oh breath, and breathe upon these slain that they may live." For the high moral grace we see the cautious and calculating worldliness; for the manly Christian poverty an emulous madness of desire for wealth; for the strong Christian self-denial a spreading cancer of effeminate luxury; for the sweet Christian nobleness, and the life hid with Christ in God, a meanness and feebleness of purpose which recall the very letter of the serpent-sentence, "Upon thy belly shalt thou go, and dust shalt thou eat all the days of thy life." Alas, we see around us a hollow Christianity, more of the lips than of the life; a Christianity whose intense inspiring power over the hearts of society has well-nigh dwindled into a convention and a name. And unless a revival of true faith call forth a nobler energy, a more transforming purpose, an intenser work among the multitudes of believers, a voice must sound forth once more which shall shake the nations, a voice of summons to the gathering battle, a voice which shall cry, not in gentle whispers, but like the trump of the archangel and the voice of God, "Let the dead bury their dead, follow thou me."

1. And whither then must we follow Christ? In spirit, if not in letter, we must follow Him along the road He trod on earth, and that was a road of self-abnegation, of poverty, of homelessness, of the base man's hatred and the proud man's scorn. Let us not disguise it; it is no primrose path of dalliance, but a hard road, hard and yet happy, and all the highest and the noblest of earth have trodden it; all who have regarded the things eternal not as things future, but merely as the unseen realities about them now. Yet oh how busy, how widespread, how multitudinous are the claims, the interests, the arguments of this world of death; how feverish the eagerness with which they are pursued; how intense and incessant the cares with which they are accompanied. Now the command is clear and plain. We cannot serve God and mammon; if we follow Christ in anything but in name, we must sit loose to the

world and the world's interests; we must be
content, if need be, with the beatitudes of poverty and persecution. For easy wealth and
epicurean self-indulgence, though we see in them
but little to reprobate, Christ had nothing but
that thunder-clap of judgment, and the silence
which followed it, "Thou fool, this night;" nothing but the lurid picture of one carried from
purple and fine linen to burning thirst and tormenting flame. And why is this? Is it because the infinite King of heaven grudges one
poor enjoyment to atoms such as we? No, but
because the prosperity of fools destroys them;
because these coarse luxuries of the body, these
evil joys of the mind[1], have no happiness in
them, and yet, such as they are, make the heart
soft and surfeited and vulnerable, unworthy to
enjoy His holiness, unfit to do His work. If
Christ's warnings needed confirmation, the experience of myriads has confirmed them: every
page of history and experience is full of the
wail of sickened worldlings and disappointed
kings. "All is vanity and vexation of spirit,"
said the wearied Solomon. "Out of fifty years
of a reign, peaceful, victorious, and pre-eminently

[1] Virgil places the "mala mentis gaudia," with Fear, and
Disease, and Hunger, at the entrance of Tartarus. *Æn.* VI. 278.

splendid, I can count but fourteen days of pure and genuine happiness," wrote Abdalrahman the Magnificent. "I have seen the silly round of business and of pleasure, and have done with it all," said the eloquent and stately Bolingbroke; "I have enjoyed all the pleasures of the world, and know their futility, and do not regret their loss." "There is nothing in the world worth living for," sighed the greatest man of modern days, as he rode through London streets. And of all earthly gauds it is pre-eminently true; God never constituted the lowest human soul so low as that it should find sufficiency in them. But of the Christian life it is not true. There are things infinitely worth living for. Integrity, and truth, and high aims, and largeness of heart, and love to our fellow-men, and a sense that God is with us—these things do sweeten even the bitter cup of life. "Happiness," it has been said, "may fly away, pleasure pall or cease to be obtainable, friends prove treacherous, and fame turn to infamy, but the power to serve God never fails, and the love to Him is never rejected."

If then we would follow Christ, we must shake off the baser objects of earthly desire as nothing better than the dust which gathers upon the cereclothes of mortality. So Christ taught us, and so He lived. Has it ever occurred to you, my brethren, that all which we know of nearly all except three years of His mortal life, from earliest boyhood to full manhood, from the glimpse which we catch of the child in the temple to Him who was baptized of John in Jordan, is contained in one single word, a word which no pious fraud has excluded from the Gospel of St Mark, though it has attempted to do so, a word which lights up, as with one broad flash, the unrecorded obscurity,— ὁ τέκτων[1], "the carpenter." "Is not this the carpenter?" Yes, the home of a Galilæan peasant, mean and poor, containing probably but a single room, and no furniture except a mat, and some clay vessels, and a painted wooden chest;—yes, the shop and the employ of a carpenter in the most despised village, of the despised province, of a despised and conquered land, this was the trade, this the home, while He had a home, of our Lord and Master, the

---

[1] Mark vi. 3, Οὐχ οὗτός ἐστιν ὁ τέκτων; The attempts both textual and exegetical to get rid of this memorable testimony, shew how deeply it is required. "*Working in a humble trade, to serve his own and his mother's needs*, He grew to the state of a man." Bp. Jer. Taylor, *Credenda*. (*Opp*. VII. 162, ed. Eden.)

Son of Man, and for thirty long years of obscure toil it sufficed Him. What a lesson of divine humility! We are heady, highminded, anxious; we lade ourselves with gilded dross; we daub ourselves with thick clay; we live and move and have our being in the very atmosphere of the infinitely little. Not so He whom we are bidden to follow; for Him the shop of the carpenter sufficed. No fierce ambition agitated His calm soul; no savage indignation lacerated His trustful heart; as now in His glory, so then in His humiliation, His soul was where he has bidden us ascend with Him in heavenly places. And when in the hungry wilderness the kingdoms of the world and the glory of them were lying at his feet, poor though He was and homeless He spurned them from Him without a thought, as wholly beneath Him and unworthy of His regard. Well might He do so: for in truth at that moment there was living one to whom Satan had given them, an undisputed despot, an emperor deified and unapproachable, "at once a priest, an atheist, and a god[1]." And at that very moment, wearied and disgusted with the cares of government, he had flung them off to make his secure re-

---

[1] The expression occurs in an early French work of Gibbon.

tirement in a delicious islet in the loveliest spot of earth; and there in its purple grottoes, surrounded by a crystal sea, he had wooed every luxury, and exhausted every Circean cup that could be conceived by the fertile inventors of evil things. And what came of it all? Let the historian answer that he was "tristissimus, ut constat, hominum[1]," confessedly the most gloomy-hearted of mankind; let *himself* answer who wrote to his fawning senate from his corrupted home: "May all the gods and goddesses, Conscript Fathers, destroy me worse than by that death I daily feel, if I know what, or how to write to you." "Thus," says Tacitus[2], "neither his fortune nor his solitude protected him from the acknowledged anguish of a sin-tormented soul." Yet who that looks at the pride, and the pleasure-seeking, and the mammon-worship of not a few in our great guilty cities, in the things they hunt after, and the

[1] Plin. *Hist. Nat.* XXVIII. 5.
[2] Tac. *Ann.* VI. 6. "'Quid scribam vobis, Patres Conscripti, aut quomodo scribam, aut quid omnino non scribam hoc tempore, di me deæque pejus perdant quam perire me cotidie sentio, si scio.' Adeo facinora et flagitia sua ipsi quoque in supplicium verterant....Quippe Tiberium non fortuna, non solitudines protegebant, quin tormenta pectoris suasque ipse pœnas fateretur."

things they love, would not suppose that their ideal was the Roman emperor rather than the Crucified; that they were followers rather of Tiberius than of Christ? Oh that there were more to set the open example of ruining, if need be, over and again, in any righteous cause, what their friends are pleased to call their *interests*; of openly repudiating, for the sake of truth, or of freedom, or of conscience, both wealth and all that leads to it; more who would adopt the prayer of St Thomas of Aquinas, "Give me, oh Lord, a noble heart which no earthly affection can draw down[1];" more who were ready to treat their money as contemptuously as St Edmund treated it, who leaving it always loose upon his window-sill would often smear it over with earth, saying, "Ashes to ashes, dust to dust." Former ages were more fruitful in such examples than our own; and if they be not higher, better, nobler, wiser examples than the mammon-worship of our own, then not only is all Scripture false, but

> "The pillared firmament is rottenness,
> And earth's base built on stubble."

2. First then in self-denial; and secondly,

[1] "Da mihi Domine cor nobile, quod nulla deorsum trahat terrena affectio." See *Christian Schools and Scholars*, II. 80.

you must follow Christ on the road of toil. Here too the manual labour and the mission labour of His own life are our example; and were it possible to overlook its meaning, His own words would emphatically supply it. But it is not possible to misread lessons so clear and so heart-searching as those of the two sons and the labourers in the vineyard, and the unprofitable servant, and the stern apologue of the barren trees. It was the first law of Eden, '*work;*' and though the work was changed to toil by a penal decree, even that toil by faithful obedience has been transformed into an honour and a blessing. "It is," as St Chrysostom calls it, "a bitter arrow from the gentle hand of God." But then the work must be approached in a right spirit, must be work in God's vineyard, and work for God. Thousands of men work, nay, toil, nay, grind and slave with a blind groping illiberal absorption at their often vulgar and mechanical routine; not for duty, or for the glory of God, or for the blessing of man, but simply to further their own emmet interests. Such work followed in such a spirit is but a little less baneful than idleness; if it does not corrupt the habits, it ossifies the heart. Unblessed of God, it is often burned up in a moment, after it has been followed for a life, and even when most successful it can bring neither happiness here nor hope hereafter. But, on the other hand, few earthly paths are more rich in intrinsic and immediate blessing than when, with earnest undivided hearts, with lofty unselfish purpose, we devote our lives to God's service. The man who does it may know well, and know long beforehand, that he shall never live to see the fruit of his labours; he may know that they will cost him strong contempt, and secret dislike, and incessant opposition; he may know that they will ruin his earthly prospects, and leave him with ample cause for anxiety and care; but yet such a man, if he trust in God, if he be trying, however poorly, to follow Christ, will not lack of inward consolation, which is loftier and sweeter than happiness itself. He will have no time for evil thoughts; every day he will work as if he had to live for ever; he will live as if he had to die at once[1]; and when he lies down at night in happy and trustful weariness, the angels of God will breathe over him an evening blessing, and shut to the doors of his heart. Till at last the weary day is over, and it ringeth to evensong:

[1] The favourite motto of St Edmund of Canterbury.

the work is done, the rest is prepared for him in heavenly mansions, and God giveth His beloved sleep.

To such a life you are called, and happy will it be for you if you obey the calling now. These bright years of college life may be to you inestimably precious; years of large growth in knowledge, and nobility, and self-control; years above all of growth in grace, and the knowledge of our Lord and Saviour Jesus Christ, which, though they will speed away like a dream when one awaketh, may supply you with inexhaustible sources of inward serenity for the years of heavier responsibility and sterner care. But, on the other hand, they may be emphatically 'years which the locust hath eaten'; years of debt, and dissipation, and extravagance, and frivolity, in which the youth uses his earliest liberty to offer to Satan the very firstfruits of his life; years such as one of our own poets has described of

> Idleness, halting with his weary clog,
> And poor misguided Shame, and witless Fear,
> And *simple Pleasure, foraging for death*.

And since the yesterdays of life are ever the

[1] Wordsworth, *The Prelude;* Cowper gives a very similar picture in the *The Task*, Bk. II.

parents of its to-morrows, there will always be too much reason to dread that these years, if thus changed from a blessing to a curse, will be the neglected avenue to an unprofitable life. An University, in its very conception, is a place for intellectual energy, directed to the glory of God, and the service of mankind; and if *any* man who neglects to train and cultivate his reason to the utmost is neglecting a simple and elementary duty which devolves on him in virtue of his mental and moral constitution, he is doubly guilty who neglects it *here*. Life is no mere game, and there *are* such entities as the intellect and the soul. If any one among you be degrading a great University into a scene of amusement, and nothing more; if he be wholly and openly sacrificing its high aims to the poor ambitions of a bodily exercise, in which after all man can never attain the powers of some of his meanest congeners, he is living unworthily of himself, unworthily of the great society to which he belongs, unworthily of the high demands of the Christian calling. The days are long past for gentlemanly ignorance; and he who has no ambition beyond the strenuous idleness of sport, is living for an excellence which is neither noble nor eternal,—for that which a few passing years shall unstring to feebleness, and a few years more dissolve to dust. Let him consider carefully whether he be following Christ's command, or whether to him belongs the solemn warning that "He who wandereth from the way of understanding, shall abide in the congregation of the dead."

3. Whether such a warning be necessary or needless, *you* know, my brethren, better than I; but let me hasten to say, thirdly, that he who would follow Christ must not only follow Him on the path of self-denial and of labour, but must follow Him also in the strength of *Enthusiasm*, must be baptised with the Holy Ghost and with fire. And herein too he must let the dead bury their dead. For the dead of this world hate this fiery spirit. "Above all no zeal," said the witty, crafty, successful statesman[1]; "fervent in spirit," said St Paul, or, as it should be rather rendered, "boiling in spirit[2]." It was not the word of a fastidious Atticist, or long-robed Pharisee, but rather one of those words that were thunders, one of the words that have hands and feet. And never was it

---

[1] Prince Talleyrand.
[2] ζέοντες τῷ πνεύματι, Rom. xii. 11. Cf. Acts xviii. 25. (Æsch. *Theb.* 708).

more needed than now; for never more than now did the world hate enthusiasm, and never was it more certain that by a noble enthusiasm it can alone be saved. For it is an age of unbelief, of hollowness, of cynicism; and these are the inevitable symptoms of decay. And decaying times need no smooth and drowsy voices, no conventional remedies, no flattering words. They need the living zeal that cannot sleep and settle on its lees, but which reels and staggers as with an invincible exaltation. The Hebrew word for prophet comes from a root that means to bubble like water on the flame[1]; and even the heathen imagined their seers as convulsed with the descending deity[2], and speaking only with frenzied lips the utterances that reached through innumerable years[3]. All this is strange to us; but it was not strange to St Paul, who was caught up to the third heaven, whether in the body or out of the body he could not tell; nor have these records of overpowering religious emotion been strange to many of those who, as though heaven's own lightning had

---

[1] נָבִיא from נָבָא *i. q.* נָבַע, *ebullivit.* 1 Sam. xviii. 16.

[2] Virg. *Æn.* VI. 45, 77. Lucan, *Phars.* v. 161. Plato, *Phædr.* p. 244.

[3] Heraclitus, *ap. Plut.* 2, 397 A.

flashed upon their faces, have become fusile throughout their whole being with the spirit of their Lord. Upon these souls, so wild, disordered, and yet so full of heaven, these souls that yield themselves like the strings of a harp to unseen players, we look down with a superior pity. Let us spare our contemptuous pity: the icy, glassy surface of our religious life is in no sort of danger of being swept by such tornadoes of spiritual emotion; but, oh, better is the clearing hurricane than the brooding pestilence; better the rush of the resistless torrent than the stagnancy of the putrid marsh. And though "enthusiast" be now a term of ridicule, though men in general seem to have adopted the inscription which may be seen in one of our southern abbeys, "*Any one who leaves the trodden path will be prosecuted* [1];" though it has been well described as the tendency of the day "to tame goodness and greatness out of their splendid passion, and stamp virtue itself into coinage of convenience;" yet without enthusiasm the world would long ago have been that barren plain in which, if I may borrow the

[1] The Cistercian Abbey at Netley near Southampton. The inscription is alluded to by Montalembert in his *Monks of the West.*

eloquent image of a modern statesman, "every mole-hill is a mountain, and every thistle a forest-tree." No deed of permanent greatness, no deed of regenerating force, can be achieved without it. By it the great forerunner stood up undaunted before the murderous tyrant and the adulterous queen; by it the Prophets and Apostles poured forth the messages which are still so pregnant with etherial fire; by it the martyrs and confessors made the emblem of a slave's death triumph over brutal armies and pagan emperors, and with "the irresistible might of weakness" shook the world. What was it but enthusiasm which inspired Origen the Adamantine, when, at the age of fourteen, he stretched forth a hand that longed for the crown of martyrdom? or Athanasius, when, at the Council of Nice, he rose up in a flame of zeal to denounce the giant heretic? or Luther, when going to face angry priests and threatening princes, he said that, if there were devils on every tile of the roofs of Worms, he would go there still? or Milton, when in his great pure youth he looked at abuses "with such an eye as struck Gehazi with leprosy, and Simon Magus with a curse"? or Whitfield, when, 'amid the pelting scorn of half an age,' he stood up at taverns and drunken fairs to preach the love of God to low women and degraded men? or Henry Martyn when, with strange folly as men thought, he left the brilliant prospects of a Cambridge senior wranglership, to preach and fail among the heathen, and to die a few years afterwards in lonely anguish, vainly trying to cool his fevered head by thrusting it among the damp boxes of his luggage? Why, these are the men who in their eccentricity of goodness, their fanaticism of faith, tower above the dead and sluggish level of ordinary Christianity, as some volcano of the West—an Orizaba or a Chimborazo—which rears its majestic summit into the still depths of the aerial ocean, whose sides are clothed with every season and every clime, and whose burning crown shines forth like a beacon to the mariner over leagues of the rolling and barren sea. And when our grovelling comforts are ended, when our poor accumulations are scattered, when our petty self-importances are forgotten or remembered only with a smile, and when *we* stand afar off among the dense common universal herd of those who may have loved God a little, but who loved mammon much,—these men, and such as these, aye, some of those who have been scorned as the very dregs and outcasts of the earth, "the faithful who were not famous," common, vulgar, unknown people, of whom bishops might very humbly have asked a blessing,—before kings, and conquerors, and priests, and learned men, shall be beckoned into the nearer presence, into the more glorious felicity of that Saviour who chose not His companions among Pharisees and formalists, but honoured with the harvest of regenerated nations the passionate zeal of Peter the fisherman, and the burning love of Paul and John.

If you would obey your Saviour's summons, you too must catch the same kindling love. But if not, if you want to eat and drink and make money and be successful, if you want to walk in tame smooth avenues, answering the world according to its idols, and never letting the stroke of your challenge ring on the broad shield of its hypocrisies, if, in short, you would live as though you were your own, and Christ had not bought you with His blood,—why then you must remain in the congregation of the dead. You may live a decent life, but it will not be a noble one. You will in heart prefer Mammon to Christ; you will deliberately prefer mean successes to splendid failures. Not for you will be the glory of consecrated knowledge, or the rich blessings of him who turns a soul from the error of his ways; not for you the steady love of good even if it be persecuted, or the steady scorn of evil even if it be enthroned,—but for you the frivolous insipidity of unreverend amusements,—the dull and discontented mind ignoble when with others, wretched when alone. Great deeds will be done, but you will not be at the doing of them; high thoughts uttered, but they shall wake no echo in the seared conscience and the sodden heart. Beyond you shall sweep the godlike procession of the nobly virtuous and the greatly wise, but you shall not be of them. And so flake after flake, and fold on fold, the chilling cares of an unprofitable and unpitied life will fall upon you, and your souls will be grey with age and satiety and weariness, long years before the grey hairs crown your heads. Successful you may be, honoured you may be, rich you may be, *but you will be dead.* Your course will be strewn even from youth with the white ashes of burnt-out passions, or, if you escape this swifter destiny, you will still be heavy, and clogged, and, surfeited, and, in the scornful intensity of the Psalmist's image, "*Your hearts will be fat as brawn.*"

But, in conclusion, if you follow Christ, what shall be your reward? And here let us not be mistaken; Christianity is no far-sighted prudence[1], no vulgar aiming at a mere absence of disappointment and of pain; if you serve with a selfish eye to the reward your service will not be accepted; you must love the battle not the victory, the work not the success; you must be prepared to perish, the forlorn hope of humanity, in the yet unconquered breach; you must be prepared, again and again, "to give up your broken sword to Fate the conqueror with a humble and a manly heart." As the world goes, your reward shall be nothing—not the palace or the equipage, not the marble monument or the wreath of fame;—these may be won by "intense selfishness, intense worldliness, intense hardness of heart," but *your* nobler reward shall be the bleeding feet which yet are beautiful upon the mountains, and the aching brow which shall have an aureole for crown. Successful? nay such a man may be miserable,—miserable as many a Prophet has been before him, amid the shout of the world's hatred and the sneers of its merciless contempt—and yet "In the willing agony he plunges and is blest[2]." He will thank

---

[1] Froude.   [2] Newman's Poems.

God daily, from his inmost heart, that he is thought worthy of that high suffering; nor would he change it for anything the world could give, or anything which it can take away. "Felix est qui sic miser est;"—the breath of God shall be to him as "a moist whistling wind" amid the glare of the streaming flame[1], and in the world's burnt wilderness his food shall be manna from the Paradise of God.

And surely, brethren, such lessons should be easier in a place like this, where not only is Christ's example daily set before you, but where His steps have been followed so often in Christ-like lives. This is no vulgar home in which it is your high privilege to dwell, but a home haunted by the spirits of the immortal and the wise. In our chapels the martyrs have worshipped, in our cloisters the saints have trod. From our halls their honoured and familiar faces look down upon us with a grace of more distinct humanity. It was here, in the quiet court of

---

[1] "So that the flame streamed forth from the furnace forty and nine cubits ... But the angel of the Lord came down into the oven ...... and made the midst of the furnace as it had been a moist whistling wind, so that the fire touched them not at all, neither hurt, nor troubled them." *Song of The Three Children*, 24—27.

Pembroke, that Ridley paced up and down, Greek Testament in hand, learning by heart the Epistles of St Paul; it was here, in Caius College, that Bp Jeremy Taylor learnt, in the sweetness of humility, that fervent yet tender eloquence which has all the melody of a lyric song; it was here, in Christ's College, that Milton fed his young and fiery heart with the passionate scorn of all things base; it was here, in the noble courts of Trinity College, that Bacon and Newton and Ray learnt that if we "toil in God's works with the sweat of our brow, He will make us partakers of His vision and His Sabbath[1]." Let us live worthy of these famous men, and the fathers who begat us; let *us* too strive to be of those, into whom the Spirit of God entering in all ages, has made them Sons of God and Prophets. These are as the beacon-heights, which, from generation to generation, have caught and reflected back the risen light of the Sun of Righteousness; it is good to gaze upon their brightness; but it is better far to fix our eyes upon the source from which it sprang, and, "with open face, reflecting as in a glass the glory of the Lord, to be changed into the same image from glory to glory." So may we all—with willing

[1] Lord Bacon's Prayer.

self-abandonment, with long toil, with burning zeal,—through praise or blame, through success or failure, in peace or in agony of heart,—follow Christ now, that we may see His face hereafter, and, whithersoever He goeth, be not found absent from His side.

IV.

RESURRECTION FROM THE DEAD.

(Preached before Harrow School, June 28, 1863.)

Rom. viii. 21.—"The creature itself also shall be delivered from the bondage of corruption."

"I KNOW that ye seek Jesus who was crucified. He is not here; He is risen, as He said." So spake the sweet angel voices to those devoted women whose love made them the last beside the cross of Jesus, and the earliest at His tomb. So spake the sweet angel voices, and their words roll to us with the divine echoes of joy and hope over the long interspace of 1800 years. Hardly less sweet are these memories of Christ's Resurrection to us who have reached the age of manhood or declining years, than are the merry bells and blithe carols that tell of the Nativity to the mirthful and the young. To them in the bright morning of life belong especially the rejoicings which fitly commemorate that holy infancy of Jesus, so full of favour with God and man; to us, who have all drunk some drops of His bitter cup, and felt some sparks of His fiery baptism, belong rather the triumphs and the hopes which, as our years draw onward and pass into the ever-deepening shade, remind us, with stronger significance, that our Lord and Master died as we must soon die, and that He put His foot upon the skull of death, that He might still the groan of a travailing creation, and take from us all dread of the conquered foe.

We are told that most savage nations live in a constant horror of death; their life is one long flight from it; it poisons their happiness; it bursts like a ghastly phantom upon their moments of peace. It is not death the agony that they shudder at, though there may be something terrible in that, but death the mystery, and "next to God the most infinite of mysteries;" death that slips the last cable of the soul, and sets it afloat on the shoreless sea of an eternal world; there it is that lies for them "the mute, ineffable, voiceless horror before which all human courage is abashed." Can you wonder at this continuous dread? They know of no world beyond the grave, and what would life be without the trust in that? How purposeless and mean, how weary and hopeless; a journey leading nowhither; a gate opening upon nothing; a ship sent forth only that she may founder in the bare unknown deeps. Look steadily at life, and consider what it is: how changeful, how short, how sorrowful. A light and thoughtless youth, of which the beauty and brightness pass rapidly away; and after that, chance, and change, and bereavement; cravings that meet with no fulfilment; the dying away of hopes, the disappointment of ambition,—a disappointment, perhaps, more bitter when it is gratified than when it fails; the struggle for a livelihood, the cares of a family, the deceitfulness of friendship, the decay and weakness of health and the faculties, as inevitable old age comes on; and all the while heard at every silent interval with a plainness that creeps along the nerves, as though our ears caught the pacing of some ghostly tread in the far-off corridors of some lonely haunted house—all the while the monotonous echoing of death's mysterious footfall, heard louder and louder, as day by day he approaches nearer and yet more near. And all this for so short a time that our petty schemes are broken off perpetually like a weaver's thread, and the meanest works of our hands survive us, and last on for other generations to which our very names shall be covered with darkness. "And is this all? Is this then the period of our being? Must we end here? Did we come into the world only to make our way through the press, amid many jostlings and hard struggles, with at best only a few brief deceitful pleasures interspersed, and so go out of it again?" Alas for man if this were all, and nought beyond, oh earth!

And then again, if there be no resurrection of the dead, how infinitely pathetic, how quite unspeakably heartrending, would be the phenomena of death itself. "If Christ be not risen, then is our preaching vain; and your faith is also vain; and we are found false witnesses of God; and ye are yet in your sins; and"—all this is terrible enough, but mark the pathos of the climax, a pathos too deep for tears—"and then they also that are fallen asleep in Christ are perished." Perished! what a world of desolate anguish, what sighs of unutterable despair, lie hid in that strange word. Most of you are too young to have ever stood, as all the eldest of us have, by the bedside of death; but none of you are too young to feel how awful such a scene would be if we did not believe, and know, that Christ has risen from the dead. There on that low bed lies one we loved, for whom our whole hearts yearned, to whom our whole affections clung; he was noble and good, he was one of the very few who loved us, and he would have undergone for us any sacrifice, and he had borne bravely and meekly the buffets of the world. It was a short life, hardly chequered (good and beautiful and upright as it was), hardly chequered with any sunshine amid its shade: and now it is over; it ends here; the bright eye is dull and glazed; the gentle face is white and cold; the good brave heart has ceased to beat. He has no more a part in anything that is done under the sun. The day was when he would have sprung to meet us, his whole face brightened at our approach; and now he lies there, cold to the voice of our affection, unmoved by our hot tears, with all the light of the soul quenched within him; gone, if there be no resurrection, to a dreary land where all things are forgotten; all that was good in him, all that was great in him, perished for ever, as we and ours must perish soon. Oh, if there were no resurrection, how could we bear it? would not the thought crush us down for very grief into the same open grave?

Many of you will have read the famous vision of him who saw a bridge of threescore and ten arches, which spanned the rolling waters of a prodigious tide, and how the Genius said to him, "The bridge thou seest is Human Life; consider it attentively." And as I looked more attentively I saw several of the passengers dropping through the bridge into the great tide that flowed underneath it; and upon examination perceived that there were innumerable trap-doors, concealed in the bridge, which the passengers no sooner trod upon, but they fell through them into the tide and immediately disappeared. My heart was filled with a deep melancholy to see several dropping unexpectedly in the midst of mirth and jollity, and catching at everything that stood by them to save themselves. Multitudes were very busy in the pursuit of bubbles that glittered in their eyes and danced before them; but often when they thought themselves within reach of them, their footing failed, and down they sunk. "Alas!" said I, "man was made in vain! how is he given away to misery and mortality! tortured in life and swallowed up in death!"

And consider how frightful it would then be to live, as we *are* living in a world, in an

universe of death. Frightful, if there be no resurrection; but, thank God, *we believe in the resurrection of the dead.* Many a time have such thoughts swept across my mind, as I have stood gazing on the rich landscape from the summit of our churchyard-hill; never I think more overwhelmingly than they did but two days back, troubling every chord of thought into a sweet though melancholy music which I vainly endeavour to recall. It was one of those golden summer evenings for whose peaceful loveliness, so sweet in its influence upon the anxious heart, we ought ever to thank God. The sun was setting, not in torrid and crimson splendour, but in a haze of soft light, which bathed the green fields in its quiet lustre. From the cricket-field below, the pleasant evening breeze brought to my ears the sounds of continuous enjoyment,— shout after shout, and peal on peal, of happy laughter. It was natural, it was harmless, that among those who were enjoying that hour of innocent gladness, death should be the very remotest of all thoughts. But it could not be so with me. I had just heard of the death of one who was a boy here but three years back. And around me the dead were lying, into whose ears the sound of laughter cannot come;

and nearest to me, at my feet, lay the mortal body of another also who but a short time back was one of you. But two short years ago I well remembered to have seen him at that annual holiday so long looked forward to; there he had not only been mirthful among the mirthful, and gay among the gay, but he had attracted my special notice and attention by the unusual exuberance of his mirth, by the exciting unchecked flow of his natural gaiety. I little thought then that I should so soon see the flowers blossoming upon his grave. Sad indeed, beyond all sadness, if the bright river of human life had no other ending save in that dark sea. But even then I remembered that it was not so; that for the body there is a resurrection, for the soul an immortality; that death and the worm are not the universal conquerors; that death and sin are not the powers or the realities of the universe, but lying rebels which for our sakes God hath vanquished and trampled under foot; that with a body the same though glorified, with a soul the same though infinitely enlarged, we shall live when time itself shall be no more; the same,—but baptized, we trust, in the river of the water of life, and with all its many many blots and stains washed white in the precious blood of Christ the Lamb. And so at last, stately, and full of wonder, and full of music, as though uttered by the voices of the Cherubim, the words of revelation crowded upon my memory, "We shall not all sleep, but we shall all be changed; in a moment, in the twinkling of an eye, at the last trump: for the trumpet shall sound, and the dead shall be raised incorruptible, and we shall be changed. For this corruptible must put on incorruption, and this mortal must put on immortality." Even so as we had heard the words, and read them in dim churches with eyes made blind with tears;— and thinking of them, even while we recall our own beloved ones who sleep under the sod far away in English villages or Indian churchyards, can we not rise above all the dust and turmoil of this wretched world, and do not our hearts add, as with a cymbal-clang of exultation, "O death, where is thy sting? O grave, where is thy victory?"

Yes, Christ is risen. O how do those words change the whole aspect of human life! The sunlight that gleams forth after the world has been drenched, and dashed, and terrified with the black thunder-drops, reawakening the song of birds and reilluminating the bloom of the folded flowers, does not more gloriously transfigure the landscape than those words transfigure the life of man. Nothing short of this could be our pledge and proof that we also shall arise. We are not left to dim intimations of it from the reminiscences of childhood; vague hopes of it in exalted moments; splendid guesses of it in ancient pages; faint analogies of it from the dawn of day, and the renovation of spring, and the quickened grain, and the butterfly shaking itself free of the enclosing chrysalis to wave its wings in the glories of summer light: all this might create a longing, the sense of some far-off possibility in a few chosen souls, but not for all the weary and suffering sons of humanity a permanent and ennobling conviction, a sure and certain hope. But Christ is risen, and we have it now; a thought to comfort us in the gloom of adversity, a belief to raise us into the high privilege of sons of God. They that are fallen asleep in Christ are not perished. Look into the Saviour's empty and angel-haunted tomb; He hath burst for us the bonds of the prison-house; He hath shattered at a touch the iron bars and brazen gates; He hath rifled the house of the spoiler, and torn away the serpent's sting; " He is not here, He is risen as He said." They that sleep in all those narrow graves shall wake again, shall rise again. Weep not, oh widowed wife, for him whose image was in thy heart; for thou shalt see him again. Weep not, oh father, for that gallant son, whose lifeblood welled out as he lay face upward on the field of death. Weep not, oh orphan boy, for the sainted mother, whose kiss shall never again be warm upon thy brow. Thy dead men shall live; they that sleep in the dust of the earth shall arise; out of the dust of the earth shall they unfold the wings wrapped within them, and rise redeemed from earth, and fly under the sunlight, and shake from their stained cerements the ashes of mortality and death. In innumerable myriads from the earth, and from the river, and from the rolling waves of the mighty sea, shall they start up at the sounding of that angel trumpet; from peaceful churchyards, from bloody battle-fields, from the catacomb and from the pyramid, from the marble monument and the mountain-cave, great and small, saint and prophet and apostle, and thronging multitudes of unknown martyrs and unrecorded heroes, in every age and every climate, on whose forehead was the Lamb's seal—they shall come forth from the power of Death and Hell. What a mighty victory! what a giant spoiling! what a trampling of the last enemy beneath the feet! Aye, Death smote for ages God's fair creation, he lifted up his hand against the Lord's anointed, he seemed as irresistible as terrible; and yet not kings only and mighty men, but the soul of the meanest beggar that ever died of want in the crowded city street, and the soul of the tenderest newborn infant that passed away like a thin breath of air a thousand years ago, shall be delivered safe and uninjured, yea, glorified and immortal, out of his armed and icy hand! What a hope, I say again, what a change in the thought of life! Bravely and happily let us walk through this Dark Valley; for though the rocks overshadow, and the Phantom haunts it, at the end of it is a door of hope—a door of Immortality that opens on the gardens of heaven, and the trees and streams of life. A dim, weary, troubled life here perhaps, if God sees fit, ended by a spasm, a struggle, an agony,—and then to have the whole soul flooded by the sense of a newer and grander being, and our tears wiped away by God's own hand. This is the Christian's hope, and truly herein Christ maketh us more than conquerors; more than conquerors, for we not only triumph over the enemy, but profit by him, wringing out of his curse a blessing; out of his prison a coronation and a home. "It is sown in corruption, it is raised in incorruption; it is sown in dishonour, it is raised in glory; it is sown in weakness, it is raised in power; it is sown a natural body, it is raised a spiritual body."

Entering, my brethren as we all are on a season of unusual holiday, and unusual excitement, a season which might well tempt you to think that life was meant for pleasure, and for idleness, and for sunshine only, I have been influenced irresistibly to turn your attention to those mighty thoughts, and those mighty themes, which are best fitted to remind us of the solemn grandeur and awful reality of life. For sobriety is the girdle of all innocent enjoyment, and the amethyst which can alone preserve you from the intoxication of excess. Nor am I anxious now, even if the time permitted me, to impress on you those vast lessons which flow naturally and at once from truths like these. To the Holy Spirit of God I pray that He may write with His own finger even on the stoniest hearts the truth that if your bodies or souls be now mastered by evil passions, with that same dishallowed body, with that same desecrated soul, unless it be cleansed, you will stand before the burning eye of God; that if you are sowing to the flesh, in that flesh and of that flesh shall you reap corruption; that whatsoever things you have done in the body, those very same things, not other things, you will receive. O let not one of those who hear me forget this; and thou that hast been false to the simple, and cruel to the timid; thou that hast hindered the diligent, and corrupted the innocent, and thwarted the good, thinkest thou not that if there be one thing more damning than another, it will be, when amid the infinite judgment hall, one whom thou knowest and shalt recognise, will arise to point at thee the finger of condemnation, and raising the voice, whose wailing thou hast often caused, until it peals above the sentence of a thousand dooms, shall say "*I* have perished in my unrepented sins, and shall *he* escape who first planted in my breast the seeds of hell?"

It was over such as these that the very lips of love pronounced their immortality to be a curse, saying, "It were well for that man if he had never been born." My brethren, what shall become of such as these? Who knoweth? Curtains of impenetrable darkness, gulfs of fathomless mystery conceal them from us, and we know not. Let those who will deal out upon them the precise form and fact of their damnation, and assert its finality, and with the hands of human feebleness trifle with the very thunderbolts of heaven. Let others, if they will, condemn those who refuse to dogmatise when God has not spoken, and brand with their reproach of heretic the men who will not bar up against their brethren the irrevocable gates of hell. For me, I will never assert that of which neither I, nor any man, knows or can know anything beyond the very little which God has positively revealed. The form, the fashion, the duration, of that which may be hereafter I know not; but this I do know, and have said before, that Heaven and Hell are not distant localities, not golden cities in the far-off blue, or lakes of brimstone in the central fire, but that they are now, and that they are here. The pure, the peaceful, the loving, the earnest heart, that is heaven now; the guilty, the coward, the useless, the corrupted, the envious, the discontented heart, that is hell now, and, till purged and cleansed, can never be anything but a hell, which the worm and the fire can make no worse. Yes, the Eternal is not opposite to the Temporal, but to the Visible; it is not a period, but a condition; not a locality, but a state; not a thing of the future, but of the for-ever. Let us live with the sense of it about us now, and then we cannot live those utterly dreary, empty, idle, unprofitable, vicious lives which we sometimes see. The eternal things are all around us. Let us then live in purity, knowing that no step that defileth can pass over the golden streets. Let us live in love, lest we blush, with burning shame, to find that God honours, and the Lamb of God receives into his bosom, those whom we coldly neglected, or wickedly despised. Let us live in humility, lest God punish our pride and leave us in horrible dispraise. So will Eternity unveil itself to us more and more in our daily walk, "So will the Love, and the Goodness, and the Truth which lie at the foundation of the Universe come out to us through all the thick clouds which our selfishness, and the selfishness of men have raised to hide them from us. We shall learn that they belong to us, and that there is in them a power to make us like to them, and to make our acts in conformity to them[1]." This shall make us noble and happy in life; this shall strengthen us to smile at death; this shall

[1] Prof. Maurice, in a Sermon on 2 Cor. iv. 18, which is one of the noblest and loftiest sermons either of ancient or modern times which it was ever my happiness to read.

cause us to live all our days in the continual light of those two most marvellous of all Christian truths,

The resurrection of the body—the immortality of the Soul.

V.

ASCENSION WITH CHRIST.

(Preached before Harrow School on Ascension Day 1865.)

ACTS i. 9.—"And a cloud received him out of their sight."

AND that cloud still remains. To *their* eyes doubtless it was luminous as the floor of heaven, —soft and beautiful as those that lie cradled near the setting sun, and do but vail its too blinding splendour; but to the eyes of the world, and oftentimes to our own, it has grown thicker, and blacker, and more vast; it has rolled its darkness over the blue sky; it has blotted out the light of day; not even the rainbow circles it; it has become a cloud of wrath and terror, and no gleam save that of the lightning tears a way out of its lurid depths. It is no mere fleeting mist which has hidden Christ the Sun of Righteousness from our eyes, but an earthborn fog, bred in the dismal region of unbelief, reeking upwards from the abysses of human guilt; sin is its very substance, and an unhallowed pride, and a dreary science, and a godless criticism, and an unredeemable despair, have all added fold on fold to that midnight screen. So that now we see not in its brightness that beloved face, marred more than the face of any man with sorrow for our sakes,—that face like our own face, bends down no longer to listen to our prayers; no longer, as upon the dying martyr, does it beam the tenderness of its compassion over the trials of our daily life; no longer, as on "the fusile Apostle", does it flash the sense of unutterable conviction on our doubting souls. Men have long been asking 'where is the promise of His coming?' And as century after century, millennium after millennium, has sped by in its deep unbroken silence,—as no voice from heaven has made itself heard during long æons of ignorance, of error, and of crime,—as no new word of revelation has stilled the passions of fanatic enthusiasm, and the battle-cry of deluded sects,—as the world has sunk more and more into the dead and dreary level of a life given up to its farm and its merchandise,—men have learnt to say in their hearts 'There is no God,' or, if there is, He has withdrawn Himself far away into His inmost heaven, and cares nothing for such worms, such atoms as men are, nor do His ears hear the cry of their lamentation, nor do His eyes behold the scarlet of their sins. And thus have men lost the sense that a Man like themselves, but divine, immortal, infinite, loves them and is loved by them; that a Voice like their own voice comes through the thunder; that a hand like their own shall fling open to them the gate of life;—and losing this they have lost with it all the charm, and all the sunlight, and all the dignity of life. In the night there is no gracious presence to enlighten; in the storm no gentle voice to utter 'It is I, be not afraid.' The cloud has hidden Christ out of their sight. Lord, on this Ascension day may it not be so with us; may the dark clouds of sin, and of unbelief, that hide thee from us be rolled away; may we see thy face, and see Thee as thou art, and seeing Thee be changed into thy likeness from glory to glory!

Yes, may we see Him; and then we too shall be full of joy, as were the holy Apostles when those glittering angels told them that He should come again. Then shall the sky be dark no longer, but bright as with the light of seven suns; then shall the Voice of God be hushed no more, but heard in every murmur of the world and every echo of the soul. Then nothing shall conquer, nothing shall affright us; if it please the Lord to bruise us with many troubles, even then we shall not quail, for He who liveth and was dead has borne them all. And if looking upon "that hideous thing a naked human heart" we are appalled to think that all these evil monsters which lurk in its sunless caverns, are ever bare before the Father of Lights,—or if, again, while we gaze on the great sins of society, on the hidden cancers that eat it away, on the crimes and miseries that ever seethe amid the moral corruption of its swarming myriads, we are half tempted to atheism or to despair, then we are comforted, even to exultation, by the thought that "the very nature which we see, which we feel to be capable of such infinite degradation, your nature and mine, has been taken, redeemed, justified, glorified by the Son of Man, and that in that same nature, undivested of a single attribute save sin, human yet perfect, He stands as our High Priest and Representative at the right hand of God." Feel then, my brethren even to the youngest of you, feel, I pray you, with great joy that Ascension Day is a day of triumph, of glorious triumph, for which the mightiest clang of the whole world's minstrelsy and music were not too loud. For what have we to fear any longer? the only enemies we had ever need to fear were Sin, and Death, and Hell ; and look how high the heaven is from the earth, so far hath God removed our *Sins* from us ; and *Hell* we are told shall deliver up her dead, and be flung into a lake of fire; and, putting all enemies beneath his feet, Christ shall crush last the skull of Death. It is our pledge of victory in the Armageddon of the world ; the victory of truth over lies, of God's love over the devil's hate, of the slave over his oppressor, of divine glory over human degradation, of the spirit over the flesh, of God's transcendent power and mercy over man's corrupt and fallen will. Enter into the spirit of your own beautiful hymns which catch that thunder tone of triumph,—

> Now empty are the courts of death,
>   And crushed thy sting, despair,
> And roses bloom in the desert tomb,
>   For Jesus hath been there!
>
> And he hath tamed the strength of hell,
>   And dragged him through the sky,
> And captive behind his chariot-wheel
>   He hath bound captivity.
>
> God is gone up with a merry noise
>   Of saints that sing on high;
> With his own right hand and his holy arm
>   He hath won the victory.

Bear with me, then, my brethren, while very briefly and simply I point out to you, without attempting fully to enforce or to expand, the obvious lessons which result at once from Christ's Ascension; may we so realise them that the cloud which hides Him from us shall pass away.

1. And the first is heavenly-mindedness. 'Lift up your heads, oh ye gates; and be ye lift up ye everlasting doors; and the King of glory shall come in;' yes, but not He alone. When the triumphs of the chariots of God, even thousands of angels, swept behind Him in their unseen procession, the everlasting portals closed not after them; they are open still, open to us, and to our race, and through them pass, and shall pass till the end of time, the thronging souls of the redeemed. He went to prepare a place for those whom He loved; He went up on high, He led captivity captive, to receive gifts for men, "yea even for his enemies, that the Lord God might dwell among them." He went but as the great forerunner of his people, and we must follow in his course; where the Head is there should the members be; and our treasure, our life, our affection are meant to be with Him at the right hand of God. O how long then shall our hearts be grovelling in the world; how long

shall they be tossed like bubbles on the waves of its unrest; how long shall they be covered with the dust of its meanness and the stain of its sins: shall they never unfold the wings wrapped within them, and thither ascend, and shake the mire of earthliness from the white robes of spiritual resurrection? Shall they thus stoop, and pine, and waste away for ever? O rather let us hear the cries that come to us from heaven above and from the earth beneath, from the works of nature, and the voices of conscience, and from the wail of the weary, and from all the graves of men, the cry of *Sursum corda*, 'Lift up your hearts;' and from every one of us let the answer be 'We lift them up unto the Lord.'

2. And the second lesson is a lesson of simple duty. In that Epistle which I have already quoted so often, which is emphatically the Epistle of the Ascension, and of which the Ascension is the very idea and motive, I mean the Epistle to the Ephesians, this is the aspect of the doctrine which is always urged. Read it for yourselves and see. Because Christ is very high exalted, because we are raised up together with Him and sit together in heavenly places, therefore we are told in it to be lowly,

and meek, and to forbear one another in love, to put off the old man which is corrupt according to the deceitful lusts, to put away theft, and lying, and corrupt communication out of our mouths, and foolishness, and filthy talking, and inconvenient jesting, and the fellowship with those unfruitful works of darkness and secrecy of which it is a shame even to speak; for now being light in the Lord, ye are to walk as children of the light. You see the simplest, the plainest, the vulgarest morality if you will, is also the loftiest and the most sublime. You are not bidden to the martyr's agony, or to the hermit's cell; you are bidden only to live your ordinary lives, to go through the trivial round, the common task, as the servants of Him who looketh down on you from his lofty throne; to abstain from lying, and evil speaking, and youthful lusts, because Christ your king and captain hath ascended into the heavens, and no unclean person or idolater hath any inheritance in the kingdom of Christ or of God. It is the same plain and unvarnished and homely lesson which is taught in two of those glorious Psalms which the Church has appointed for the service of to-day. "Lord, who shall dwell in thy tabernacle, or who shall rest upon thy holy hill?" is it only the lofty, the unapproachable, the devoted, the timely-happy? no, but common men who by God's grace have lived their common lives in the paths of purity and duty, the lowly, the undeceitful, the unmalicious, the uncorrupt. Who shall ascend into the hill of the Lord, or who shall rise up in his holy place? Even he that hath clean hands and a pure heart; "he who doeth the thing which is right, and speaketh the truth from his heart. He who doeth these things shall never fall."

3. And the third is a lesson of holy fear. My brethren, how are you living? What kind of lives are yours? What things are most often on your thoughts and lips? are your minds set upon right, oh ye congregation? If so your souls are delivered for ever from craven fear, for He that is very high exalted defendeth you as with a shield, keepeth you as the apple of His eye, treasureth you as the jewels of the Lord, bindeth up your names in the bundle of life. But, if not—if your's is the wicked boldness which bids you defy God and walk after your own lusts—if your's is the soul-corrupting ideal of the world, scorning meekness, and diligence, and purity, and faith—if pride, and passion, and pleasure are your gods—if your's are deadly habits

> "Sported like a crown
> Upon the insolent aspiring brow
> Of spurious notions,"

then fear, and tremble; yea, every soul among that godless band tremble and shiver as the skeleton leaves of the naked grove that sigh, and tremble, and shiver in the November wind. Fear, for your sin will find you out; fear, for the root of your prosperity shall be as rottenness, and the blossom of your strength and beauty shall go up as dust. Fear, for you have made God your enemy; fear, for from the throne whereon He reigns, far above all principality and power and every name that is named, His scorching eye, which is as a flame of fire, burns into the unbared secrets of your souls; fear, for though hand join in hand your wickedness shall not be unpunished; fear, for death is nigh, and after death the judgment and the eternity; fear, for to you the throne of the Ascended Saviour shall be more terrible than flaming peaks of Sinai; fear, for as He ascended, so shall He one day descend to awful judgment, 'thundering omnipotent vengeance on the astonished ear,' dashing His foes to pieces like a potter's vessel with His iron rod, charioted on the rolling clouds and armed with the consuming fires, with that face before which the heaven and the earth shall flee away. Will the world's banded effeminacies, will the world's gilded lures, will the world's delicate pleasures, will the world's insolent ideal, serve you then? Oh if you be an impenitent and hardened sinner, and will continue impenitent and hardened still, then *fear;* for then to you the lesson of Christ's Ascension is a lesson of wrath and doom.

4. But lastly, if you be loving justice and mercy, and walking humbly with your God, if you be striving, however faintly, to be true and pure and good, then the lesson of the Ascension is a lesson of hope. It is a pledge to us of that forgiveness which Christ died to win. You may have fallen very low; the white robes of your baptismal innocence may have contracted many and many a stain; yet you may be full of hope: "though ye have lien among the pots, yet shall ye be as the wings of a dove which is covered with silver wings, and her feathers like gold." For Christ is our Intercessor. Once in the year, washed, and crowned, and clothed in fine white linen, bearing in his hand the incense of kindling perfumes, sprinkling the blood of the sacrifice upon the consecrated gold, passed the Jewish High Priest through the embroidered curtain

into the Holiest Place, and then, reclad in the splendid vestures of priesthood, in blue and purple and crimson, woven with pomegranates and fringed with bells, he came forth to bless the people, while on his breast shone the Urim and Thummim ardent with oracular gems. But this ceremonial of gorgeous significance was but the antetype of a truer propitiation. For us, in the shining vesture of a stainless life, with the nobler sacrifice of His own blood, and the more fragrant incense of His own prayers, has passed on this day through the blue and starry Vail of Heaven our great High Priest for ever to the throne of his never-ending rule. And therefore when we are summoned to the bar of God's Judgment-seat, we may hope: for the soft rainbow like unto an emerald encircles it, and we have an Intercessor; humble yet unabashed may we stand where the very seraphs must vail their faces with their wings, for He is by our side. And it shall be with us as with Joshua the High Priest in Zechariah's vision, when he stood before God, and Satan stood at his right hand to resist him: "And the Lord said unto Satan, The Lord rebuke thee; even the Lord that hath chosen Jerusalem, rebuke thee: is not this a brand plucked from the burning? Now Joshua was clothed with filthy garments, and stood before the angel. And he said unto those which stood before him, Take away the filthy garments from him; and unto him he said, Behold, I have caused thine iniquity to pass from thee, and I will clothe thee with change of raiment....So they set a fair mitre upon his head, and clothed him with garments, and the angel of the Lord stood by." Oh with the thought of an Intercessor such as this, to the skirts of whose garment we may cling and be safe, who will save us from our sins, and hide our shameful nakedness with His own white robe, oh with such thoughts as this is not the lesson of the Ascension, for those who love, for those who try to love their Lord, is it not a lesson of infinite peace and hope?

Oh my young brethren, if you forget, as you will forget at the first light word which meets your ears after you have left the chapel doors, these teachings of heavenly-mindedness, of duty, of fear, of hope, yet take with you, I pray you even to the youngest, this one simple thought; that Christ your King, your Saviour, your High Priest, who wears your nature, who knows your temptations, who mourns over your sins, who reads your hearts, is living still, living in heaven, watching you with love and hope, drawing you to himself, turning away your eyes from the bewildering magic, and the crushing disappointment, and the scathing curse of a world that ruins and deceives; searching, even at this moment, with love or grief the most secret thoughts of your very hearts. Do you think that you can conceal them, if they are thoughts of sin and shame? oh no! the cloud, that has received Him out of your sight is no cloud to Him; oh pray that it may be no cloud to us, no cloud to you. Believe me then will life itself be different to you, and lit with the light of heaven.

> —"Believe thou, oh my soul,
> Life is a vision shadowy of truth;
> And vice, and anguish, and the wormy grave,
> Shapes of a dream! The veiling clouds retire,
> And lo! the Throne of the redeeming God,
> Forth flashing unimaginable day,
> Wraps in one blaze earth, heaven, and deepest hell."

VI.

THE IMMORTALITY AND THE MEANNESS OF MAN.

(Preached at Nottingham, during the Meeting of the British Association, August 1866.)

Ps. viii 4.—"What is man, that thou art mindful of him? and the son of man, that thou visitest him?"

MANY of you may have seen last year the painting of a great artist in which he represents King David sitting alone on his palace-roof during the last flush of a summer-day. The once fair and ruddy face is aged and sorrowful, the once bright locks are streaked with silver, the once smooth forehead is ploughed with the furrows of care. His own hands have eased his brow of the glittering circlet of sovereignty, which is lying neglected beside his feet, and the arm that smote the Philistine rests wearily on the parapet of the roof. Far away, into one deep gleam of unbroken blue, some doves are winging their soft flight, and the King as he follows them with his wistful gaze, seems to be murmuring to himself, 'O that I had wings like a dove, for then would I flee away and be at rest;'—or, meditating it may be on his own stained and sin-bewildered life, he is inspired with the yearning prophecy, "Though ye have lien among the pots, yet shall ye be as the wings of a dove, that is covered with silver wings, and her feathers like gold."

On some such evening as the painter has embodied, but in a brighter and more hopeful mood, David had again been sitting at eventide upon his palace-roof, and the sun had set, and from the bulwarks and battlements of Jerusalem, and from the olives that rested in grey clouds over the hills around, the last blush of evening had faded, and overhead the moon had begun to shine, and the stars to gather and gather for the mighty march of their unnumbered hosts, until the whole heavens seemed bursting into starlit depths. How did David feel, as he gazed on that soul-annihilating spectacle? did his mortal spirit reel and stagger under the sense of infinitude? was he like the modern poet, half-crushed to gaze on those

> Innumerable, pitiless, passionless eyes,
> Cold fires, yet with power to burn and brand
> His nothingness into man?

Let this Psalm answer;—for, as he was musing the fire burned, and he burst into those rapt and glowing words—words which come surging upon the memory of many of us on the rolling waves of organ-music and choral song,—"O Lord, our Governour, how excellent is thy name in all the world, thou that hast set thy glory above the heavens;—when I consider thy heavens, the work of thy fingers, the moon and the stars which thou hast ordained, what is man that thou art mindful of him, and the son of man that thou visitest him?"—And then, in an instant, as with a mighty reflux of thought, the answer comes, What is he? not one to quail before the thought of immensity, but to pervade it with his mighty destinies! not one to be crushed before the dread glory of the unintelligent creation, but to be its lord and king, not one to worship the orbs of heaven, but to weigh them and measure them, and discover the constituents of which they are made. "Thou madest him a little lower than the angels;" no, not than the angels, as our English Version has it, but thou madest him a little lower than God, "thou hast crowned him with glory and honour; thou madest him to have dominion over the works of thy hands, thou hast put all things under his feet."

Very different is the response to the same question in that Psalm (the 144th) which David seems to have written, not in the quiet hour of meditation, but in the proud moment of victory and success. There too he asks 'What is man?' but there the answer comes, (more like the wail of a dying penitent than the song of a triumphant king), "man is like a thing of nought, his time passeth away like a shadow;" and then, as though longing to be delivered from the whole mean and malignant crew of enemies and blasphemers that encircles him, he cries, "Bow thy heavens, oh Lord, and come down: touch the mountains, and they shall smoke: cast forth thy lightning, and tear them, shoot out thine arrows, and consume them." It is the same when on the lips of the ruined Job the same question is repeated; and it is as though both Job and David were to cry in the spirit of the modern singer,

"Let the heavens burst and drown with deluging storms
The feeble vassals of wine, and anger, and lust,
The little hearts that know not how to forgive.
Arise, my God, and strike, for we hold thee just,—
We are not worthy to live."

All Scripture is full of the same sharp contrasts. Formed out of the dust of the ground, yet made in the image and similitude of God;

children of the Most Highest, yet crushed before the moth;—drinking in iniquity like water, yet filled with the inspiration of the Almighty which giveth him understanding;—a worm and a thing of nought, yet with a destiny higher than the sons of light;—there is in man's nature a terrible dualism, 'the angel has him by the hand or the serpent by the heart;' he may rise to the heights of heaven, he may sink to the abyss of hell. Through all literature, ancient and modern, runs the same antithesis, from the 'man is a god on earth' of the Roman orator, to the 'man is the shadow of a dream' of the Greek tragedians; from the stately utterance of our great dramatist, "What a piece of work is man! how noble in reason! how infinite in faculty! in form and moving how express and admirable! in action how like an angel! in apprehension how like a god," down to that late bitter condemnation of another, "However we brave it out, we men are a little breed."

Nor is it in the thoughts of others alone that we find such contradictions; they are patent enough to our own. On the one hand, we are amazed at man's greatness, on the other, we blush for his degradation; on the one hand we see him as the lord of Science, binding the wayward winds in the white wings of his vessels, and kindling his silver beacons on the wave-tormented crags, as though to light up the broad ocean as the highway for his commerce, the lord who has subdued the all-shattering electric flash into a harmless vassal to girdle his habitable globe, and carry his messages even under the raging seas, and has bidden the imprisoned vapour speed him as a slave over the wastes of sandy deserts and through the heart of iron hills; and on the other we see him sunk into a degradation lower than that of beasts that perish, disinherited of all the radiance of his origin, the only creature that thwarts the purposes and violates the majesty of his Creator, the lowest because the guiltiest, the guiltiest because the most responsible of all that God has made;—so that when we gaze first on the glories of his dominion and then on him who was made its monarch, it is as when one wanders through a pyramid, passing through pictured corridor to pictured corridor, and from granite hall to granite hall, only to see enshrined in the last dim chamber the mummy of a senseless animal, or the handful of charred ashes which are all that remains of some nameless king.

For alas! when we look around us how little we see of a life in accordance with the splendid dignity, with the immortal hopes, of one whom God's own hand crowned with the diadem of honour. Little surely that is high, little that is heroic, little that is valorous, little that is charitable; common-place, conventional lives; petty aims, petty interests, petty faults, dwarfed natures, and ever dwindling achievements, and everywhere over the dead level of routine and mediocrity a dense undergrowth of paltry vices. This is not an age of great crimes, but an age of little meannesses; an age too timid for individuality, too calculating for enthusiasm. There are few murders, but plenty of malice; few thefts, but abundance of avarice; little true charity, but large ostentatious philanthropy; rare positive lies, but floods of timid trickery; little open hatred, but oceans of secret blame. "Wo unto us! the crown is fallen from our heads, for we have sinned." Oh we need the lightning flash to burn away as tow the bonds of those feeble interests which tie down the energies of our souls; oh we need the wild fearless voice of some indignant prophet to rouse our enfeebled natures out of the sleek dream of their unheroic repose. Better by far that God's hand should shatter the sea of glass beneath our cautious footsteps, and let the nether fires glare in our very faces; better by far that He should open the windows of heaven, and break up the fountains of the great deep; better by far that He should shake down, and level with the dust the crumbling edifice of our insignificant ambitions; better by far that He should unmoor us from our smooth anchorage on that muddy sea which has long ceased to reflect heaven's azure or the countenance of God, and toss, and beat, and buffet our struggling despairing souls amid all His storms to force out whatever of noble they still retain,—than that He should suffer those souls to rot away piecemeal amid the hollow comforts of life, and to lose all that is divine, and manly, and royal within us, in getting, and spending, and putting out on good security, and laying by, and settling on our lees, and taking this world as it is for our all in all.

Such then are the contrasts between the magnificence of our human heritage and the too often grovelling tenor of our human lives; and their reconciliation is no mystery, but a commonplace. In the one we contemplate man as he may be, in the other as he is. The former, my brethren, is the nobler contemplation; it is wiser to think of our possible exaltation than of our actual fall. It is better to bear in mind the glory we might bear with us, and the divine altar from whose brightness the flame of our souls was lit, than to conceive of ourselves as a mean, a worthless, and a ruined herd;—it is better with David to lift up our eyes, undaunted, even to the starry vault of heaven, and to believe that on the very throne of the omnipotent is the likeness of a human form, than to regard ourselves with the diseased and anguished Job, as the valueless playthings of a divine irony, and the scorned slaves of an unmerciful decree. For as our thoughts are we shall be; and if they are fixed on glory and immortality, with Christ in heavenly places, there is more hope that we too shall in heart and mind thither ascend. Oh reverence yourselves, encourage in yourselves, not as a feeling of pride, since it crushes all pride, and annihilates a conceited self-satisfaction into a divine and modest humility, but, as an incentive to all purity and to all praise, cherish in yourselves the thought of your exalted origin from God, and of that lofty destiny which may lead you through the grave and gate of death, to stand undazzled before His throne. Read, legibly emblazoned in the heraldry of the soul, the proofs of its glorious genealogy, and the right to rise far above the interests of earth; claim fearlessly your great privilege as the children of a king, claim it as your talisman against all weakness and all degradation, till your lives catch something of that glory which is visible in the example of Him who redeemed them, as the face of Moses shone with a divine and dazzling lustre, as he returned down the flaming mountain from high communings with his Father and his God.

But there are certain enemies which will assail us, some now, some hereafter, all perhaps at some time or other of our lives. Against these foes, foes that soil the white robes of our immortality, and abase the towering stature of manhood into the dust, against these foes I would now warn you.

1. The first of them is Care.

In one of our cathedrals is a nameless grave, and on the slab which covers it, is carved, without a date and without a record, but one single word. It is the word *Miserrimus*, 'most wretched.' This and nothing more. It is the self-chosen memorial of one who would leave behind him no other history: there, in its mute appeal against heaven, there, in its silent blasphemy against a God of love, it lies in the quiet cloister beside the noble pile, and the sunbeam falls athwart it and the sound of children's voices are heard as they play around it, and the foot of many a heedless passenger is arrested ere it falls on the terrible epitaph. Yet how many of those who tread upon it might assume it to themselves: for it is the epitome of a careworn life, and than a careworn life nothing is more common. The gay, epicurean, lyric poet of ancient Rome, sings even in his light strains, of 'diseased care climbing the brazen trireme, and sitting triumphant behind the knight;' and modern myriads may tell you of cares haunting them in countless swarms from sunrise to sunset, nay even 'scaring the midnight pillow,' and sitting heavy on the breast that has begun to heave already with the throes of death! cares for our livelihood, cares for our health, cares for our prosperity, cares for our incomes, cares more anxious than any others, about our children and our families, cares meanest of all others, as to what people will think of us or say of us, cares whether we shall succeed or no, cares whether our little comforts will last or no; cares, out of a haunting past, cares, in a restless present, cares about an uncertain future,—oh it is a chaos, a weltering sea of cares for him who suffers himself to be choked therein. They fill healthy life with the unsubstantial phantoms of disease, they jangle its peaceful melodies into a tuneless discord, they plough with harrows of iron the brows which were once bright with baptismal dew. From how many have they torn the diadem to brand in its place the festering stigma of the slave; from how many have they taken 'the freshness of the meadow, the coolness of the stream;' in how many have they quenched 'bright thoughts, clear deeds, the constancy, the fidelity, the bounty, the generous honesty which are the germs of noble minds,' and in which it was once said that 'the heroic English gentleman hath no peer'? Yet we might shake them off for ever; by sitting more loosely to the things of earth, by learning to despise the gilded dust which debases all who love it and set store by it, we might recover our manhood, and be free. The pestilent malaria does not creep with more certainty out of the stagnant swamp over the doomed city, than does that fatal blight which exhales over the soul from the undrained marshes of worldly care. O that we could all wring this black drop out of our souls. Then, if cares came, we could lay them all on Him who would bear for us their intolerable burden, and, after the very heaviest misfortune which could befall us, sorrowful it may be, but undebased,

"We might take up our burden of life again,
Not saying even It might have been."

Why should we be care-stricken? what business have we to be sad in the sunshine? we have nothing to do with the past, nothing to do with the future; we have to do with the present only, and that even in the hour of trial we are by God's grace strong enough to bear.

2. But there is another enemy to the true glory of manhood of which I would warn you—an enemy which will assail you no less certainly than care, I mean Worldliness.

And of worldliness I accept no such cheap and vulgar definition as that which makes it consist in going to races, and theatres, and balls. No, I mean something infinitely deeper than this. I mean living for what is temporal, and not for what is eternal, a crime of which not the publicans only, but many a sleek Pharisee is guilty. To live as thousands live, mainly it would seem to store up their little dues, slowly or quickly to scrape themselves up a competence and leave the rest of their substance to their babes, to join in the race for wealth, to live without public spirit, without love to man, with no care but for our own selfish comforts, grandeurs, or interests, to take the print of a mammon-worshipping age, and so to live dismal, illiberal, acquisitive lives, is a terrible danger to us all. And oh what a great blank of the soul comes upon the man who accepts this life; how all the ardours of his early enthusiasm die away; how all that was free, and delicate, and noble, and attractive about him, all artless simplicity, all the tenderness, all the romance, all the chivalry, all the poetry of his existence gets congealed and hardened into conceit and commonplace; how in his easy life evils come upon him which as has been well said "vex less but mortify more, which suck the blood though they do not shed it, and ossify the heart though they do not torture it." The rust and the canker eat away all of the little soul that is left, and the scurf of a heartless conventionality lies thick all over the daily life. Men become like the corpse of the ancient Scythian lord, which was carried around, in its stately chariot, from house to house, and the banquet spread before the glazed eyes in the houses of its friends: so of these worldly men—they are rich, they are feasted, they are at ease, they are successful, they are honoured, but, they are dead.

My brethren, however poor or insignificant, thank God, I envy you not the greatest wealth, I envy you not the highest rank to which any one of you were born. They may be a splendid boon ; they may be a fatal curse. If they are to make a narrow life span the horizon of your hopes, and the turbid world yield you the only joys for which you care, if they are to make you lounge through an idle or fashionable life in the dull round of insipid pleasures and satiating excitements, if they are to make you turn your attention to dress, and equipages, and servants, and the heavy adjuncts of a vulgar display, then for my own part, sooner than change with you, I had rather be the meanest Christian workman on whose brow the sweatdrops must stand thick, each day, ere he can earn his daily bread; I had rather be the most poor and toilworn fisherman, who draws his precarious food from the troubled waters, and whose shipwrecked boat and drowned corpse are at last flung up without pity, like a plaything of which the waves are tired, high upon the hungry and stony beach. Nay even as a matter of this world's life, I believe that so I should be happier than you in a life of eating, and drinking, and dressing, and hunting, and doing nothing. I should at least have the bright eye of health, and the brawny arm of strength, and the fearless heart of independence, and the dauntless brow of honest innocence, and the home unvulgarized by useless conventionalities and joyless joys, and the simple, unsophisticated, unsated heart, the wellspring of trustfulness and peace. But, how much more, if I add to these the hopes which the worldly life loses for ever? I would not sell one, the smallest, of those hopes, for the brightest coronet or the stateliest castle you could give me. I would say, as a happy and high-minded writer of this age has said of them, "Lead, lead me on, my hopes! I know that ye are true and not vain. Vanish from my eyes day after day, but arise in new forms. I will follow your holy deception; follow till ye have brought me to the feet of my Father in Heaven, where I shall find you all with folded wings, spangling the sapphire dusk, whereon stands His throne, which is our Home."

3. I should not be true to my duty if I did not, in very few words, warn you of one more enemy to your immortal nature, perhaps the most virulent, and the deadliest of all, I mean Evil Passion.

I need not define it; it is to suffer the lower, the meaner, the animal part of your nature to triumph, and to guide the chariot of the soul, of which God has made Reason and Conscience the sole safe charioteers. My brethren, Care may drag us down to earth; Worldliness may chain us to its trough; but Sensuality permanently degrades the soul, tears off its wings, and trails them in the mire. But, believe me,—and I venture to ask your earnest and solemn attention to what I say,—God has not made it difficult for the simple and manly heart to put a curb on evil passions; if you will remember the lessons learnt at your mother's knee, if you will turn with pity and abhorrence from the conversation of the corrupt and base, if you will regard with loathing and anguish the thought of degrading yourselves, whose mortal bodies are the Temples of the Holy Ghost, it is not difficult for any one of you to live, with a white and unstained soul, from happy boyhood to noble youth, from noble youth to godlike manhood, unassailed by leprous thoughts, beyond earshot of "the flapping of unclean wings." But, for those who have not resisted the gradual growth of evil passions in their own hearts, then, I do not deny it, it is difficult—nay it involves perhaps a lifelong struggle and a lifelong watchfulness to recover the once-lost jewel of immortal innocence. Yet, if you would not be ruined, ruined for this world, and ruined for the next, on that struggle you must enter. In God's name then, take heart of courage; God and your Saviour, and the Holy Spirit of God, will help you, and will lend you their omnipotent power to pluck away your soul lest it be lost, lost for ever, in that fatal path on which some unhappy feet begin to tread so young, which leads nevertheless to that gate on which is written,

"All hope abandon ye who enter here."

Now in conclusion:—What is man? the true answer, 'A little lower than God, crowned with glory and honour,' came but in part to David under that starlit sky: it came with fuller assurance, it came with a Symphony of louder, more triumphant, more immortal exultation, not to a crowned king, but, 1000 years after, to humble shepherds under another starlit sky, keeping watch over their flocks by night. For they were told by the angel-voices that the God-man was born: oh if you would see the ideal of manhood, look to Him; care fretted him not, for that Lamb of God lived from childhood in the green pastures and beside the still waters of his Father's love; worldliness debased Him not, for He despised the kingdoms of the world, and the glory of them when they lay outspread in their dazzling glory before His feet; passion never assaulted Him, for it is only the meanest and the dissolutest souls that passion long enslaves. But, though He felt not the yoke of these temptations, He saw them in others, and with a divine pity pitied them. To the careworn He said, 'Come unto me, and I will give you rest;' to the worldly He said 'Lay not up for yourselves treasures upon earth...but lay up for yourselves treasures in heaven, where neither rust nor moth doth corrupt, and where thieves do not break through nor steal;' to the most stained and fallen and corrupted He said, 'Neither do I condemn thee; go and sin no more.' He healed the ravages which sin and shame had left upon their faces; He cast out the devils which care and lust had introduced into their souls. Let Him, our Lord, our Hope, our Saviour, let Him be our ideal, and not the ideal of the world; let His, and not the example of the world, be our example: so shall we attain the full height of our destiny, so shall we, partakers of His redemption, and heirs of His immortality, after a godly life here live with God hereafter, the tears wiped from our faces, the scars of sin and sorrow healed in our souls, not a little lower, but higher, than the angels, crowned with a glory and honour which can never fade or be dimmed again, and with Death itself, the last of all our enemies, vanquished and crushed beneath our feet.

VII.

RIGHTEOUSNESS THE STRENGTH OF NATIONS.

(Preached before the National Rifle Association, in the Volunteer Camp at Wimbledon, July 15, 1866.)

1 Cor. xvi. 13.—"Quit you like men, be strong."

SURELY the time at which we are assembled gives to this noble exhortation an unwonted emphasis. Meeting as we do at a moment when the battle-fields of Europe are still encumbered with their unburied slain,—meeting at the close of a few days during which the great boundaries of Europe have been altered, perhaps for ever,—fresh from the spectacle of a brave and military nation, with an army the best disciplined in Europe, yet forced after one day of raging battle to succumb in hopeless ruin to a surer weapon, —while the messages of battle are being daily flashed to our quiet homes, and the destiny of empires is being weighed in the balances of war, —surely I say at such a time, when our eyes are open to the possibilities of the future, and our blood stirred by the tidings of 400,000 gallant men wrestling in a gigantic struggle,—the command must come with a more thrilling emphasis, *Quit you like men, be strong*. The camp, indeed, in which *we* are gathered is a peaceful camp, nor is the heather we tread on wet with blood; but over two other and vaster camps on this very summer-day may be hanging the smoke of battle, and in other ears on this quiet Sabbath may be thundering the roar of artillery and the shock of strife. With what widely different thoughts and feelings, if they be gathered for worship, must the worshippers be actuated in those other camps,—the one intoxicated with the triumph of victory, the other prostrate in humiliation and despair. But for *us*, thank God, there is neither the dangerous flush of victory, nor the burning anguish of shame. Never for centuries has our national existence been imperilled; never for centuries has our flag been trampled, or an enemy set hostile foot on our inviolate shore. And to-day, though our gathering bear the aspect of war, it is a gathering subservient to the purest interests of peace, and our thoughts are not of defiance but of defence; our purpose not a purpose of aggression or of aggrandisement, but the calm and fearless attitude of the strong man armed.

Yet the tidings of the last few days force us to a serious and sober estimate of our actual position. Happily we have no cause to blush for the memories thus evoked. We call to mind how, six years ago, there was some dim menace, some uncertain whisper of danger or of invasion. Founded or unfounded, that mere whisper of peril, that intangible rumour of attack, was enough; at once the slumbering embers of a patriotism, which *seemed* only to be buried under the ashes of self-interest, burst into a flame, and, with an ardour which some nicknamed a panic, the passionate manhood of England sprang to its feet. The foolish ridiculed it as a mania, the frivolous sneered at it as an illusion; but wise statesmen approved, and greyhaired veterans generously welcomed it; and if it were a panic it was a panic, not turbulent, transitory, and irregular, but disciplined with the soberest precision and developed into the solidest results. And as the yew-tree used in old days to be planted in the very shadow of the churches, so that our ancestors might at any moment cut their national weapon from ground hallowed by God's worship and their fathers' graves, so now that National Church, for whom, weakened though she be by factions, and though her voice have lost something of the noble and the ringing tone which it had of yore, yet for whom we have *not* lost as a nation our honour and our love, came forward to cheer the movement with her encouragement,—to lend to it the sanction of her most solemn services, and to bless it with her uplifted hand.

That was six years ago, when many said with a sneer that the mania would be evanescent, yet we are here to-day, and trust to be here for many years. Sirs, had it been evanescent it would have been contemptible. But it sprang from causes holier and deeper than a fugitive alarm. We did not wish to bequeath to our children a tarnished name, an abnegated mission, a glory obscured or shorn away. We knew that a great nation, if she cannot (which is best) be loved, must at least be honoured and feared. The effort was made, and at once the waning star of England shone with new lustre among the nations. Our volunteers, if they did not save us from aggression, yet, without controversy, won us respect. They were a witness against the base old scandal that we are a nation who care only for the counter and the till; they were a witness that, though not military, neither were we pusillanimous, nor would we suffer our love of peace to degenerate into fear of war, or to become a gilded name for sensuality, for corruption, and for death. They proved that the very poorest of our sons yet knew that he had a stake,—ay, and a stake dear as life,—in his native land, though he owned no furrow of her soil. But had the movement been shortlived, it would have sunk us lower than it has ever raised us. It would have shown that we were only capable of spasmodic efforts, and that though, by a divine instinct, we might feel some pale and colourless affection, if for nothing better in England, yet at least for her sweet green fields and wave-washed barriers, yet it was not a love noble enough or strong enough to make us sacrifice for her sake our money or our ease, or consecrate to her service one hour of the many which we devote to Mammon or slumber away in rest.

An institution so rich in blessings,—in blessings which it is hardly possible to exaggerate,—as is this germ of war in the heart of peace, should not and must not die away. It is a blessing that men,—and above all men engaged in the race for wealth,—should be awoke continually from lowthoughted dreams. It is a blessing that dead and selfish hearts should be stirred to passion by an inspiring sense of national unison. It is a blessing that high and low, rich and poor, the learned and the ignorant, the noble and the working man, should find their interests not antagonistic but identical, and should stand side by side in a cordial brotherhood, and animated by a common cause. It is an infinite blessing, both to our soldiers and to ourselves, that our defence should be no mere dangerous trade delegated into a few hands, but that our soldiers should be citizens and our citizens soldiers, a strong barrier at once against popular anarchy and tyrannous monopoly, united in the defence of England's liberty and England's fame. It is an infinite blessing that thousands, in the midst of money-getting and toil-worn lives, should be strengthened by a manly exercise, and inspired by an elevating thought, so that they may not feel themselves mere slaves, chained to the car of Mammon and ever stifled by the noise and dust of its grinding wheels,—but,—scorning that base ideal of sluggish and easy prosperity which makes men fit to be nothing better than a tyrant's slaves,—should take conspicuous part in a service, unpaid indeed by material rewards, but richly paid by a nation's gratitude, and richly contributing to a nation's praise.

Nor is it a blessing only;—let us face the stern, plain, unvarnished fact, that though it is a free service it is a political necessity,—a necessity even if England never dreams of anything higher than her own defence. For England is no longer the mistress of the seas, nor is the white wake of her vessels any longer "the avenue to her palace-front," along which no enemy may approach. At this very moment a steam-ram floats in her waters which no one of her vessels could resist, and armies are armed with a gun which at the present moment no soldiers of hers could overcome. Are then the glory and the power and the 1000 years of her splendid pre-eminence to lie at the mercy of steam-rams and needle-guns? They would do so, even more than they do now, but for our volunteers. It is not that we have lost one atom of confidence in our gallant army. No, they on many a bloody field have vindicated their hereditary valour; and the men who fought at Balaclava and Inkermann, and formed that "thin red line" which charged up the hills of Alma, and marched under the burning sun of

India to Lucknow and Cawnpore, as they are the sons of those who fought at Vittoria and Waterloo, so are they no degenerate descendants of the heroes who won at Crecy and at Azincour. But can a handful of 50,000, which, small as it is, could hardly be concentrated without difficulty and delay, meet those 500,000 who could, at very brief notice, be poured upon her shores? And at a time when the political horizon is rarely free from thunderous clouds,—at a time when rumours of war, like "the mighty succession of billows which roll shoreward, and roar, and strike, and are dissipated," again and again have swept us into war, or agitated us into ignoble hurry and undignified alarm,—does it do at such a time to indulge in utopian dreams as to the possibilities of perpetual peace? No, we are by no means too secure, and that we should be secure impregnably is a duty which England owes to her God, to the world, and to herself. The battle-brunt of an indomitable heroism,—the firm solidity of a valour inspired by the sense of duty,—a patriotism which can be as little shaken as the rocks which gird it round,—the traditional grandeur of "a proud and haughty nation, fierce in arms,"—yes, on these we might reckon to face that tremendous front of war, which on almost any day might be arrayed against us by the envy, the anger, or the hate of other lands;—but what are these ideal entities before the whirling blasts of an irresistible artillery,—what are these if our little army could not reckon on the aid of 200,000 brother citizens, to screen their terrible advance to the final struggle behind "a vail of impenetrable fire?"

Yes, every one of you in his peaceful but serviceable manhood tends directly to the security of England; but, I ask, will it finally content you that England shall be secure, and nothing more? Is her glory, her dignity, her influence in the mighty destiny of nations—are these nothing to you; mere impalpable things which you cannot clutch, mere airy fantasies not to be mentioned by practical men, forsooth, in the same breath as taxes and merchandise and wealth? Are you content that her voice should be hushed for ever, which once thundered words of awful weight at the council-board of nations? Are you content that she should but selfishly clutch and tighten the sword in its scabbard which she once wielded in many a generous cause? It is our glory to hate aggression and the lust of empire; but shall it be our glory to lose all chivalry of sentiment, all 'sensibility of honour?' If so, England may indeed grow richer, but her riches will be garnered for her enemies, and her isolation may only tend to make her sink hereafter in unassisted perplexity to an unpitied fall. Oh! proclaim it not yet that you will have peace at any price. Your theory of non-intervention may be a right and manly and unselfish one, but do not stretch it till it cracks. Hide it as yet from the nations of Europe that we prefer the gilded reality of our wealth to that exploded old-fashioned fantastic enthusiasm for England's honour. If it be our pride to hold aloof from mere foreign dissensions, if the progressive interests of our vast empire make it a necessity that England should be no longer for influence in Europe the England of Elizabeth or of Cromwell, yet at least let it be understood that the day may come again, ay and that soon, when she will fight with the invincible majesty of her noblest days. Not yet will she learn to stare without a blow at the struggles of the helpless and the agony of the oppressed. Though it is ever her boast that while there are 6,000,000 soldiers in Europe she has but half a million for the whole of her vast domain—not yet will she tamely abdicate her place in the vanguard of the world's righteous progress. Not yet will she erase the lion from her unconquered banner, nor for the ensign of Judah which was the lion's whelp, and the blessing of Judah which was "the sceptre" and "the hand upon the neck of his enemies," will she choose the mean banner and the mean blessing of Issachar[1]—a blessing more like a curse—"to be an ass crouching between two burdens; and he saw that rest was good and the land that it was pleasant, and he bowed his shoulder to the yoke, and became a servant unto tribute." If her moral influence be inevitably weakened by the duty or the expedience of her material inaction, yet let us prove it by our deeds that that inaction is not another name for mere selfishness, and that if any presume upon it too far, the day may come when the lordly heart and giant energy of England shall reawaken with a shout. In the words of our greatest poet, "Methinks I see a noble and puissant nation, rousing herself like a strong man after sleep, and shaking her invincible locks,—methinks I see her as an eagle, mewing her mighty youth and kindling her undazzled eye at the full midday beam, while the whole

---

[1] See Lord Bacon's Essay on the true Greatness of Kingdoms.

noise of timorous and flocking birds, with those also that love the twilight, flutter about, amazed at what she means!"

My brethren, if themes like these tend to awaken us from that worst and widest of all our vices, our deep-rooted individual selfishness, they need no apology; still less do they need it *here* and *now*. Nothing is more pitiful than a life spent in thinking of nothing but self, yes, even in thinking of nothing but one's own soul; nothing is more ghastly and revolting than the thought of the one thousand millions of human beings who are now living on the surface of the globe, if they be but one thousand millions of separate atoms toiling, less nobly than the very emmets on an anthill, for their individual gains. May such a spirit—though it has been often fostered by the teachers of Christianity—be ever alien to the spirit of England, as it is alien to the spirit of Christianity itself. That spirit teaches us that we are not our own, nor are our lives our own; that spirit bids us to "quit us like men, and be strong," not to moulder away the faculties which God has intrusted to us in the desert or the cell, but to rise from our mere personal interests to those of our Church, and of our nation, and through our nation to the interests of the world. The philosopher who denies that Christianity has recognized the virtue of patriotism has not represented it aright, for Christianity is no dull system of formal ethics, but a living impulse, and one that speaks as loudly in patriotism as in all the other virtues which it has inspired. And patriotism may sometimes demand, and demand imperiously, the sacrifice of war. I know not how men can take the Bible in their hands, the Bible which they profess to adore, and of which whole books clang with the sounds of sword and shield,—the Bible wherein is such fiery intermingling of indignation and righteous wrath with peace and love,—the Bible of which whole chapters are like the battle of the warrior with its confused noise and garments rolled in blood,—and yet deny that "agonies of pain and blood shed in rivers are less evils than the soul spotted and bewildered with sin," and that rather than a corrupt, a rotten, and a mammon-worshipping peace, we had better by far have

" War with a thousand battles and shaking a hundred thrones."

This is an instinctive feeling, and it is one that belongs to the best part of our nature; it is instinctive, and, like all our nobler instincts, it has the sanction of Christianity. Christianity is no emasculated religion, no effeminate and silken system of bigots and of priests, nay, it is pre-eminently a strong and manly religion, and because manly, godlike. "Quit you like men;" virtue is manliness; and therefore valour, and chivalry, and passion, and enthusiasm, and gallantry, and strength of purpose, and a burning resentment against lies and cruelty and wrong are no mean parts, but rather essential elements of a lofty virtue. Say what you will, but no coward, no soft, pitiful, creeping character could ever be truly Christian; for Christianity exorcises that spirit of craven fear, and brands as contemptible the soul that wastes the glory of life with no higher object than eagerly to surround itself with comforts and greedily to heap up gain.

But the fact of your presence here speaks better things for you, and it is an augury of hope for our native land. There are those who say that her day is gone;—not because of the corruptions within her, not because of her criminal population, not because of her neglected outcasts, not because of her spoliations, her covetousness, or her greed,—but because of the possible exhaustion of her great fields of coal, and because nature supplies no substitute for the stored up decay of those primeval forests, which as they grew and perished long myriads of millenniums back, were even then preparing the earth in the designs of an unchanging Creator for the maintenance and happiness of man. My brethren, it may be, or it may not be, that our coal will fail us before a hundred years have passed; if so let us use those hundred years in building our greatness on a fairer and less perishable basis, for though we may grow poorer and weaker, yet no nation can perish and pass away into contempt and ruin for any other cause but for her sins. And England's true greatness, much more her sole greatness, lies in something better than her coal. Not in that, though it may have contributed to her wealth and strength—not in that, but in whatever there be of truth, of purity, of nobleness, of honour in the bosom of her sons, lies the real glory and the future hope of our native land. Though her soldiers and her volunteers were ten times in number what they are, the enemy would no more fear them than a lion fears whole flocks of sheep, unless there were in them that animating courage which suffices not only for the flash of transient valour, but for the long heroism of steadfast endurance. If you would see the star of her destiny, look for it in the heart of your brethren, look for it in your own. As volunteers you have the high privilege, the inestimable honour of definitely, distinctly, immediately, serving your native land; be grateful to God for this high privilege, as your country is grateful from her heart to you. But forget not that there are ways in which you can serve your country even more,—ay indefinitely, infinitely, more. The large majority of you, and of your leaders, are yet in the flush of youth, or the noble prime of early manhood: Oh how much you may do for England! You have come forward to help and to defend, to honour and to elevate her: Oh would to God that each and every one of you would take the solemn and heart-spoken vow to save and to ennoble her not only now, not only thus,—not only when your uniform is on, not only when the rifle is in your hands,—but far away, each one of you in your own loved homes, in your peaceful villages or stirring towns, or it may be hereafter in far-off colonies and the islands of the sea. You serve your country acceptably in the camp, and at the drill, and when your keen eye is on the centre at the range,—and she thanks you, and her wives and her maidens honour and bless you: But oh! you may serve her more, infinitely more, if you will serve her not only in public but alone, not only in your corps but in your lives; if you will devote, not some certain hours, but your very hearts to her service, whether it be in the senate or in the factory, whether it be in the artist's studio or the lawyer's chambers, or the workman's cottage, or the merchant's shop. There, and not here only,—there, in the secret hour of temptation and the unseen crisis of strife—there, in your closet, with no eye upon your struggling soul save the unsleeping eye of God,—"Quit you like men, be strong." To you, as to a new order of knighthood that has sprung up among us,—to the clearness of your consciences, to the cleanness of your hands in God's eyesight, to the pure and high purposes which, in the very "teeth of clenched antagonisms" may inspire and animate your noble lives—to you, I say, we look to guard and purify the true lifesprings of our national existence. But if otherwise, if your ranks be filled with those who have not learned to conquer their own passions and themselves,—why then, if you have not this iron of right and truth, and chastity in the blood of manhood, neither your skill nor your numbers will much avail. For when the hour comes, as come it may, when you or your children shall be called to holiday exercises no longer, but to the deathful roar of the perilous fight, when every ringing whizz of the bullet involves not a smile of triumph, but a ghastly and murderous wound, it will be too late then: —the strength will be gone from the nerveless arm, and the courage from the enervated soul, and there will be neither might nor heroism in the hearts charred to dust with the fires of passion, and rotten to the core with the sins of youth. My brethren, I honestly believe that in this sense also, the sense of fighting against all wickedness, whether without you or within, all of you wish, many of you strive, to be true soldiers. The fact that for a space of six years, out of 200,000 so very few have brought dishonour upon their uniform,—the fact that the spectacle of a Volunteer in disgrace is so rare as to excite marked and special reprobation whenever it does occur,—the fact that in this camp, out of 1,200 men gathered from every rank, and from every quarter, there has arisen, during so many years, no single cause for complaint of drunkenness, of insubordination, of violence, of unseemliness,—these happy and hopeful facts entitle us to assume that, in donning his uniform, a Volunteer does feel, as he ought to feel, that he is acquiring a new and powerful incentive to that high self-respect which shall teach him to rise above the meanness and degradation of a sinful selfishness, and to regard his mortal body as the Temple of the Holy Spirit of God.

For, to sum up in one last word;—not only on the fields of Europe now, but ever and everywhere a mighty battle is raging round us, a battle in which we all are Volunteers, ay, and enrolled Soldiers on either side,—the great silent internal battle, of lust and purity, of truth and falsehood, of right and wrong. It needs no splendid occasion, no stately amphitheatre, no pomp and prodigality of outward circumstances; —for its seat is in the human heart. But its effects and issues are in the world. Wherever the haunted conscience, or the desecrated frame, have driven men into madness or suicide,— wherever the root of a youthful life has been as bitterness, and its blossom has gone up as dust, —wherever the drunkard quakes in the loathly feebleness of retributive disease,—wherever in the lazar-house, scorned of man, and forsaken (it might seem) of God, lie the miserable victims of calculating passions, who once wore the sweet rose of innocence, and once were, what but for men's sins they yet might have been, fair human beings with the grace of matronhood upon their foreheads and the dew of God upon their souls,—wherever some lost wretch creeps to the black river-side under the midnight, and there is a dull splash, and all is done,—there, in every sob, and every shriek, and in every murky ripple of the disturbed wave, are the sounds of this battle;—and its dead lie thick in all our streets, and their blood, the blood of their murdered souls, which is spattered on many a young man's heart, and the crimson spots of which may perhaps even now be staining some haunted conscience here,—cries aloud to God for vengeance. These are the victims slain in the battle against God; oh! young Volunteers of England, take your part for God in that great battle-field. Be, as I said before, for I trust that the expression may linger in your minds, be a Christian order of knighthood, sworn by a vow, unspoken indeed yet sacred as that of the knights of old. If we be not Christ's soldiers, ready to follow him to the death, if we refuse to receive his counsels, if we delight to break his laws;—then little indeed can our arms avail, and the crown must fall from our brows, for we have sinned. Oh! deliver your souls, a pure, a fresh, and a noble gift, to Him; oh, listen to the daily summons wherewith He bids you resist his foes. If the sons of England win in that fight, then no other can injure their native land. Such sons will defend and dignify her more ten thousandfold than whole fleets of iron-plated vessels and batteries bristling on every promontory with ponderous guns. The land that is given over to lust, and softness, and luxury, and greed, that land has the law of weakness within herself, and the sentence of pitiless destruction, blazing to her condemnation in every line of the historic page; but that nation whose soldiers are also good servants and soldiers of Jesus Christ, has nothing to fear in the Armageddon of a whole world banded against her with unrighteous arms. If she sink even for a time, she can only sink to rise again more glorious, as a happy, a godly, a christian people,—even as the sun sinks but for a time in the ocean's bed only to rise once more in greater splendour and

"FLAME IN THE FOREHEAD OF THE
MORNING SKY."

VIII.

THE HISTORY AND HOPES OF A PUBLIC SCHOOL.

(Preached before Harrow School on Founder's Day, Oct. 6, 1859.)

ISAIAH liv. 11—13.—*Behold, I will lay thy stones with fair colours, and will lay thy foundations with sapphires. And I will make thy windows of agates, and thy gates of carbuncles, and all thy borders of pleasant stones. And all thy children shall be taught of the Lord; and great shall be the peace of thy children.*

SUCH was the splendid picture which rose before the mind of the Hebrew poet, when earnest faith and fervent aspiration clothed themselves in the language of prophecy. Such too is the vision which every true heart among us would fain contemplate when we look forwards to the future; and it is a condition which yet may be realised by united exertion and humble prayer.

We have met together, my brethren, to do honour to the religious memory of a good man, and to remind ourselves of the relation in which we stand to a great community. The name of

John Lyon—of little note to the world in general—is full of significance to us. To-day at least our thoughts should be occupied not with ourselves or our own interests, but with Harrow and its interests, and the duties we owe to one another, and to this our common home. And of the thousand thoughts that rush to our minds, on which we might dwell with profit, it is difficult to select the most useful and the most opportune. One who speaks on such an occasion, and in the honour of such an institution, may well shrink from the responsibility laid upon him;—may he not also hope that words however imperfect, however hastily thrown together, may, if spoken from a sincere affection and a loyal heart, be received with kindly consideration, and by a sympathising audience, for the sake of the theme by which they are inspired?

And I know not how better to fulfil the object of Founder's Day than by asking you to glance with me first at the past history of Harrow School; secondly at its one object and purpose; and lastly at one or two considerations which seem naturally to flow from our present connection with so famous, so permanent, and so honoured a Foundation. May God's good Spirit be with us, and bless the word spoken to every heart.

And *First*, of the past history of Harrow School.

In the fifteenth and sixteenth centuries there was a mighty awakening of the human mind. Europe was stirred to its depths by new knowledge, and as its first vernal influences chased away the cold mists of ignorance and superstition a thousand intellects sprang into freedom, and a thousand utterances burst into eloquence and song.

It was a noble period;—the period of giant Progress, of conscious liberty, of golden hope. In England a sour-hearted and bigot Queen had attempted to bind men's souls in the iron network of Popery, and the blood of five martyr-Bishops[1] had hissed in the fires of persecution. But Mary had been succeeded by another Queen of royal talents and lion heart, under whose enlightened and fostering care thought and learning flourished, and whose throne was girt by men around whose brows the honours of poet, statesman, and philosopher were often garlanded in a single wreath. Never before was the glory of England more pre-eminent; and the fair fame which had been obscured for a moment, had

---

[1] Cranmer, Hooper, Ridley, Latimer, Farrar.

risen once more, like the sun out of the ocean waves.

It was during this period some 290[1] years ago that an honest yeoman, living in the fields of Preston in Harrow parish, was led to meditate over the causes which had produced for his age and country such magnificent results. Those causes were not far to seek; they were universally recognised. It was the forgotten learning and neglected thought of the old world which breathed fresh vigour into the languid intellect of Europe. Men began to see that they were far behind the ages which had preceded them, and that in their hands the torch of knowledge was burning low; and from the songs which had once thrilled into the heart of youthful nations, and the eloquence which had once fulmined over the waves of a 'fierce democratie,' they caught once more the flame of freedom and the passion of awakening strength. The renewed study of the Classics,—the very study in which you are now trained,—led to the Revival of Literature; and literature was synonymous with thought, with energy, with life. The Queen herself set the example of earnest

[1] John Lyon obtained his charter from Queen Elizabeth in 1571.

study;—unlike the would-be fine-gentlemen of modern days, who know no condition but that of ignorance, and honour no life but a life of mental sloth,—she studied Greek and Latin diligently, even when burdened with the cares of sovereignty,—and read hard, "no young student at an University more daily or more duly[1]."

The Harrow yeoman saw that Language was the best instrument for training the intellect, and for furthering thereby the interests and the happiness of the human race: and unknown as he was, he determined to secure for his own village the advantages of that education which had been so prolific in mighty consequences. Now John Lyon was a simple yeoman, or small farmer; there was nothing in his rank or position to command respect: he did not even write 'gentleman' after his name, and had we met him in the streets we should have regarded him as an ordinary man. But he was not deterred by his obscurity from the endeavour to do good in his generation. Instead of spending his fortune for personal aggrandisement or immediate comfort he founded with it a Grammar School and drew up a few simple regulations for its future governance,—regulations wisely embrac-

---

[1] Bacon, *Advancement of Learning.*

ing the threefold scope of education, moral, intellectual, physical; the perfection of the soul, the mind, the body,—and, in their due harmony and subordination, the perfection of the living man. One of those regulations was characteristic,—and I recommend it to your earnest thoughts; it was in the common spirit of the time, "aut disce aut discede[1]"—it provided expressly that the idle or the incapable should not be permitted to stay for more than a year in Harrow School. This was neither the time, nor this the place for idlers and triflers. No cumbrous, no barren, no injurious stem was to take from the fruitful branches the richness of the soil. In John Lyon's heritage the axe was to be at the root of the barren trees.

So John Lyon founded Harrow Grammar School. A Grammar School!—it may sound a humble designation; but it is what Harrow is and what all the great schools are, and it is a title which, when understood rightly, is not to be despised. For he who has learnt grammar has gained the very key of language, and the inmost secret of the mighty mystery of speech. He has learnt to use and to value the noblest of

[1] A motto found in several Grammar Schools—as Winchester, St Paul's, &c.

human gifts;—the gift whereby man is raised above the beasts;—the gift whereby soul speaks to soul;—the gift whereby mere pulses of articulated air become breathing thoughts and burning words;—the gift whereby, like the vibration of a silver chord, emotions thrill from heart to heart;—the gift whereby we understand the affections of men and give expression to the worship of God;—the gift whereby the lip of divine inspiration, uttering things simple and unperfumed and unadorned, reacheth with its passionate voice through a thousand generations by the help of the Word of God[1].

And when,—a few years after Harrow was founded and as yet perhaps but a dozen village lads sat on the benches of a single room,—the Invincible Armada came sweeping with its broad crescent-line the waters of our seas, and, aided by the storms of God, our few ships met and shattered it, and drove back its ducal leader in defeat and shame, John Lyon must have exulted at this fresh proof of English prowess, and must have prayed—for he was a God-fearing man—

---

[1] Compare the noble fragment of Heraclitus, preserved in Plutarch: Πολυμαθίη οὐ διδάσκει· ἡ δὲ Σίβυλλα μαινομένῳ στόματι ἁπλᾶ καὶ ἀκαλλώπιστα καὶ ἀμύριστα φθεγγομένη μυρίων ἐτῶν διέρχεται διὰ τὸν Θεόν.

that some of the young scholars of his new school, whom he was providing with sound learning and religious education, might in their turn become brave and loyal and freedom-loving Englishmen, might one day play their parts too as nobly and manfully in the great battle of the world.

The little seed which John Lyon planted, grew and flourished, and the hopes and fears of generations took shelter under the shadow of its boughs. Not from a single village,—but from north to south and east to west of a great united kingdom;—not from a few struggling village families, but from the many homes and hearths of stately houses, the sons of England were to be gathered as one family, in strange but beautiful unity, under the village yeoman's roof. The Lord had built the house, and their labour was not lost that built it. That element of strength—God's blessing sought in prayer—is a mightier buttress than the labours of nations who toiled for centuries at the houses of pride or the haunts of pleasure, the palaces of Nineveh, and the hanging gardens of Semiramis.

And Harrow continued to grow and flourish. England went through strange and troublous times; one king was executed for trammelling liberty; another king was driven a fugitive for tampering with religion; thrones tottered and dynasties were changed,—but whether England was annexing new kingdoms, or winning fresh empires, or losing the government of mighty continents;—whether she was trembling under the fury of persecution or swept by the hot flames of civil war,—the School continued stable amid troubles, and permanent amid change; year by year old Harrovians were taking their places in the ranks of life as good men, and brave, and honourable and true,—and year by year the Harrow boys were shooting for the silver arrow in the playing-fields, and winning the well-earned prize in the quiet school-room. It continued, I say, to grow and flourish, and, as we may remember with honest gratitude, it was but last term that it attained the zenith of a long-continuing prosperity, and the maximum of numbers which had long steadily increased.

And now if John Lyon could rise from his grave in the churchyard, and shake off the dust of centuries from his cerecloth, and walk among us,—if we could take him to the Fourth form room and shew him the names of poet and statesman and warrior carved by their own boyish hands upon the oaken panels—if we could shew him that

> "Great men have been among us,—hands that penned
> And tongues that uttered wisdom[1];"

how from his village school were sent forth poets of undying memory, great divines, learned scholars, governors who ruled millions of new subjects in distant provinces, eloquent orators who have held listening senates breathless at their voice,—statesmen who have been the foremost to guide the destiny of civilised nations,—mighty warriors who have rolled the tempestuous thunders of victory over land and sea,—if we could shew him that his foundation has gained royal patronage, and risen to unquestioned preeminence, and become "a name and a power" in English education for ever;—think you not that his whole heart would rejoice within him, and that from the past history of Harrow School, and the mighty results springing from God's blessing on small causes, he would wish you to learn at least this great lesson—which his own act, though done by a common yeoman, so gloriously exemplifies—the great lesson that

"GOOD DEEDS CANNOT DIE."

And in this long stability of Harrow School

---

[1] Wordsworth.

we see the pledge of its future permanence. In the language of one whose name will be identified with Harrow for many a generation, "an institution like this, when it has once taken deep root, is a permanent—almost an indestructible thing. It cannot in days of humiliation quietly die out and be forgotten. In shame or in honour it exists, and must exist. It may either rise from point to point till it becomes one of the very greatest of the educational institutions of England, or else it may sink into a deep obscurity and be known only as the wreck and failure of a school[1]." What shall be the fate of Harrow, my brethren, rests in *your* hands; a single generation may decide it. Our own hold on the school may be very short; the average time of a boy's stay here is less than five years, but the good or the harm he may do during those few years is simply incalculable. Although in five years from this time hardly one of you will be sitting on those benches, yet as you yourselves will have carried hence lifelong reminiscences, so also those then sitting in your places will be suffering from the sins which *you* have committed, or reaping the blessings of which *you*

[1] See Dr Vaughan's *Sermon on the Vocation of a Public School*, (Repton Tercentenary).

have sown the seed. For the time being you are Harrow School; and this congregation—ever varying in its constituent elements—is the common representative of a thousand successors. As the waves pass but the river is perpetual, so the members of a great school are perpetually dissolving and being recomposed, but the school continues still. And it is mainly guided and moulded by a powerful tradition to the strength of which every single boy appreciably contributes. When we have gone, our work has not gone; it still continues to widen its concentric circles of influence; for good or for evil it witnesseth against us still. Harrow boys of this generation, answer me—for I answer not the question for you either way—has the honour of Harrow risen or fallen in your hands? What has *your* work been? Have you strengthened the good tradition, or added virulence to the evil? Have you brightened the name of Harrow, or even for a moment clouded it? Think of it yourselves, and, if the answer be unfavourable, think of it, I pray you, with burning shame. Supposing any one of you were the last living scion of an ancient and noble house, what would be your feelings if you brought on that honourable lineage a lasting, an irreparable disgrace?

Yet the blot on the white scutcheon of an illustrious line is as nothing to any shame or disgrace brought through your weakness or wickedness upon the reputation of a noble school,—a school, the name of which, if you but do your duty, must and will shed more honour on the majority of *you*, than you will ever shed on it.

And yet to reflect some lustre on the place of your education,—so to live that generations to come of Harrow boys shall say of you hereafter "He, too, was a Harrow boy,"—is to an ardent and generous spirit one of the most legitimate incentives to an upright and honourable course. You cannot all be great; probably very few of you will attain to greatness; but none the less you may do your duty right royally in the obscurest position, and still be counted in the long list of Harrow worthies. They whose names are graven on yonder brazen tablets were not great or famous men; but they died in the brave and manly performance of duty, and therefore we record them as our honoured sons, and never read their names without an emotion of sorrowing pride. Even supposing God has cast your lot in some unknown and common institution, it would have been your duty to honour, to cherish, to upraise it; but he has cast your lot in one of the very highest, that confesses itself second in honour unto none. A pride in it, if it be a manly pride, is not only pardonable but right, not only excusable but desirable. This school, and not another, claims your loyal allegiance; to this school, and not another, is your chivalrous devotion due. "*Spartam nactus es, hanc exorna*[1]." If Harrow be failing in anything, endow it with fresh advantages; fence it round with yet more gallant institutes; store it with yet more precious memorials;—drive manfully away the evils, if they yet exist, which if they do exist, are now forced to skulk in its darkest corners; above all, remember that eloquent advice, which you heard so recently, "to make every bedside an altar too," and pray for Harrow with genuine affection, till the light of God's own countenance streams over it in a living flood.

For turning, *Secondly*, to the object and purpose of a public school, let me tell you that it is worthy of all your pride, and of all your affection. Its object and purpose is to prepare the boy to become an intelligent and worthy man; to provide for the health and vigour of his body;

[1] "Quod reliquum est Σπάρταν ἔλαχες ταύταν κόσμει."—Cic. *Epp. ad Att.* IV. 6.

to foster his opening intelligence and teach him the value of time, and save him from the disgrace and stagnation of idleness and ignorance; above all, to see that he grows pure, virtuous, manly, a gentleman and a Christian; in one word, its object is, in the often, but never too-often, quoted language of our daily prayer, to train him that he may be "a profitable member of the Church and Commonwealth, and at last a partaker of the immortal glory of the resurrection."

And however much they may fall short of this glorious ideal, the public schools of England have done their work so well as at least to be counted, and worthily counted, among our English institutions, and to be regarded by all Europe with envy and admiration. Let me translate to you the opinion of a distinguished and competent authority. "There is," says the Comte de Montalembert, "in England a spectacle even rarer and more magnificent than that of her Parliament,—it is her public schools. Under the modest name of schools are included three or four vast foundations, among which Eton and Harrow hold the first rank, which receive all the highborn sons of English families, and offer them, under eminent direction, an education at once classical and manly. Identified in some sort by their date with national history, they offer to their scholars as their first influence the memory of the great men who have preceded them on those benches which they have quitted to preside over the destinies of the vastest empire under the sun. These boys enjoy a liberty strange in our eyes. Without surveillance, without any other restrictions than those imposed by certain traditional usages, and that self-respect with which every Englishman is penetrated, they commence with an impetuous and precocious force their apprenticeship in self-government. Early as they are accustomed to liberty, one observes among them neither rudeness nor grossness, and when we see them at their games we can understand the saying of the Duke of Wellington, when—revisiting in the decline of life the fair scenes of his education and recalling the sports of his boyhood, and finding the same precocious vigour in the sons of his comrades—he exclaimed aloud, *It is here that Waterloo was won*[1]*.*"

But, my brethren, although I hold no distinctions between "secular" and "religious," and do

[1] *De l'Avenir Politique de l'Angleterre*, ch. XI. Les Ecoles (freely paraphrased).

not for a moment apologise for introducing subjects usually foreign to a pulpit, let me not forget that it is *here—here* in God's house—that we must look for the culminating influence of the public school,—I mean the discipline of the heart. Strength and health and beauty and even knowledge are but as the dust of the balance in comparison with holiness; and better, far better, that we should send from among us one *good* boy than fifty clever boys or strong boys or well-taught boys. My brethren, if Harrow has been honoured and successful, I believe that the secret of it is to be found in this place of worship, and in the steady unswerving endeavour as our first and main object to keep the love of God ever in your minds, and the example of Christ ever before your memories and your hearts. You have been under a pious and a prayerful guidance, and we never enter on our common studies in the morning or close them at night, without the earnest prayer (in which many youthful hearts join I trust continually) that God's blessing may rest upon our labours. None will accuse me, my brethren, of ignoring the dangers and the temptations of a public school, but I believe that if, which God forbid, there be any thoroughly bad hearts in the midst of us, they are bad, not *because of* Harrow, but *in spite of* it. And if our pious founder could return once more into the midst of us; if he could gaze with delight on this fair chapel with the names of the brave and warrior dead recorded on its walls, and with the story of kings and prophets and of the life of the Son of God Himself streaming in glorious colours from its painted windows;—if Sunday by Sunday he could take part for a while in its hallowed ministrations, and listen to the sweet sounds of its "Solemn Psalms and silver litanies;" if he could hear with what passionate earnestness and varied power, with what faithfulness, and fearlessness, yea with what tears of genuine emotion, God's precepts are urged upon you, and Christ's atonement pointed out as at once the one means of forgiveness and the only remedy for sin;—then would he not say that if you fall your blood is on your own heads and we are free? Yes, imagine him to come in here in his simple yeoman's dress, and to walk up that aisle—(a better and wiser man perhaps for all his low station than the noblest here)— and imagine him to be endowed with voice once more to tell you one lesson about his school; would it not be this?—

"If you fall at Harrow School,—if you came to it bright and happy, and leave it with but few lessons save those of sin and sorrow,—blame yourselves, your own warped natures, your own weak hearts, your own wandering desires, your own forgetfulness of God, and not the nurse who would have trained you in all godliness, and who taught you to fold your hands in prayer. Remember ye, Harrow boys who leave Harrow worse than when you came, remember ye that Samuel and the sons of Eli were nurtured in the same tabernacle precincts; the light of the sanctuary lamp fell on the boyhood of them both, and the glow of the same Shechinah flowed for both through the purple of the embroidered vail. Samuel heard God's voice, and became a prophet of the Highest, while the sons of Eli were sons of Belial, and were filling God's courts with violent rapine and brutal lust. Was it then the Temple that corrupted the sons of Eli? Nay, not more than it is your school which ruins you."

I have been speaking to you as a body, now lastly bear with me in patience on this solemn occasion while I speak to you a few words as individuals.

I have said that each boy here has some

share, and an appreciable share, in creating that tradition which permeates the whole life of a public school, and if I might particularise further I should say that to do his work rightly a boy has need of three great virtues or principles of action,—*Diligence, Manliness, Decision.* Of Diligence it has often been our privilege to speak from this place before, and to point out the duty and necessity of it for all who would serve God or benefit mankind : of Manliness too we have spoken continually, and shewn you that precocious vice is its deadly and spurious counterfeit, and that it is only possible to the pure in heart ; but of Decision let me speak one word again. My brethren, if you would do your duty by your school, *you must substitute active enmity with evil, for passive pursuit of good.* At whatever cost, you must make vice impossible at least in your presence. You must not be afraid of the contemptible sneer of a degraded companion, but rather be afraid of judgment, be afraid of sin, be afraid of conscience, be afraid of eternity, be afraid of God. You say the task of rooting out all evil from the midst of a large school is difficult, is painful ; yes it may be, just as it is painful to cauterise a poisoned wound, and yet the wound must be cauterised if you would not have the whole body cankered and killed. But do not talk of difficulty: the greater the difficulty, the greater is the honour, the greater the necessity; it is not because it is difficult that you do not dare, but it is difficult because, and only because, you do not dare[1]. But difficult or not, believe me it is your duty, and it will be successful. The youngest boy, the most recent arrival, must take his side at once, and, if any one would trifle with his simplicity, let him know that he will do so at his peril. Do not fear that your influence will be small; no influence is small; but, even if it were, the aggregate of small influences is far more irresistible than the most vigorous and heroic of isolated efforts.

The temple of the Lord, the temple of the Lord, the temple of the Lord are these! the whole is God's building, built on Christ as the foundation,—and each member should be a living stone; a stone of fair colours in the spiritual edifice. Are there not such among you? yes, thank God, there are,—boys who do honour to this place,—diligent, honest, pure-hearted, happy, strong, — because temperance and sobermind-

[1] "Non quia difficilia non sunt audemus, sed quia non audemus difficilia sunt."

edness are strength,—beautiful of countenance, because beauty is but "the sacrament of goodness,"—courteous and noble, because virtue is the true nobility and noble manners are but the fruit of noble minds. These are the stones of fair colours on the sapphire-founded shrine ;— varying in their order, varying in their brightness, but all beautiful, all worthy of being built on the precious corner stone of Christ ;—let one represent the amethyst of temperance, and another the pearl of purity, and another the ruby of fiery zeal; but each in his own order, each a jewel of the Lord, each shining with the lustre of the firmament, and as the stars for ever and ever. Give us but this for all alike and we will not imagine an ideal Utopia, or an Atalantis sunk beneath the waves. Give us but a school like this, and we ask no brighter temple, no holier sanctuary, no happier home. Give us but this, and content with God's presence here, we will not yearn for palaces of emerald and chrysolite, for walls of jasper or streets of gold. The ideal, translated into fact, will be a diviner spectacle than the most radiant combination of material images can adequately shadow forth.

"O thou afflicted, tossed with tempest but not comforted, behold, I will lay thy stones with fair colours, and lay thy foundations with sapphires. And I will make thy windows of agates, and thy gates of carbuncles, and all thy borders of pleasant stones. And all thy children shall be taught of the Lord, and great shall be the peace of thy children."

God grant that this may prove to be for us also the language of prophecy, and that the prophecy of to-day may be the history of to-morrow!

ΤΩ ΘΕΩ ΔΟΞΑ.

IX.

CHURCH SERVICES.

(Preached in the Parish Church of Doncaster, at the Choral Festival, 1867.)

Ps. cxxii. 1. (Prayer Book Version.)—"I was glad when they said unto me, We will go into the house of the Lord."

So spake of old a warrior-prophet, a poet-king; but his words sound in many ears like a satire now. "Glad when they said unto me"?—nay rather is not God's service too generally thought of, and spoken of,—spoken of openly in conversation, in magazines, in newspapers—as the weariest and dreariest of all conventionalities, to be avoided as often as possible, to be endured, if at all, rather out of a sense of decency, than from a feeling of delight? We hear much of the overweening length and many repetitions of our services;—much of the tedium of sermons to intellectual men;—much of wrangling and dissension where all should be love and peace,—

but little indeed of David's rapture as he draws near to the altars of his God and King; little of washing the hands in innocency, and closing the heart in silence, as we enter God's sanctuary;—little indeed of preferring to be a doorkeeper in the House of the Lord to dwelling in the tents of ungodliness.

Surely, my brethren, it is a sad thing that this olden rapture, this olden enthusiasm, should have died away. Many of you, I trust, have felt to-day that a day spent like this—a day spent in God's courts—is better than a thousand. In this weary world, what with our sins and what with our sorrows, there are not so many sources of innocent joy that we can afford to let any one of them be lost. The loss may have arisen in part because we have so little understood how to make the Sabbath a delight, Holy of the Lord, and honourable; in part from the deadness and coldness of spirit that has in many places insensibly benumbed our gatherings; in part from the misfortune of that exclusive system which, while for the rich it has afforded ample and luxurious accommodation, has said to the poor man "Stand thou there, or sit here under my footstool;"—in part from causes that lie far deeper and have spread far more widely than, any of these. But, be those causes what they may, since they tend to rob us of some of the sweetest and brightest moments of our lives, let us, in our own hearts at least, strive to counteract them. Gathered to-day in this beautiful house of God, so happy in the fair order of its services, let us strive to learn how we may realise some of these lost blessings; how we may learn when, Sabbath after Sabbath, our day and our thoughts, and our prayers are undisturbed, —when, hand in hand, with our little ones we pass through the green mounds where the bones of our fathers lie,—when, within the sacred precincts, we bow our heads in solemn prayer, and shut out the vain noises of the world,—we may learn to be enriched by all those sweet and softening influences, and not suffer them to fall like the dew of God upon hard and barren ground. Assuredly this effort will be its own reward. We shall soon thankfully regard our Sundays as a blessed and recurring truce amid the trials of our earthly warfare,—a truce of God between our nobler selves and those evil powers or mean cares which annoy and beset us; a bright interspace of rest and calm in which we may creep nearer to the Great Light, and see, with eyes less troubled and less clouded, our Father's face. Then, what Elim was to the weary and fainting Israelites as they rested beneath its overshadowing palms, that, week by week, will the Sunday be to us,—a sapphire fountain wherein to quench our thirst for all high and holy things amid this earthly wilderness of deceitful images and burning sands, amid this daily dusty path of little anxieties and corroding cares.

And if I mistake not, my brethren, this refreshful influence will be mainly connected with the Divine worship of our Church. It is one of our great blessings that in England there is not a town, not a village, scarcely even a hamlet, throughout its length and breadth, which is left without its appointed place for the sacred ordinances of our religion. Never, probably, have we passed a Sunday in England, without hearing the music of village chimes, rising and falling from the green valleys or scented fields; and even in the great dim cities the noisy wheels of work are silenced, and the sound of church bells falls pleasantly on our ears. And in most places these national churches are, as they ever ought to be, the chief centres of attraction and of reverence; in many they have remained unshaken amid changing dynasties and changing ages; under their elms generation after generation has grown up and gone to rest,—and their spire, pointing heavenwards from amid its clustering trees, has been the last sight which the village-boy has seen, the last reminder he has had of the lessons of home, as he started forth upon his journey into the world. They may be poor and mean in outward structure and inward decoration; but to all true and faithful hearts they will still remain, in the words of St Chrysostom, "the place of angels and archangels, the court of God, and the image of heaven." A thousand memories make them dear to us:—there the pure and solemn melodies of human instruments and human song have soothed and elevated our souls;—there, it may be, like lightning from on high, some message of God has burst with its revealing blaze into our hearts, and we have heard his still small voice stirring the inmost depth of our being ;—there we have risen on the wings of passionate supplication till we felt as though we were "kneeling on the sapphire dusk whereon stands His throne;"—there we have felt ourselves one of His great human family, while it was borne in upon us that, not only under that quiet roof,—but far away from the deck of sailing vessels, and from churches built of coral in the islands of the sea, and where the light glows from the painted windows of stately minsters, and where the sunset streams over men of other races from under the woven branches of pine and palm, as though all the nations of Humanity were kneeling to grasp at one moment the hem of His robe,—the voices of ten thousand worshippers were all arising with ours in the same hallowed words into the listening ears of the Lord of Sabaoth. Long may such associations be blended together, in one hallowing bond, to add dearness and interest to our public worship, and I pray to God's Holy Spirit—to that Holy Spirit who not only mitred the brows of the Apostles with cloven flame, but who can ordain strength even out of feeble and alien lips—I pray that He may so bless our thoughts to-day that the services of our Church, and the House of God wherein they are offered, and the Book of Common Prayer in which they are contained, may win henceforth a yet deeper and livelier significance in all our minds.

And first what a blessing it is to possess this Book of Common Prayer; what a blessing that we are not left at the mercy of one man's feeble utterances, dictated by the narrow limits of his own individuality, and marred, as they often might be, by the poverty, the earthliness, or even the insincerity, of his mind. No; our prayers, so simple, so noble, so eloquent, are the grandest outpouring of those many wants which the long sufferings and the long experience of humanity have taught us to feel and know. In our own private prayers we must have often been haunted by an uneasy consciousness that, after all, it might prove better for us if our wishes were not granted,—and we must have often felt the need of adding to our petitions,

> "Not what we wish, but what we want,
>   Thy favouring grace supply;
> The good, unasked, in mercy grant,
>   The ill, though asked, deny:—"

but assuredly you will not find one doubtful or dangerous petition, not one to which the heart cannot assent and consent, in the many litanies of this precious book. They were composed and uttered, not by men dwarfed with the miserable narrowness of party spirit, or swallowed up in worldly cares, but by those virgin souls who lived in the purple dawn of Christian enthusiasm, in the early glow of Christian love. These prayers, and such as these, were uttered by the confessors from the dungeon and the catacomb; and these, or such as these, the martyrs breathed when they lifted their thin hands in adoration out of the quivering flames. And this is why we find in these prayers—the costly legacy of their sorrows and their triumphs —the bright Christian hope which recognises all men without distinction as the sons of a common Father, and the heirs of a common promise. Among professing Christians, how often do we catch an echo of that wretched language of the Pharisee, "Stand aside, for I am holier than thou." But in our Prayer-book, thank God, there is no trace of this self-satisfaction, no trace of the self-soothing and trenchant division between the world and the saints. No, in the prayers of that book we all, the very proudest of us, must come before God as sinners; yet all, the very meanest of us, as children too; all of us as brethren of Christ, and children of our most merciful Father,—all of us as equally guilty, yet all as equally redeemed. The priest and the publican, the Magdalen and the Pharisee, united in one common Saviour, must approach in the same words the footstool and the mercy-seat of the same God. O let us thank God for this hallowed Book of Common Prayer: —for this pure golden censer which, refined in the sevenfold fires of affliction, has gleamed so brightly from the days of the Apostles in the hands of his greatest saints,—for 'this golden censer which was purged at the Reformation from all its dross[1],' and in which have mingled together, amid the storms and agitations of a thousand years, those voices of true supplication which rise like the richest of all incense through the hands of the great High Priest before the throne.

We begin our service with a word of admonition to solemnise our thoughts; then comes an exhortation to remind us where we are; and this is followed by a confession of our sins, by the authoritative promise of forgiveness; and by the words of that Divine petition wherewith our Lord taught his disciples to pray. And after this we are in a fit mood for the Canticle and the Psalm. Now the necessity of exhortation, of confession, and of absolution, are plain to every mind; but this weekly and daily use of the Psalms of David has been censured, by more than one eminent thinker[2], as indiscriminate and absurd. My brethren, when our hearts are rightly attuned to the spirit of devotion, do we really find it so? It is true that different Psalms are the echo of different moods; and the

[1] Stowell.   [2] Especially by Baron von Bunsen.

wild utterance of anguish wherewith the soul cries "out of the depths" to the living God, requires a different condition of mind for its realisation to that wherein David bids "take the Psalm, and bring hither the tabret, the merry harp with the lute." But surely this is the very reason why the Psalms, when many are assembled, contain something suitable for the varying moods of every worshipper. They are the echoes of a deep and passionate emotion; the records of a struggling yet noble life; and because they came fresh and burning from the heart, they will enter fresh and burning into it, and will cause to vibrate for ever the finest and most musical chords of human sympathy. Of David, it might be truly said as of the angel of Mohametan legend, that his heartstrings were a lute. He learnt in suffering what he taught in song. Through all that wonderful and moving life of his; from the time when, as a boy, he lived among his mountain flocks, and smote the lion and the bear, to the glorious youth, in which he slew the giant, and lulled with his melodies the evil spirit which vexed the dark soul of his king,—through all the long reign which dawned in fame, and splendour, and manhood, and set in dotage, and tears, and blood,—

this man, who, though he had sunk into abhorred acts of lust and murder, was yet counted among the saints of God, has left us in these Psalms, as on a harp with a thousand strings, the thrilling record of every sublime thought, of every troubled moment, of every fiery experience which swept over the horizon of his soul. He was a sinner indeed, but it is

> "the sin which practice burns into the blood,
> And not the one dark hour that brings remorse
> That stamps us after of whose fold we be:"

and these Psalms are the living picture of a heart which, in spite of all its awful failures, was yet longing, yearning, praying continually, with all its energies and through all its agonies, for that which was noble, and pure, and good: and therefore so long as our souls also live and struggle and fail, so long will these Psalms of David supply us with the fittest language in which to find vent for our experiences; so long will they cheer the depression of the mournful, and cheek the carelessness of the mirthful; so long will they teach us how best to pray against our temptations, how best to bewail our sins.

And you, my brethren, in rendering those Psalms into music, and so singing merrily unto God your strength, are uttering them as David meant them to be uttered. Oh be sure that yours is a holy ministry, and let the youngest boy in those village choirs who can use the sweet voice which God has given him in praise and giving thanks, feel happy that God accepts this service at his hands. For the influence of music is powerful and holy; and, in the words of an old Father, they must have hearts very dry and tough for whom the sweetness and softness of that which toucheth the ear, does not convey as it were by stealth, the treasure of good things into man's mind. "They must have hearts very dry and tough," says Hooker, "from whom the melody of the Psalms doth not sometimes draw that wherein a religious soul delighteth;" and have your hearts never leapt within you, my brethren, when, with the rolling tones of organ music and choral song, you sang in passionate exultation, "O praise the Lord of heaven; praise him in the height; praise him all ye angels of his; praise him all his host. Praise him sun and moon; praise him all ye stars and light"? or have you never thrilled with sudden emotion at the swelling jubilance of the strains which tell how God scattered his enemies as stubble before the wind—" the tabernacles of the Edomites and Ishmaelites, the Moabites and Hagarens; Gebal and Ammon and Amalek; the Philistines also with them that dwell at Tyrus." Those who, in a world of sorrow and mammon-worship, are glad and thankful for any noble pleasure which can raise and inspire the soul above its low-thoughted cares,—which can breathe into it, even for an hour, something of that high happiness which God intended for every innocent heart,—will rejoice to hear the powers of music dedicated to God's praise, and will be sure that He who made the common air thrill with ten thousand melodies, will not be displeased that our worship upon earth should catch some faint echo of that "sevenfold chorus of Hallelujahs and harping symphonies" wherewith the song of angels encircles His heavenly throne.

And so we come to the Lessons for morning and evening service; and these chapters, selected as they are from the very grandest portions of Holy Writ,—forming as they do the most priceless jewels of that inestimable treasure-house,—may well be ranked among the most blessed parts of our Sunday Service. Oh learn, my brethren,—above all learn in these days in which too often the Bible is degraded into a wrangling-ground for sectarian differences,—

learn to love and reverence it aright. May it ever be associated in our minds with all things which are "soft and gentle and pure and penitent and good." In its words, while yet we were helpless infants, we were admitted into that fold whereof Christ is the good Shepherd; out of its words a mother—now it may be a saint in heaven—taught us at her knee to be early accustomed to the story of our Saviour's love. In its words of mystery and beauty, we received the blessing of God as we stood beside the marriage-altar. In its words of healing and hope we found the thoughts of consolation and the promises of immortality, when Death broke pitilessly into the circle of our beloved. We have read its words with eyes blinded by tears in old churches far away; and its words have breathed into our souls a sweet and healing calm even as we leant over the open grave where we had just laid our best beloved into the dust. Never shall we know until the last great day what life histories hang upon its every page. It is like that tree of northern fable, whose leaves were the lives of men. How often, in crucial moments of temptation, have its remembered words prevented the commission of some dread crime; how often, flashing into the memory, has it awakened the slumbering conscience with thunder-crashes of remorse. How often has the drowning sailor thought of it when, in some lone sea, the breaker swept him from the stranded vessel into the seething depths; how often the dying soldier, as he lay face upwards, in the cold moonlight, on the battle-field, with the life-blood ebbing from his wounds; and men and women, on peaceful deathbeds, die most often with its words upon their lips, when they turn from their sobbing families to wet the pillow with their weak tears and die. Oh let us treasure, let us love the words which come to us hallowed and intensified with such wondrous associations of childhood and innocence, of marriage and sickness, of eternity and death.

And those hymns which you sing,—embalming some of the holiest thoughts of some of the holiest men,—my brethren, how happy, how truly delightful, a part of God's services are they! What a page of the soul's story would that be which should tell us the origin of our favourite hymns! "God is our refuge in distress" sprang like a spark of fire from the glowing soul of Luther in the year when the Princes of Germany presented to the Diet of Spires that celebrated Protest from which is derived the name of Protestant. "Lo, he comes in clouds descending" expresses the thought of Cennick during the tumults and horrors of European war. "Jerusalem the Golden" echoes in Dr Neale's translation the immortal yearnings of Bernard of Cluny. "O for a closer walk with God" is the deep sigh of Cowper when the cloud of insanity was overshadowing one of the tenderest and sweetest of Christian souls. "From Greenland's icy mountains" tells of that bright philanthropy which sent the noble spirit of Heber from all his high English prospects to die in his Indian bishopric. "Oft in sorrow, oft in woe" was written in fragments on the backs of the mathematical papers of Henry Kirke White, when that eagle intellect was already being pierced by a shaft winged from its own plumes.

> "Abide with me, fast falls the eveningtide,
> The darkness deepens, Lord, with me abide;
> When other comforts fail, and helpers flee,
> Friend of the friendless, oh abide with me,"

was written by Henry Lyte, when the deep chill waters of death's river were beginning already to close around him. And yet more various than the circumstances under which hymns have been written, are the circumstances under which they have been sung. It was after having sung a hymn that our dear and blessed Lord crossed the brook Kedron to enter on his agony in the garden of Gethsemane; it was with hymns that Paul and Silas, their backs scorched and bleeding with Roman rods, solaced their midnight solitude in the dungeon of Philippi; it was the song of boy singers with their hymnal that woke up the fasting Luther from his dangerous swoon in the cell of Erfurdt; it was a little girl singing a hymn on the doorstep of her home that comforted the banished Melancthon in the streets of Weimar; it was with hymns that the camp of William the Conqueror resounded on the eve of that great battle that changed for centuries the destinies of England; they rang in the sweet valleys of the Vaudois while they were being deluged with innocent blood; they have given enthusiasm to the warrior as he rode to danger; they have cheered the martyr's soul in the hour of death. We probably all know cases of the deep root they strike in the memory:—one such instance among many came not long ago to my knowledge. By one of those mysterious Providences, which shew our utter ignorance of the divine ways, it was God's will to call to Himself the soul of a young and hopeful boy—as young and as full of hope as some of you—and that, not down the lingering declivities of disease, but by the sharp stroke of sudden accident. It was in the hymns stored up in his memory that the dying boy found his main consolation. The last hour drew nigh, and he asked his young sister to sing for him that earnest and favourite hymn of Toplady's, which has breathed calm over the tossed soul of so many a penitent:

> "Rock of ages, cleft for me,
> Let me hide myself in thee:"

but, as her voice first wavered and then broke down with tears, sweetly and almost steadily the voice of the dying sufferer arose; sweetly it lingered on the lines of comfort, and even while it lingered, the silver cord was loosed, the golden bowl broken, and in the very words which he had been uttering, the "eyelids closed in death," and the young spirit had "risen to worlds unknown," to hide in that Rock whereon his trust was stayed.

It is not my purpose, brethren, to go through the rest of our service,—to dwell on those other prayers that may kindle our darkening souls as the embers of a fire are kindled by breath of air; on those commandments which remind us of the fiery majesty of the moral law; or on that Holy Sacrament, which at its every recurrence should bring home to us more deeply that "Man doth not live by bread alone, but by every word that proceedeth out of the mouth of God." But let me, selecting but one more topic, pass at once to say a few words on that portion of the Service to which so many attach an exaggerated importance, and so many an exaggerated contempt.

"Resort to sermons," says the old poet of our Church, "but to prayers most,—praying's the end of preaching." But yet it is too much of a modern and unchristian fashion to disparage or discredit this ordinance in itself. True it is,— and it would be absurd to deny or conceal the inevitable fact,—that from the pulpit are spoken many trite, many fatiguing, and many unprofitable words. True it is, that not to one in ten thousand, that to a few only in a generation, is it given by the grace of God

> "To preach as one who ne'er should preach again,
> And as a dying man to dying men;"

to stand forth like a heavenly archer, and to hurl into the dark heart arrows of lightnings; to wield the Word of God as that which indeed it is, a hammer to dash in pieces the flinty conscience; a fire to devour the stubble of human deceitfulness; a sword to pierce the soul, and to divide in sunder the very joints and marrow. But what then, my brethren? Does the unprofitableness, does what St Paul calls the foolishness of our preaching arise solely or mainly from the weakness of the preacher? Has the listlessness, the weariness, the wilful inattention of the congregation nothing to do with it? Is the failure of the sermon the fault of Paul who preached, or of Eutychus who slept? How can the words of the preacher stir your conscience, how can they touch your heart, if you settle yourselves down into supercilious indifference, with a predetermination not to be converted, not to be instructed, not to be aroused,—if you cover yourselves and your sins with that triple panoply of ice and steel, wherein is not even one joint of the harness through which the arrow of conviction can wing its way? You blame the preacher, my brethren, but was it that he did not sow good seed, or was it that it fell on the stony and trodden ground? Was it that he was ineffective, or that your own hearts were preoccupied and dead? You listened—aye, you listened critically, impatiently, unconcernedly—but where was the meek heart and due reverence, where was the humble spirit and the childlike faith? Ah, sirs, let us be humble listeners. Let us try to regard the preacher with the kindness and forbearance due to a brother,—our brother indeed in sins, in infirmities, in all sad experience,—our inferior, it may be, in utterance, in knowledge, and even in every spiritual grace,—but still to one who has been set apart as the ambassador of God, and who, however feeble, may yet have some special message of God for our individual souls. Aye, and the Word of God has not lost its power, nor the arm of God is not shortened. These despised sermons may perhaps be, and I believe that they often are, the invisible links of that golden chain which keeps our souls from falling into utter forgetfulness of God.

I have spoken, then, my brethren, of the Sabbaths we keep—their peace and calm; of the Services in which we join—their beauty and refreshfulness; of the hymns and psalms, which inspire us with their ennobling music; of the hallowed earthly temples wherein we meet for the worship of God. Before you leave this church you will have the opportunity of assisting by your contributions a gathering intended to add to the beauty, to the solemnity, to the happiness of our weekly Services; and that opportunity I trust and I am sure that you will not neglect;—but oh remember, in conclusion, that all these are but what we make them. Not by singing "Lord, Lord," but by doing the will of Christ, shall you enjoy a foretaste of heaven. No number of Hallelujahs, sung with an unloving heart, can bring you one step nearer to the throne;—and he who chants the Trisagion of the Seraphim with lips uncircumcised, offers a service as little pleasing as the blasphemy of the condemned. The very prayer of such an one is turned into sin. Oh remember, then, that your duty may become your danger; the happy privilege may be changed into the terrible stumblingblock. Your Sabbaths, your songs, your Services,—these may be to you a crystal river of unreproved enjoyment; they *may* become turbid and wearisome, an unprofitable burden, an idle form. But, for the heart which is cleansed and calm, not these only but life itself becomes a Sabbath, whose inward rest no agitations can disturb; a Service which no weariness can invade; a Hymn on which no discord can jar; a Temple of God, about which indeed the clouds may roll, but of which no clouds can quench the Light of that Presence which shines within. Only through that heart can you see God. "Through the glass darkly," it has been said, "but except through the glass in no wise. A tremulous crystal, waved as water, poured out upon the ground: you may despise it, defile it, pollute it, at your pleasure and at your peril: for on the peace of those weak waves must all the heaven you shall ever gain be first seen; and through such purity as you can win for those dark waves, must all the light of the risen Sun of Righteousness be bent down by faint refraction. Cleanse them, and calm them as you love your life."

X.

GOD'S BANQUET AND THE WORLD'S.

(Preached before Harrow School, January 15, 1863.)

LUKE xv. 16.—"And he would fain have filled his belly with the husks that the swine did eat: and no man gave unto him."

THERE are two banquets ever outspread before you,—God's banquet and the World's. The fair linen cloth upon yonder altar, covering the broken bread and the sacramental wine, reminds you of one image of that table which God provides us in the wilderness of life. The bread from heaven,—the meat which consists in doing the will of God,—the well-spring of water that excludes all thirst, and springs up into everlasting life,—the tree of life blossoming with twelve manner of immortal fruits, and every fruit an innocence or a virtue;—these are the few and simple types of God's banquet,—of that marriage supper of the King's Son to which the voice of God invites continually His children in the world.

The few and simple types,—there is no luxury here, no alluring splendour, no regal magnificence. Far more outwardly gorgeous, far more dazzling in its voluptuous pomp, is the gay banquet of the world. Wealth lavishes upon it her silver and gold,—art degrades for its adornment the mystery of soft colours, and perfect forms,— beauty wears beside it her most dangerous smile,—sinful mirth laughs loudly at its reckless orgies. Over that table pride waves her haughtiest banners, and the trumpets of ambition breathe out their most maddening notes. It is a banquet of the world's best, which she offers to her votaries first; every day she is offering it to you.

These are the two banquets; but mark the difference between them. Eat of the bread of life, and you shall hunger no more; drink of its crystal river, and you cannot thirst again. The soul eats and drinks thereof, and it is satisfied for ever. But, sit down at the world's feast, and what follows? You eat, and ever as the food grows coarser and scantier, the craving hunger gnaws you with keener pangs; you drink, till the wine cup is drawn down to the lees, but the bitter draught only scorches the parched throat. You are hardly seated there, when, as though an enchanter waved his wand, you behold it all in its true light; you are sitting amid the gilded relics of corruption; for beauty there is burning, the riches are corrupted, the garments moth-eaten, the gold and silver is red with the canker and the rust. You would not have believed it before; for everything was masked and counterfeit, and the triple veil of folly and sensuality were bound upon your eyes. You would not believe it before, but you see it now. You look round you, and none but the Dead are there.

Many of you, still under the spell of enchantment, are sitting, I say, at this banquet now; many who have gone from the midst of us are among its weary guests. It hath never wanted its countless revellers. But, because its seductiveness is so strong, and because till you have seen its horror no hand can tear you from its allurements, and because to-day you are invited to another and a purer feast, listen to me while, following the teaching of our Lord and Master, I tell you the history of one who accepted that fatal invitation. It is the life-history of one,—and if of one, then it is also the life-history of countless human souls. Perhaps it is the history of some of those souls that are looking at me even now with the eyes of youth.

It is no far-fetched story; the very youngest boy here knows it well; the sun never shines at morning without flinging the picture of it in colours of blue and crimson from the chancel windows on the chapel-floor, yet it happens that during more than seven years I remember but once to have heard it made the subject of a sermon from this place, though it is the most divinely tender, the most awfully pathetic of the Parables of Christ, the Parable of the Prodigal Son.

"A certain man had two sons; and the younger of them said to his father, Father, give me the portion of goods that falleth to me. And he divided unto them his living." *We* are those children, and to us does God our Father divide His gracious and glorious gifts. To all of us He gives this earth, with its daily miracles of beauty and power; to all of us the sunrise and the sunset, the flowers and the dew of heaven, the mountains and rivers, the sky and fields. To all of us the healthy airs of day, and the soft sleep of night; to each of us a home, and the sweet voice of friend or brother, of wife or child; to each of us the perfect round of life's changing seasons, and the sweet mystery of death, and the hope of heaven beyond. And to *you* many special and precious gifts; the glories of living, "the luxury of sight and sound, the golden hours of youth," the inestimable gem of Time; to many of you rank and wealth, strength of arm, advantage of position, power of mind. These are God's talents; the inheritance He divides among us at our birth. He gives them to us,— for what purpose? To bury, or hide, or squander them in self-seeking, in self-indulgence, for self-glory? Nay, not so! They are His, not ours; given, not earned; nay, rather lent, not given,— lent us for His service, to be used for His glory with contentedness, with industry, with love.

Alas! it was not so that the young prodigal used his. We have looked on the picture of his home; now mark his departure from it. "And not many days after the younger son gathered all together, and took his journey into a far country." Not many days after; sad words, full of mournful meaning! Still in his glad boyhood, but a few days after he had received the gifts of life, he seeks to leave his father's home. All its sweet memories, all its yearning affections, all its loving faces, are nothing to him. He spurns its pure and holy atmosphere, its gentle and wholesome discipline, its secure and necessary restraint; he has never felt the graceful beauty of obedience, the rich blessing of youthful dependancy. What does he care for all that? He wants to follow the bent of his wild wayward passions. His inmost heart burns for a spurious liberty, a ruinous license to have his own way. He will be a god, knowing good and evil. His father, you see, does not oppose him; his heart may ache for it, yet he must let him eat of the fruit of his own works, and be filled with his own devices. The wilful must have their own way; they must learn by their own experience both as a punishment and as a cure. When an eager boy mounts the chariot of life, and hurls reason from the seat, and casts the reins to passion, he must be swept away by the wild career of those fiery steeds, till their brief strength is broken, and he is flung down shattered and bleeding into the mire beneath their hoofs.

And so, gathering all together, his youth, his health, his beauty, his riches, the poor deluded boy, amid parting tears and the waving of farewell hands, rides away lighthearted from father and from home. Do you blame and scorn the gay young fool? Do you say that he must have been some "warped slip of the wilderness," and no true scion of the old stock? Nay, but is it not what we all have done? Do we not all, as soon almost as we are born, go astray and speak lies, and inflame ourselves with our own idols under every green tree? Are we not daily living among sons who have forgotten and flung to the winds all the pure and tender lessons of childhood and home? Have we not all known many "a younker and prodigal" who, not in a figure but in fact, has turned his back on the home of his infancy, who has left his weeping mother and family, and forsaking the guide of his youth, and forgetting the covenant of his God, has plunged up to the lips in the giddy vortex of vice and sin, and come back, if at all, only as "a forlorn and desperate castaway"? Have we forgotten that the first boy born into the world was also the first murderer, and was driven forth from the presence of God with a brand upon his brow?

He rode forth into "a far country"—alas! how far from heaven and from home—how different are the sights and sounds of it from all that he has heard and seen before! In old days the young knights rode forth to do justice and redress wrong,—and that was a noble and a hopeful starting. But this young prodigal's riding forth,—it was all meanness, and sadness, and misery. Look for nothing brave or manly there. From innocence to sin, from sin to sorrow,—there was no beauty in that path. To be the slave of Satan, to follow the whisper of temptation in the black and dark night,—there was nothing but abomination in that errand. A bird hasting to the snare, an ox led to destruction, are the fit emblems of that pilgrimage. The roads are different, but all deadly; one leads to madness, one to suicide, one to sudden destruction, one to open shame; but they all sweep through the valley of the shadow, they all end in the chambers of death and hell.

And what does the youth do in this far country? It is a short and simple description; he "wastes his substance with riotous living." You have seen the home, and the departure,—fill up the third scene as you will. Give the prodigal all the benefit of his brief pleasuring. Let the meteor-lights of delusive happiness dance before him in all their dangerous splendour. This is the brief madness of the prodigal's delirious dream. Imagine the unhappy youth lying at the glittering feast, with his eyes sparkling and the crown of roses twined around his hair. Let the mirth be furious, and the revels long and loud. Add if you will the dulcet flatteries of a false friendship, aye, and the base lures of a simulated love. Let Vice wear for a time the bewitching mask which has made him turn away from the pure face of Virtue to gaze upon her. These are the pleasures of sin for a season; for sin, like many another poison, is sweet to the taste at first. If it were not who would taste it? Who would ever have been tempted by the Lamia of ancient fable, if a semblance of beauty did not conceal the venomous fangs and the serpent folds? Let the prodigal have this scene to himself; no man has ever enjoyed it long! The next feast at which we shall meet him will be a different one from this.

He "wasted" his substance with riotous living, so that we are not surprised to hear that he had soon "spent all." There is no moderation in that career. It is an amazing thing how men *do* waste the gifts of life: nay, "waste" is a slight word,—how they squander, lavish, spill, devour them,—how they empty themselves of all that is pure and noble in life, as when one wipeth out a dish and turneth it upside down. Soon, very soon, the prodigal found that the bare materials of pleasure are gone; marvellously soon his youth is consumed, his strength sapped, his beauty withered, his wealth devastated, satiety has seized him like a perpetual sickness; his very sense of enjoyment is blunted and palled. The disenchantment comes wonderfully early: long before youth is over, the very capacity for real joy is gone. The youth feels that he is killing himself, and that he has killed already every healthy and true pleasure within him. The devil promises, but he does not care to pay; he who sells himself to a liar, must not be surprised that he has earned, as his sole reward, a lie. Sin gives even her poor poisonous pleasures only grudgingly: —enough to tempt, not enough to appease; enough to enflame and corrode for a lifetime the vitiated taste, not enough to give a sense of satisfaction for a single day. She promises rapture; she gives the only thing she has to give, and that is her own disgustful presence, and the Death which dogs her footsteps, and notches his arrow against her upon the twanging string.

So there arose a mighty famine in that land; there always has been a famine in that far land. Before the spirit is quite quenched, and the soul quite carnalised, there is a craving for higher and better things, which cannot now be realized; and when the spirit is quenched, and the soul is embruted, there is a famine even of that false food which is not bread, and thirst for those stolen waters which only make the thirst more hot. It is a gaunt hungry land that land of sin, peopled only by divers diseases and sundry kinds of death. And its famine-stricken inhabitants are forced from worse to worse; to pleasure of a baser and baser sort, to sins of a deeper and deeper degradation, which yet, to their unhappy minds, are ever more and more vapid and tasteless. Nothing is more mournfully instructive than "the dirges which the tired children of this world are ever wailing forth over the departed gladness of their youth." It has been with them like a fevered dream; they have dreamt of eating, and when they awake, lo! they are hungry. Looking around them they have nothing to shew as an equivalent for their own ruin; where are all those hours of folly and of pleasure and of sin? They have not left even a trace behind. For what, after all, have they sold themselves? It is as though they were sitting down in the ashes of a palace which their own hands have burnt. He "began to be in want." No wonder; it is a passage from ten thousand biographies. Let me put beside it but one familiar page from real life. There was one whose name is often shewn to strangers carved by his own hand on our schoolroom wall, but of whom alas! we have no reason to be proud. Well, he had well-nigh every gift that God could give him. He was young; he was beautiful; he was rich; he bore a noble name; he excelled in all feats of athletic power; he had burning within him the light of a glorious genius. Fortune seemed to have showered upon him, with both hands, her brightest stars. The world lay like a path of light before him, where he might take his ease and enjoyment to the full. Well, he tried the experiment, and how did this one of yourselves, even this poet of your own, write, long before he had attained the full flower of life in its prime of manhood? These are his words:—

> "My days are in the yellow leaf,
>   The flowers, the fruits of love are gone,
> The worm, the canker, and the grief,
>   Are mine alone.
>
> The fire that on my bosom preys,
>   Is lone as some volcanic isle;
> No torch is lighted at its blaze,—
>   A funeral pile."

You see it is the old old story over again; the prodigal's famine in the land of sin. That fire which preys on the bosom of the guilty—what is it? Is it not most often "that infernal fire, whose fuel is gluttony, whose flame is pride, whose sparkles are wanton words, whose ashes are uncleanness, whose end is hell[1]?"

Yes! for in the next and fourth scene the Prodigal has lost every germ of self-respect, and is abased even unto hell. "And he went and joined himself unto a citizen of that country; and he sent him into his fields to feed swine." There is no lighted banquet here, no crown of roses, or smiles of pleasure,—no wreathing perfumes or intoxicating draughts;—no, the fourth scene is rags, famine, beggary, loneliness; and therewith an occupation, which was degrading even to filthy and witless Gadarenes, but which to a Jewish ear carried a sickening sense of disgust and detestation, which made it represent the last depth of hopeless squalor. What a hideous fall for the rich and gay boy who, so short a time before, had ridden forth in hope and beauty, from the peaceful abundance of his father's home, to "enjoy life," to be "independent," to be "free!" Where were all his friends and flatterers,—the partners of his prosperity, the boon companions of his mirthful orgies? They, like his riches, had departed from him.

[1] St Augustine.

True friendship is not purchased thus; it is an attribute of virtue and righteousness, and can only be cemented between high and noble minds. Even the good man, who alone knows what a sacred thing true friendship is, may miss this blessing, and be forced to walk in utter loneliness through the dreary intercourse of daily life, scorning that hollow simulacrum with which conventionality desecrates the great name of friend; but if the good man *may*, the bad man *must* miss it. Partnership in pleasure, association in vice and crime, is no bond of union, but the sure source of ultimate aversion. Those who flatter and spoil you,—those who encourage you in sin and sneer at you in what is right,—those for the fear of whom or the approval of whom you sell your birthright of innocence, and fling the jewel of early piety under the feet of dogs,—these never will or can be your friends. They only despise you for your weakness, and you will soon learn to hate them for the wrong they do. You are only their dupe, to be first lowered to their own level, then tossed aside with scorn. When they are tired of your companionship, they will only laugh at your calamities; when you have ceased to serve their purposes, they will send you to feed swine.

And so, step by step, we have come to that climax of the poor youth's history, which is contained in the text, every word of which strikes the ear like the echo of some unfathomable despair; "*and he would fain have filled his belly with the husks that the swine did eat, and no man gave unto him.*" "He would fain;" why what a strange, unearthly, unnatural longing is this, and what a sore sore famine it must have been that caused it! The day had been when this boy had lived abundantly on pure and wholesome food; had known what it was to wear the best robe and the jewelled ring, and feed in innocent merriment upon the fatted calf; but now we have filth, and abasement, desertion, rags, beggary, and a hunger that crumbles and parches up the very strings of life. Oh! that gnawing hunger, gnawing like a viper at the secret heart; the hunger that nothing can appease, nothing allay, nothing satisfy; the hunger so corrupt that it cannot taste the food of virtue, and gasps in vain even for the filthy husks that in the hour of famine feed the unclean beast, that hunger which is worse than hell itself, and which is all the after-taste which can be ever left by the world's feasts; how at one touch does our Lord set it before us, compressing into a word the history of all erring souls, the fate of sinful nations and sinful men! "He would fain have filled his belly." You know that when the hunters of Ceylon can get no food, they eat the bark of trees as a substitute for food; so with the prodigal: there is no question now of satisfying the appetite, but only of "filling the belly." And why?—for this awful reason; because when the pleasures of sin have long long ceased to be pleasures, they have not ceased to haunt and tear the hungry soul; they leave behind them the fiery brood of evil habits, to breed in and feed upon the soul, so that the wretch longs to fill his belly, though he knows that even thus, and even with this vile food, he cannot appease the cravings of his want. And the same thing is implied by the final touch of all; the last line to this picture of anguish and degradation, that infinitely pathetic conclusion of this story of his fall, "and no man gave unto him." O sin, thou art indeed a hard master to him who serveth thee!

Thus have I traced from our Lord's Parable the history of a soul's fall. But thanks be to God, there is a most tender and touching close to this dark story, the history of a soul's recovery. God's mercy enabled this sinner to repent. God's voice found him in the bitter hankering loneliness of his pollution and distress; it came to him like the first stirrings of the vernal wind that wakes the earth from the stupefaction of winter. That dawn of repentance in the soul comes in different ways to different men. To some it comes with a sudden, overwhelming, irresistible power, in a great flash of lightning, and a sudden shuddering intuition of God's presence, as to him whose conversion the Church commemorates to-day. To others it comes by some word of Holy Writ, falling unexpectedly into some open place in the heart of stone, as a sunbeam struggles into a dark rift between the rocks. I have read of one first awoke to his desperate condition by hearing read the mere chapter of a Scripture genealogy, where many verses end with the words "and he died," which verses brought him face to face with Death and the unseen world. I have read of another who first began to think of spiritual things when his thoughts were arrested by the verse "A living dog is better than a dead lion." He might be mean and low, he knew it; but at least he was living, and the meanest living has an opportunity which may have ceased to exist for the noblest dead. But in most cases probably it is by means of evil that we learn that good is best, and through sin and sorrow and punishment we are raised into eternal life. So it was that the Prodigal was converted. Broken, humbled, ruined, the wanderer came to himself; he remembered his Father's home; and in spite of disgrace, and shame, and fear—those things which have prevented many a poor erring boy from coming back to a home which he has left—he takes the only path which the sinner has left open to himself, he gives up his sins, leaves them behind him, confesses them unreservedly, humbles himself because of them to the very dust. "He arose, and came to his Father."

And now will his father receive him? There are thousands of earthly fathers who have not done so, though the offence committed against them has been far less heinous than that of the Prodigal. One father I knew once, whose son had been sent to sea. The boy may have behaved badly, but at any rate he was illtreated, he was miserable, and he ran away from his ship to seek once more his father's home. How did his father—an old man, a clergyman, and one who had known sorrow—receive him? He took the boy to an upper room, locked him up there, gave him bread and water to eat and drink, and next morning, in spite of entreaties and of tears, took him straight back to the ship he hated, and the captain from whose persecutions he had fled. That boy never again, never again, came back to his father's home. And how could the prodigal know that he too would not be received with cruelty and punishment, perhaps with stripes and death? how could he expect aught else than to have the doors shut against him, and to be driven with infamy from the hearts he had desolated, and the home he had stained and shamed?

You know how he *was* received. In the whole round of human and divine literature there is nothing equal to that wonderful depth of impassioned and forgiving love. "And he arose, and came to his father. And when he was yet a great way off, his father saw him, and had compassion, and ran, and fell on his neck, and kissed him,"—why need I add the rest, which you all know? Oh! may every lost, every dead son here be thus alive again, be thus found! for there are prodigals here; prodigals young in years, but old in sin; unsuspected and unknown it may be, yet assuredly they are sitting here, feeling the death-hunger in their secret souls. "Go thou up into the tribunal of thy own conscience, and set thyself before thyself," and ask if it be thus with thee. And if so, as thou hast imitated the Prodigal's apostasy, even so imitate his repentance and his return. Unhappy one! though thy very mind and conscience be defiled, though these very words pierce, as with the arrow of conviction, thy guilty heart, yet even for thee, who from thy wayward childhood hast gone astray at the call of every sin, for thee, as for the publicans and sinners who heard these words of the Son of God, our Father's invitation is full and free. Oh! turn from the world's banquet, which first palls the taste and then offers its last dregs, to that pure feast of the true bread to which He still invites you. Come as the Prodigal did, even in the filthy rags, even from the swinish sty: He will not reject you, nay rather He will see you afar off, and cover your unworthiness with His own white robe, and will allay your anguish of hunger, and make the ground bright with heavenly manna for your eternal sustenance, and will cool your raging thirst with sweet large draughts of that water of the river of Life, pure as crystal, which proceedeth out of the throne of God, and of the Lamb.

XI.

THE ANIMAL AND THE SPIRITUAL.

(Preached before Harrow School on the First Sunday of the Summer Term, 1864.)

GEN. xxv. 27.—"And the boys grew, and Esau was a cunning hunter, a man of the field; and Jacob was a plain man, dwelling in tents."

THE life and the heart of man were essentially the same 4000 years ago as they are now. The hand of the sacred historian draws aside the tent-curtains of the patriarch, and shews us the same shades of character as may be seen in a modern English home. He shews us two boys at play. They are the sons of pious parents, the heirs of precious promises, the possessors of golden opportunities; but though they enjoy the same privileges, they make a very different use of them, and throughout life they follow very different paths.

1. The two boys differed as many among

you differ. Esau was full of healthy vigour and the spirit of adventure, exulting in field sports, active, muscular, with the rough aspect and bounding pulse of the free desert. Jacob was a harmless shepherd, pensive and tranquil, dwelling by the hearth, and caring only for quiet occupations. The one was never so happy as when he drank the eager mountain air, while he chased the wild roe over Judah's hills, or saw the lion leap "with bare breast and unarmed claws upon surrounding deaths;" the other never so happy as when he rested among his sheep at eventide, and saw the name of God written in starlight on the great leaves of the book of heaven, or, in the tent and at the feet of Abraham (now an old man, and full of years), listened with a beating heart to the story of the Promised Seed.

So far we know nothing wrong of Esau. In those days the chase was no idle amusement, but for those who followed it a serious and necessary employment, full of manly perils, and a means of providing for daily food. The impulses indeed of Jacob were nobler and more immortal impulses, but those of Esau, although animal, were not intrinsically immoral. Beware of idolising, beware of overvaluing, mere physical preeminence. Strength, and speed, and courage, and endurance, are blessings not lightly to be despised; but he who confines his ideal to them, as Esau did, chooses a low ideal, and one which can bring a man but little peace at the last. Esau is not a good example to imitate. His uncle Ishmael, the Bedouin chief of a roving Arab horde, was probably his model, and the Scripture calls him "a wild man," or to render it literally, "a wild ass of a man." Well, the wild ass of the desert is a gallant and dazzling creature, swift, indomitable, and strong; in these gifts even an Ishmael cannot rival, much less excel it: but is a son of Abraham, nay more, a son of God, to be content, like the ignorant savage, to take his name and to find his prototype in some unintelligent creature of the wild? Why then what a pitiful thing his life must be, hardly better than the gleaming of some gorgeous insect in an hour of summer's sun! For these bodily triumphs, if they be all that a man can look to, are only possible for a few short years, and where is he, or what pleasures has he left, when youth has glided by like a dream, and sickness, or accident, or inevitable age, have dried up his strength like a potsherd, and brought him to the gates of death? Live not in the present only, but provide for the future too. Vigour, and strength, and other physical gifts may be an innocent, nay more, a glorious, crown round the brows of manhood ; but they never can be so if they are sought exclusively, if they are not united to other and better things. In themselves there was nothing wrong in Esau's tastes ; I only say that Jacob's were of a nobler and a better kind, inasmuch as time is of infinitely less moment than eternity, inasmuch as the body is a meaner and earthlier thing than the spirit and the soul.

Yet God has given diversities of gifts, and we ought duly to value and thankfully to recognise them all. To every living being our Father in Heaven has given something which shall enable him to maintain his happiness and his self-respect; in short, to hold his own among his fellow men. One has a noble body, another a keen intellect ; one excels in the schoolroom, another in the cricket-field : each may find in the other something to admire, something to imitate, something to respect; and oh ! that each honoured each, and helped each ; for all are brethren; all sons of the same Father; all sheep of a common fold. If it were so, how far greater and happier we should be ; but alas ! it is often not so, even in the same family. It was not so in Isaac's. The parents might have been proud of the gifts of both, and have loved both alike; but instead of that there was unhappy favouritism. Isaac loved his wild and gallant boy, who brought him venison from fields which God had blessed; Rebekah folded the gentler and more thoughtful son with deeper fondness to a mother's heart. Nor was it otherwise with the brothers. Jacob might have taught to Esau a more sober wisdom, and Esau might have inspired in Jacob a healthier manliness; but instead thereof Esau hated Jacob, and Jacob despised Esau. It is one of our great dangers that we live only half lives; we do not cultivate, as we should do, every part of our moral and physical constitution:

> "In this world who can do a thing will not,
> And he who would do, cannot, I perceive:
> And so we half-men struggle."

Esau reaches but half the blessing of a man, and that the meaner and temporal half; "the other half, that he is made in the image of an invisible Being," that he has the awful gift of immortality, and a life beyond the grave, seems seldom or never to have entered into his thoughts. "Narrow life spanned his hopes and expectations; the impure earth yielded him all its joy."

2. So, side by side, these boys grew up, and the next memorable scene of their history shews us that the great peril of animal life, the peril lest it should forget God altogether, and merge into mere uncontrolled, intemperate sensuality, had happened to Esau. We see him in this scene living the lowest life to which human nature can be addicted, the mere life of the flesh, and cultivation of the bodily affections, "unreasonable, unspiritual, unenlightened." Think of it, I pray you, as I bring the scene before you. Esau, now grown up into a strong, shaggy huntsman, comes in from his day's hunting weary to death. It happens that at that moment, Jacob, sitting quietly in his tent, has been cooking pottage of lentiles. It was one of the cheapest and commonest articles of vegetable food, but to the hungry hunter the steaming mess looks so tempting and refreshing, that it fills him with voracious eagerness. Caught by its red appearance, he exclaims with the breathless impatience of a child, "Feed me, I pray, with that same red pottage," or as it is, literally translated, "Let me devour, I pray thee, that red, that red thing; for I am tired." In the unbridled passion of an animal nature, he cannot stop even to get the right word out, but can only demand the thing

by its colour—that red thing—and must have it at any cost. And then all the astute meanness of Jacob's nature displays itself; he sees his opportunity, and knowing that Esau will barter anything for the gratification of his immediate appetite, he says "Sell me to-day thy birthright." Now as the main blessing of the birthright is a spiritual blessing, and as the spiritual is not something to eat or drink or grasp with both hands, as it is not even visible, and has never helped Esau in his huntings and wild sports, he answers with contemptuous readiness, "Behold, I shall die sooner or later, and what good is this birthright to me?" Jacob seizes the advantage, makes Esau swear to the bargain, and then gives him this mess of pottage, for which the sensual hunter sells in one moment the prophecy of the far future, and the blessing of a thousand years. It did not take him many minutes to eat it; and then the Scripture adds—with a touch of that deep irony, which is all the more profound and pathetic because it has none of the world's corrosive malice in it—adds half sadly, half humorously, the leisurely description, "So he ate, and drank, and rose up, and went his way, and despised his birthright."

"He ate, and drank, and rose up, and went

his way, and despised his birthright;" and there you will say was the end of it; and so many and many a sinner has said when he shut his eyes and plunged for the first time into some sensual indulgence. But alas! there was only the beginning of it, not the end of it. The end of it was that he, with all his fine qualities, so frank, and hearty, and brave, and generous, never regained that birthright which he had despised. First came the reckless and frivolous unfaithfulness, which led him into unholy marriages with the daughters of a doomed and guilty race; then came the blessing which his folly had changed into little better than a curse, life by the bloody sword, subjection, and a home, not "*of* the fatness of the earth and the dew of heaven," but, as it should be rendered, "away from or without" the fatness and the dew, in the red rocks namely and burning wildernesses of Idumæa. Then too came the scornful name of Edom or the Red, branding him as the man who had sold his birthright with all its immortal privileges for a mere red mess; and so he passes away into the wilderness, where he lives

"as dead,
And lost to life, and use, and name, and fame;"

and when we catch the last glimmering of the clump of spears with which, in impulsive passion, he came forth to slay the brother whom with impulsive generosity he forgave, we hear nothing more of him except that from him sprung a long line of obscure dukes, who did no good to man, and of whose dynasties the only petty record snatched from fortunate oblivion, is that one of them found some hot springs[1] in the wilderness; and he, the father of them all, has no other epitaph than this—the epitaph of a lifetime recording for ever the consummated carelessness of a moment—Esau, a profane person, "who for one morsel of meat sold his birthright."

Surely a miserable fate for one who had so many manly and noble qualities; but alas! it is the very curse of sin that it does degrade and pervert, and destroy minds otherwise noble. It breaks the one weak link in a chain that otherwise may be strong and sound. That life, it has been said, must be reprobate indeed, in which sin is the narrative, and not the episode. A few fine natural qualities, like the meteoric flashes of a stormy midnight, serve but to enhance the general darkness. This is the very moral of it; Esau sets his affections on the earth,

[1] A. V. "mules."

and therefore loses even that; selling his soul
for the animal pleasures of this life, he gets less
even of those than his meaner brother. And
why? because Jacob, with all the contemptible
faults which lay on the surface of his character,
had deep within his soul the faith, the faith in
the unseen, the sense of dependence on and love
to God, which Esau did not even comprehend.
So that a crisis came in Jacob's life which at
last purged away the thick dross of his spirit,
and left that only which was pure and high:
the crisis came first when he saw that golden
ladder from heaven to earth whereon the angels
trod; and next when, by the Jabbok, his soul
wrestled so mightily in the lone agony of midnight prayer, and transformed him, as by the
touch of some celestial finger, from Jacob the
mean and cunning defrauder, into Israel the
Prince with God. To Esau no such crisis ever
came, because he was incapable of it; the crisis
of his life was the mess which he so greedily
devoured. After that, like many another fine
and generous and manly fellow after him, he
dwindled more and more into the slave of un-
ruly appetites; the indifference which ever
follows their indulgence came upon him; he
cooled more and more, and hardened more and

more in sin, till "the brood of sin had battened upon the bowels of human happiness," and the furies of an unregenerate nature had wrought their own revenge. "O horrible thought," it has been well said, "that any one for whom Christ died, any one who had a place in His Church, perhaps a share in His blessed sacraments, who has been visited by His grace, upon whom the light of Heaven has once fallen, who has lived in the tent of His chosen ones, and been borne upon the knee beside His saints—that such an one should be given up to the full possession of evil, with all that such a miserable casting away implies,—and all because one vile appetite craved for indulgence,"—all because a present gratification was preferred to all the future, and one violent lust weighed more in the soul's balance than the soul, and eternity, and virtue, and the love of God.

Surely you say, the dearest mess of pottage ever eaten! and the strangest and foolishest act ever done! no one else can ever have been so unspeakably senseless! Pardon me, my brethren, this selling of the birthright, this selling of the soul, aye, and selling it invariably for nought, is a very very common thing. If Esau sold it for a morsel of meat, why, Eve sold it for a forbidden fruit; Balaam sold it for a promise that was never fulfilled, and a death on the battlefield among the foes of God; Achan sold it for a dress which he never put on, and for some gold which lay for a few weeks under the turf of his tent-floor; Ahab sold it for a vineyard, at the gate of which the very next morning the prophet met him and made it abhorrent to him; Judas sold it for 30 pieces of silver, not one of which he ever spent, and all of which he flung down in horror a few days after on the temple pavement; the Prodigal sold it for a banquet which began with revelry and ended with the husks of swine. But what is this? need we seek for examples 2000 years ago? Has none of you then ever sold it? Each of you once had or now has a birthright;—the indwelling spirit of God,—a divine voice within you restraining you from evil, encouraging you to good,—a childish heart full of holy obedience and sweetness,—a memory unsullied as a crystal rivulet,—an innocence unstained as an angel robe,—a blush as pure as the auroral brightness, —a heart that had never known the agony of sin or shame,—this was a part of your birthright;—where is it now? That heart, whose chamber-walls glow with evil imaginations, is it there? that memory teeming with passages of sinfulness, is it there? that effeminate self-indulgence which shirks every duty, and shuns every difficulty, is it there? that disobedient, or idle, or stubborn, spirit of godlessness and sensuality—oh tell me is your birthright there? If not you must have sold it; for what then have you sold it? Ask, each of you, even to the youngest, for what was it that you sold the birthright of a child's innocence? was it for any thing better, anything more enduring, anything less shameful, than that red pottage? Even in the popular tales of the middle ages, they who sold themselves to the devil sold themselves for "some apple of Sodom which to them had but a painted rind, or fairy gold which dissolved into dust or changed to idle leaves." You think that these are mere idle stories: but it is not so; they are quite true. It is still common to sell the soul to Satan, but in these days men make no bargain. They sell the soul not for countless wealth, or boundless power, but for some one miserable besetting sin; or for the sneer of a fool; or for the temptation of some friend—aye, and what a friend! who leads them by the hand to the gates of hell; or for one indulged passion, or one wicked thought. They sell for it "all that once enriched and cheered them, yea they sell their soul; and all that they have gained by the sacrifice," and all that you have gained if you have done it, is sickness, and satiety, remorse, and spiritual death, a life blasted at the roots, a certain fearful anxiety more dismal than midnight or the grave.

Esau "ate, and drank, and rose, and went his way, and despised his birthright,"—and so the sin was very quickly finished; and as all memories of sin are as disagreeable as the nausea of drunkenness, he probably made haste to forget it. But if he had done with the sin, the sin, as has been so often said, had by no means done with him. It found him out, as sin always does; not immediately, not even in one year or two years, but a long time afterwards,—40 long years afterwards. All that time he was, it is probable, tolerably happy, as men often are when they have forgotten God, and God is gradually abandoning them, while His spirit, as in Ezekiel's vision of the desecrated Temple, removes first to the threshold, then to the East-gate, and then even to the hill beyond the city. It is astonishing how contented for a time the full meal of sin will make the hardened sensualist. But the day of judgment did come at last to

Esau, as it will come to each of us. The sins of your youth will leap out as from an ambush like deadly enemies upon your later years. The sin of his youth came to Esau, as I said, no less than 40 years afterwards. It came to him in that pathetic scene wherein the once gallant boy, who had so many generous and fascinating qualities, the favourite son who should have inherited the father's blessing, finds that blessing irrevocably forfeited, and the sin of his youth rolling back upon him with accumulations of intolerable force. " For ye know how that afterwards, when he would have inherited the blessing, he was rejected; for he found no place of repentance, though he sought it carefully with tears." And in the language of the book of Genesis, "when Esau heard the words of his father, he cried with a great and exceeding bitter cry, and said unto his father, Bless me, even me also, O my father. Hast thou not reserved a blessing for me? Hast thou but one blessing, my father? Bless me, even me also, O my father. And Esau lifted up his voice, and wept." Would to God that in the ears of each one, who, —(not, it may be, in depravity, but in mere feebleness of purpose and gaiety of heart, and forgetfulness of God,)—is selling his birthright,—

would to God that in the ears of such an one might ring the anguish of that great and exceeding bitter cry;—might rise the vision of that strong man's agony, as he lay prostrate and sobbing amid the ruins of his life.

In conclusion, to sum up the different topics on which I have touched, suffer me to give you two short words of affectionate advice.

The first—and I address it with chief earnestness to that large class among you who care more for games than they do for work—the first is this—Cultivate the whole of the nature which God has given you, and in doing so, remember that the mind is of more moment than the body, and the soul than both. That Royal Commission, whose labours have so lately seen the light, represents the English schoolboy as one in whom after 7 or 8 years of education, to quote their own words, "the average of classical knowledge is low; in arithmetic and in mathematics, in general information and in English, it is lower still," and they add these words—very solemn to those whom life has taught the awful value of time—"that of the time spent at school by the generality of boys, much is absolutely thrown away as regards intellectual progress." Yet this can only be true of boys whose idleness, and whose ignorance, is a blot on the position and character of an English gentleman, and culpable alike in the eyes of God and man. Be not deceived. To know nothing of the very things in which for years you have been instructed, is a shameful and thankless waste of opportunity and time. Let it not be true of any one of you. Choose the better, the manlier, and the wiser part. We look with confidence to those among you who are most distinguished in the games, not to lose, this term, the golden opportunity of using their influence on the side of steady diligence, manly modesty, and cheerful obedience. Set the Lord always before you; remembering that it rests in part with you to maintain the fame and the happiness of this great school now, the "ancient honours of this godly and virtuous island" hereafter.

And my second word of warning which I address to all, but more especially to the new boys, shall be very brief. It is this one word, Beware! Beware lest in a moment of weakness, and folly, and sinful forgetfulness of God, you sell your birthright, and barter your happy innocence for torment, and fear, and shame. Beware of false friends. Beware of idle moments. Beware of the beginnings of evil. Beware of loose words. Above all, and more than all, beware lest you once admit the fatal intrusion of evil thoughts. In solemn and awful earnest I would say to you,—Watch and pray, lest ye enter into temptation.

So then, cordially and affectionately greeting you, we hope that this term may be to you, and to us all, a golden time of innocent and happy summer-days. We pray that God may keep you in His safe and holy keeping; that in the moment of temptation He may both reveal to you the terrible results, and "raise up a brighter picture out of His own precious promises;" and so preserving you uncorrupted in your youth, lead you by the hand into settled manhood, and make you men great in well-doing, honest, and pure, and truthful, and diligent,—the children of God without rebuke.

XII.

ANGELS ON THE PATH OF LIFE.

(Preached on the Anniversary at Marlborough College [St Michael and All Angels], September 29, 1864.)

Gen. xxxii. 26.—"And he said, I will not let thee go, except thou bless me."

THE patriarch Jacob, amid the few and evil years of his earthly pilgrimage, was yet blessed with some peculiar marks of God's favour. Once in his early youth, when his lie to his father had brought its own punishment and he was forced to fly from the fury of his outraged brother, he lighted on a certain place, and pillowing his head upon the stones, he saw a ladder on which angels ascended and descended, and at whose summit was the Epiphany of God. In that place he vowed a vow that the Lord should be his God, and he never forgot the vow. And now he was returning, not as a wayworn wanderer with a single staff, but with wives, and children, and handmaids, and all the dignity of a pastoral prince. He had just escaped the angry pursuit of his uncle Laban, when once more, at Mahanaim "the angels of God met him." The rest of that memorable scene you learnt from this morning's lesson. Right in front of his path lay his injured brother, now grown to a powerful Emir at the head of his desert warriors. Full of terror and oppressed by a sense of former guilt, he yet took every precaution, and saw his wives, and his cattle, and his little ones, safely conducted over the deep ravine of the mountain-torrent which flowed before him. And then the day fell, and the crimson glories of sunset burned themselves away like the last watchfires of retiring angels on the western heights, and the stars came out, and the sacred darkness descended, and Jacob was left alone. Alone in doubt and terror, under the canopy of midnight, amid the silence of the hills. Doubtless it was an awful moment; doubtless the past flashed on Jacob's mind, as it will do in such crises of life, with all its follies and all its sins, its courage and endurance, its service of Mammon, and its visions of God. And then, suddenly, it became clear to him that though alone he was not alone, but ONE was with him, and until the breaking of the day he wrestled there in mysterious communion, conscious that man, mortal man, was wrestling alone with God. And, when the first gleam of dawn flushed the East, the Spirit said "Let me go, I pray thee, for the day breaketh." And he said "I will not let thee go, except thou bless me."

But, from the hour when the sudden flame of an oriental sunrise burst upon him as he passed over the hills of Penuel, lame with the terrible struggle,—from that hour Jacob was an altered man;—no longer Jacob but Israel; no longer the mean, selfish, crooked plotter, but a Prince with God, a Prince who wrestled and had prevailed. A change had passed over his being, and had glorified it; henceforth it was higher, and holier, and more devoted; until the morning of human life broadened into the perfect day, and his last words were that high strain of prophecy to sons who had multiplied into nations.

My brethren, though no vision is vouchsafed to our mortal eyes,—although the darkness does not move and flash around us with bright faces and glorious plumes,—yet angels of God are with us oftener than we know, and to the pure heart every home is a Bethel, and every path of life a Penuel, and a Mahanaim. In the outer world, and the inner world, do we see and meet continually these messengers of God. In the outer world God maketh the winds[1] His angels, and the flames of fire His messengers; the sun and the moon utter His knowledge, and the morning stars shout His praise. And in the inner world there are angels too,—the angels of youth, and of innocence, and of opportunity;— the angels of prayer, and of time, and of death;

> "*Our acts our angels are*—or good or ill,
> Our fatal shadows that walk by us still."

These too are God's messengers; these are even more to us for practical consideration than Saint Michael and all Angels; they encircle us continually with a curse or a blessing,—a blessing for those of the girded loin and the burning lamp, but a curse for the idle and the wicked, a curse for the heart of the sensual, and the life of the sluggard. To those who wrestle with them in faith and prayer, they are angels with hands full of immortal gifts;—to those who neglect or use them ill, they are angels with drawn sword and scathing flame. In speaking of them thus, I scarcely use language of allegory; but so far as I do, it is language authorised by scripture, and

[1] Psalm civ. 4, xix. 1, 2. Job xxxviii. 7.

too simple to be misunderstood. Listen then, my young brethren, while I speak of some of those angels who meet us in the path of life; and earnestly would I exhort you to wrestle with them and prevail, as Jacob did;—to wring from them the blessings they can give, crying to each one of them, "I will not let thee go, except thou bless me."

And first is the earliest angel, the angel of Youth, who even now beholds the face of your Father which is in Heaven. Do not think that you can retain him long. Very rapidly will he pass you by, and when once gone he is gone for ever. Every year that you neglect him, will fewer blessings be possible to obtain from him; fewer for the boy of sixteen than for the boy of fifteen, fewer for the boy of fifteen than for the boy of twelve. Oh! use, as wise stewards, this blessed portion of your lives. Do not spend it, as is so often done, in such a way as shall make the rest of life miserable, and the remembrance of this portion of it a sigh. Remember that as your faces are setting into the look which they shall wear in later years, so is it with your lives. Remember that "every act of yours is a seed, planted either in heaven or in hell, and producing for you there this very hour, the sweetest or the deadliest fruits." It depends on your time now, whether you form habits of truthfulness, courage, purity, self-denial;—or of falsehood, cowardice, selfishness, lust. This angel of youth can—as I have seen him lead many another before you— take you by the hand and lead you to the threshold of noble manhood, strong and patient, great in good works, irresistible in innocence, glowing with zeal, armed with the helmet of holiness and the shield of truth:—or else,—shall I tell you what he may do with you?—he may, as I have seen him do to many another before you, push you tottering out of the privileges of boyhood, useless, selfish, ignorant, degraded,— with the leprosy staining the temple-walls of your spiritual being, and in lieu of that fragrant incense of prayer and praise and pure aspirations which should be burning on the altar, only the sick fume and fetid atmosphere of a sin-polluted soul.

And next is the angel of Innocent Pleasure, —which is more especially the angel of boyhood;—not perhaps for the boyhoods of poverty and oppression, hard labour and scant food, but at any rate of yours; *your* mouths at any rate are filled with laughter, and your tongues with joy. For you that olden picture of youth is true: "he dances like a bubble nimbly and gay, and shines like a dove's neck, or the image of a rainbow, which hath no substance, and whose very imagery and colours are phantastical." "Innocent happiness," oh! what a world of meaning lies in these two words, and what a heaven on earth they signify! In manhood what memories do they recall! memories of games and triumphs, and of a light heart which knew no care, and of knowledge won, and of dear friends now perhaps lost or alienated, and of bright hopes now perhaps dimmed or dead; memories of the freshness of the dawn, and the unimaginable splendour of sunset; memories of the glory of the lily, and the song of the nightingale, and of long summer holidays when we played on the sea-shore, or roamed the mountain-side, treading ankle-deep in the purple heather, knee-deep in the tall green ferns. And oh! to have it in our power innocently to drink such deep draughts of this sweet fountain, as shall last us through all the thirsty desert of after years; as shall give us the perpetual sunshine of a merry or peaceful heart though the winds of misfortune buffet us, and the waves of sorrow are dashing at our feet. Well might you each re-echo the prayer of that English Princess[1],

---

[1] Queen Caroline Matilda of Denmark, Sister of George III.

who in the hour of temptation wrote with a diamond upon her castle window,

" O KEEP ME INNOCENT, MAKE OTHERS GREAT."

But, my brethren, trifle not with this angel. Remember that in heathen mythology the Lord of Pleasure is also the God of Death. For if you seek for happiness, as thousands of boys do, in sin, which is a transgression of God's will: in crime, which is offence against the peace or happiness of man; in vice, which is some degraded habit in your own personal life,—then sin, and vice, and crime will leave all over your souls the dark trail of guilt, which is an abiding and horrifying sense of God's wrath, and makes of all present happiness an immediate and irretrievable shipwreck. "Guilty happiness"—there is no such thing on earth. Guilty *pleasure* there is,—a flower plucked from the very brink of the precipice of hell;—a pleasure short, envenomed, ruinous in proportion to its guilt. But guilty *happiness*—no! nature knows of no such thing. There is no such thing on earth;—for guilt and misery are inseparable twins. Happy, while the soul burns with guilty secrets; happy, while he knows what he is, and loathes it, yet will not be otherwise; happy, while one and another can point to him as the cause of their ruin; happy, while he is tied hand and foot at the mercy of his sins, and the quenchless fire of remorse is burning, and the gnawing worm of conscience will not die?—No my brethren, no man can be happy thus! But you are young as yet, and innocent happiness is open to most of you. My young brethren, believe me it is a gift and grace of God;—it is a foretaste of heaven; and both now and through all your lives, may God the loving, God the merciful, God our God and Father, grant it unto you!

And then there are the angels of Time and Opportunity. They are with us now, and even now we may unclench from their conquered hands garlands of immortal flowers;—yet with beating wing and soundless footfall they are ever bearing us onward,—bearing us through a dark river and to an unknown land. Almost before you know it, you will be men. We stand with our feet in the wave, and noiselessly the river of life broadens, deepens, lengthens, rises silently to our ankles, to our knees, to our necks, flows over our heads, and hurries more and more, while we regard it not, its rapid waters, eager to sweep us on to the great eternal deeps. O reverence and use aright the hours which as they perish are imputed to you. Regard each new day—(and remember that the days of even the longest pilgrimage are still but few)—as a fresh unstained gift from God, and wrestling with it earnestly from its earliest dawn, say to it, "I will not let thee go, unless thou bless me." O hallow it while it is yet unstained and innocent in your morning prayer:—for Prayer too is an angel,—an angel whose wing is strong as an eagle's, though it be as the wings of a dove, which is covered with silver wings, and her feathers like gold;—an angel who "moves the arms of Him who moves the world;"—an angel who can even turn "pollution into purity, sinners into penitents, and penitents into saints." Be prayerful and you will be happy, and innocent, and noble too. What your prayers are, you will be. O my brethren, with deep earnestness would I urge you to pray,—habitually, reverently, trustfully to pray to your heavenly Father,—and never to rise from your knees, until you feel that you rise victorious, and that you too have been saying to God in the heartfelt purpose which gave might to the olden Patriarch, "I will not let thee go, except thou bless me."

Now these, my brethren, the angels of Youth, and Time, and Happiness, and Prayer—are angels with whom you may wrestle or no;—but there is one angel with whom we must wrestle, whether we will or no, and whose power of curse or blessing we cannot alter—even the Angel of Death. We know not when he cometh, but as surely as the leaves of your forest, which last spring you saw so young and green, and bright in the rain of golden sunshine, are now fading and falling around us, and being trodden down into the dishonoured dust,—so surely the generations of men are passing, so surely shall each of us be carried among mourners to our last long home, outstretched in the cold fixity of death. We are never left for long without such warnings. We were not left without them nine years ago when I was here, and when that painted window at the end of the chapel was put up as the memorial[1] of one of the gentlest, one of the purest, one of the holiest boys I ever knew. And again four years ago, when Death had taken from us a friend[2], whom many among us knew and loved, and who succeeded me in the office which once, to my own great happi-

---

[1] M. S. Theod. C. Stanton, qui pueritia pie, pure, amabiliter peracta, obiit in Christo. Id. Dec. MDCCCLIV. æt. xviii.

[2] Edward Lawford Brown, late Fellow of Trinity College, Cambridge, and Assistant Master at Marlborough College. The quotation is from the Funeral Sermon by the Rev. G. G. Bradley.

ness, I held in this place, you were reminded in words of solemn beauty, that "this young School is growing older, and that, like the man's life, its approach towards manhood is marked by the graves of its early friends." Alas! to the number of those graves, another has recently been added;—another grave in a far-off Indian churchyard, of one who was also a Master here[1], but who had gone to aid those great labours the thought of which fills every Marlborough boy with gratitude and pride. Of those labours two years ago he himself reminded you. Two years ago he spoke from this place those manly and therefore characteristic words about Christian Principle, which are in the hands of many of you, and which many of you must still remember; but now that voice is silent and you will see his face no more,—for under other stars, away from his own loved English home, the grass is green already upon his distant resting-place. I little thought when shortly before his departure for India he spent a Sunday with me alone in a quiet English parsonage, that I should next have to name his name as the name of one

[1] The Rev. Thomas Harris Burn, late Assistant Master of Marlborough College, and Domestic Chaplain to the Bishop of Calcutta.

whom God's hand has beckoned away, before an audience of friends whom he honoured, and of boys among whom he taught.—But Death has been far nearer to you than this: not only have you heard the sound of his approach, like the still echo of some ghostly footfall in the far-off corridors of some lonely haunted house, but he has been among you. You have seen him in the midst of you;—you have felt the gloom, you have heard the beating of his overshadowing wings;—you have seen that he sets his foot upon us in a moment, and as a child might trample out the sparks of a piece of paper, tramples out for ever our sins and sorrows, our hopes and fears. Schoolfellows whose faces you remember well, whose merry laugh you have often heard, the grasp of whose hands but a short time ago was warm in yours, have in the last months vanished from the midst of you, and others sit in their vacant places, while they have carried up with them to God and His Christ, the eyewitness report of what Marlborough boys are, and how they live among themselves. The voices then that call to you are voices from boys' graves. My brethren, do not these deaths toll in your ears with a heavy and solemn warning? do they not say to you in voices awful as the voices from the unseen world, "keep innocency, and take heed to the thing that is right, for that shall bring a man peace at the last"? O let them not call in vain. You have seen here, and we have seen at Harrow, where in the course of nine years I have grieved over the deaths not of one or two only, but of many young as you, that even a boy is not too young to say to corruption "thou art my father," to the worm "thou art my mother and my sister." Do you not see that it is not only the grass that withers, but the flower too that fades? The grass withereth, the flower fadeth; but the word of the Lord endureth for ever.

The word of the Lord endureth for ever: and therefore after death cometh the judgment. In one sense our judgment is always proceeding, always being recorded. At the foot of God's throne lies an open Book, wherein are written, in living characters for the day of witness, every secret and every open sin of our past lives; and each sinner ever bears about

> "A silent court of justice in himself,
> Himself the judge and jury, and himself
> The prisoner at the bar ever condemned;
> And that drags down his life."

But besides this, we must meet on the great Day of Wrath the Archangel of Judgment, and give an account of our deeds before God's throne, when that which was done in secret shall be revealed by fire, and proclaimed before God and all angels and all men. And when the rolling echoes of that awakening voice, and the long tumultuous blast of that archangelic trumpet, have startled the unnumbered dead from their long sleep,—when all the works of our hands have been consumed, and the petty vanities of life have been burned up, and its petty hopes and petty successes have shrunk like a gilded moth in the devouring flame, and all the lusts of the flesh, and all the lusts of the eye, and all the pride of life are but as seething "scum in the fiery surge;"—when the elements are melting with fervent heat, and the heaven is being shrivelled up like a blazing scroll,—on that day of St Michael and All Angels, where shall we be? how shall we pass through those awful scenes? The answer lies in our daily lives: look in your own hearts, my young brethren, and you will find the answer there. Think not that we shall escape among the multitude; even among the multitude our sins like Achan's shall find us out, and amid the crash of universal judgment shall peal in our ears the thunder of an individual doom. For, whatever we may have done or thought in this world, however various and multiform our lives may have been, yet in the tablets of the angel-witnesses but one brief line of record will suffice to be transcribed upon our tombs,—and that not the pompous enumeration of achievements or the heraldic blazonries of rank, but the shorter and sterner epitaph of Israelitish kings. On *their* tombs the unblushing marble might record the number of their iron chariots and golden shields, the provinces they had conquered, and the ivory palaces they had built,—but alike for their lives and for ours, alike for the life of magnificence and the life of obscurity, there is but one record which is known in heaven, and that is the short unvarnished sentence, "*He did that which was good,*" or "*He did that which was evil in the sight of the Lord.*"

O if you would meet in faith and fearlessness those last angels of Death and Judgment, see, my brethren, that ye wrestle with those other angels of Youth, of Innocence, of Time, of Opportunity, of Prayer. Ye may wrestle with them even now, and see that ye do not let them go except they bless you. Daily in this place, above all, daily in the worship of this fair house of God, and to-day on this anniversary of All

Angels, and to-day on this birthday of the School you love, do they offer you the blessings they possess,—the blessings which they offer to none more richly than to you. " What could have been done more to my vineyard, that I have not done unto it?" oh take heed lest in this day of your prosperity,—(for prosperity is more dangerous than adversity, and it is in the day of your best prosperity that we most tremble for your good)—take heed that when God looks for grapes, it doth not bring forth wild grapes. Not such the fruit it hath borne hitherto. Young as this School is,—the happier perhaps because endowed we trust with somewhat of that innocence which is the very grace of youth, and not yet hampered with the evil traditions of advancing life—young as it is, it has yet produced in large measure, those who have been and shall be "profitable members of the Church and Commonwealth, and hereafter partakers of the immortal glories of the resurrection." To your hands, to the hands of each passing school generation, its honour and its happiness are intrusted as a sacred and solemn charge; beware lest in your hands, beware lest through your sins, it acquire the tone and the tradition which may hereafter prove an ineradicable curse;—the tone and the traditions, which after all are but the moral atmosphere which the life of each boy here leaves behind, and which, if they be evil, may even poison all the happiness and all the usefulness of this school, and imperil every immortal soul committed to its charge. As yet the simplicity and purity of tone, the earnestness and manliness of character which have here been specially cultivated, that singular unitedness of mutual affection and respect which seems by God's blessing to bind together the hearts of boys and masters here like the heart of one man, are inestimable advantages if you know how to use them rightly,— advantages which must be lessened before their full value can be realised. But I cannot profess to speak impartially. Nine years ago I was one of your number; I say of *your* number, for the heart of a Marlborough master is like the heart of a Marlborough boy:—and though those nine years have brought with them other duties and other interests, they have not dimmed my gratitude or my affection for a place where I found a friend whom, like many others, I love and reverence as a father[1]; and colleagues from

---

[1] The late Lord Bishop of Calcutta, whose sudden and untimely death was felt by the author, as it was by a very large

whom I received the kindness and sympathy and forbearance of brothers; and pupils, of whom some are here present, who have since become friends on more equal terms, and who having passed through many distinctions to a useful and honourable manhood, are now fellow-labourers in the same great work, striving with you to build up in your own hearts and in the life of this great school a Temple whose entablature shall be holiness to the Lord! I return and find these friends and other friends unchanged; I find the work still continued in the same hearty, fervent, simple, unselfish spirit, and continued with rare and increasing success. Those were days of doubt, trial, and difficulty: but God blessed the work which was then undertaken for his own honour, and we all rejoice with grateful hearts to know and acknowledge that *these* are days of advance, prosperity, and triumph. *Then* the friends of this College sowed in tears, now through God's great love and mercy they reap in joy. From a full heart I

number of deeply attached friends, to be an irreparable personal loss and misfortune. It can fall to the lot of but few men to be so long and affectionately mourned as Bishop Cotton has been: to know him was at once to reverence and to love him; and I, for one, shall always reckon his warm friendship and unvarying kindness among the best blessings which life has given.

pray that these blessings may be continued. From a full heart I pray that God may lay your stones with fair colours, and your foundations with sapphires;—that all your children may be taught of the Lord, and that great may be the peace of your children. From a full heart, as one among the thousands who love this noble school, I pray that His fatherly hand may ever be over you; that His Holy Spirit may ever be with you;—and that He may so lead you in the knowledge and obedience of His word that in the end you may obtain everlasting life!

Δόξα τῷ Θεῷ.

XIII.

THEIR WORKS DO FOLLOW THEM.

(Preached at All Saints', Huntingdon, Dec. 28, 1862.)

Rev. xiv. 13.—"And their works do follow them."

To those who can read it aright, few books are more full of sublime comfort,—few books are more illuminated with the glory of a heavenly hope,—than the Revelation of St John. It is true that in the vain attempt to degrade it into a prophecy of private interpretation, it has been made the battle-field of opposing prejudices, until its value has been discredited, its meaning obscured, and those simple hearts have almost abandoned it, who dislike the noise and dust of idle controversy. But to one who reads it with a quiet and truth-loving heart, it is full of the most unspeakable wisdom. Marvellous indeed was the vision unrolled before the eyes of him whose young head had rested on the bosom of the Lord! From the sulphurous mine, from the rugged island, from the loneliness of exile, from the convict's company and the felon's chain, he is raised into the very presence of the mightiest Immortalities; the glorious spectacle of innumerable multitudes sweeps before him, and the hymns of the highest heaven melt in their speechless sweetness upon his mortal ears. True it is that there are other scenes which he must witness;—the seven great plagues, and the seven vials full of wrath, the woe-trumpets, and the scorpion army, and Death riding on his livid horse[1], and the judgment of her who was drunken with the blood of the prophets, and "the hues of earthquake and eclipse." But mingled ever with these scenes of Retribution,—preceding and following and out-dazzling them,—are the visions of the Lamb and the Lion, and the white-robed palm-bearing procession of happy human souls, and the crowned elders, and the victor angels, and Jerusalem the Golden descending out of heaven with its walls of jasper and gates of pearl. Fitly indeed do the melodies of this book rest last upon our ears; fitly does it close the gate of Revelation, which alone

---

[1] ἰδοὺ ἵππος χλωρός.—Rev. vi. 8. Not "pale," as in A. V.

displays to man one brief glimpse of the glories of Paradise. When life is weary and sad, when sorrow and selfishness are oppressive, when aspirations wax feeble and hope grows faint, I know no book so well fitted as this dying strain of revelation to raise, to ennoble, to purify, to cheer.

It is from one of these awfully intermingled visions that the words of my text are taken. Turning to the 14th chapter, you will find that grand poem which forms the epistle for the day. First, amid voices like the sound of thunders and of many waters, St John hears the voice of harpers harping with their harps,—the virgin multitude on whose forehead is the Lamb's Seal; then an angel flies through the midst of heaven having the Everlasting Gospel in his hand; a second angel cries aloud "Fallen, fallen[1] is Babylon the Great;" a third angel tells how the torment of them who worship the beast shall ascend like smoke for ever;—and then the end of the chapter is like a garment rolled and drenched in the blood of wrath; a crowned and awful figure is sitting on a white cloud, who thrusts his sharp sickle into the harvest, and wrings and

---

[1] Ἔπεσεν ἔπεσε Βαβυλὼν ἡ μεγάλη.—Rev. xiv. 8.

tramples the blood of judgment from the purple clusters of earth until the horrid seas of blood are rolling for a thousand furlongs bridle-deep; —but in the very midst, between the denunciation and the vengeance, as though a dove were floating over the waves of that crimson deluge,— a voice falls from heaven,—a sweet single voice like a falling star in a dark night, saying unto me, "Write, Blessed are the dead which die in the Lord from henceforth; yea, saith the Spirit, that they may rest from their labours; and their works do follow them."

Ah! how often have we heard those words, my brethren, as we laid our best-beloved under the sod!

There is perhaps no book from which we may learn so much about the condition of the dead as from the Book of Revelation. But after all it is but one little corner of the curtain that is lifted; let those who will lift it more if they can, and strive to peer behind it. For us let it be enough that the dead, as well as the living, are in God's hand. I ask no more. I know no more. I pretend to know no more. For us too the veil shall be one day drawn, and we too shall know. Till then, as one who from the shore watches a friend sail away towards the sunset, and the vessel sinks behind a round of lighted sea, and the sacred darkness follows, even so we look after the dead, and know little or nothing of the new strange regions which they have sought. Here we cannot know; but, as I said before, one day we too shall know; and meanwhile, in the sure and certain hope of resurrection, with these words we commend their mortal bodies to the dust.

This verse calls us to consider the dead, not in their new condition, but in their immortal memory; not as what they are in death, but as what they were in life: and not the dead generally, but the dead who die in the Lord, that is the noble dead. I say the noble dead, not the useless and the worthless dead,—" for the hope of the ungodly is like dust that is blown away with the wind; like a thin froth that is driven away with the storm; like as the smoke which is disturbed here and there with the tempest; but the righteous live for evermore, their reward also is with the Lord, and the care of them with the Most High."

And mark! it says that they are blessed that they may rest from their labours. It does not contemplate the possibility of any dead, *i.e.* of any blessed dead, who have not laboured. He whose sweet voice fell from heaven, bearing comfort to the mourning souls of earth, he knew of none such. There are none such. "Sweet is rest when work is done." But if there have been no work, there can be no rest. It was the first law that God gave in Eden, Work;—it is the last blessing that he utters, Enter, now that thy work is over, into thy rest. Here is thy place of work; the great garden of the earth to be tilled; the great vineyard of the earth to be tended, and its fruits rendered, and its waste places cleared. Work, till death release thee; then shalt thou have earned, thus only canst thou obtain, thus only couldst thou enjoy thy rest. For the idle, for the useless, for the self-indulgent, there is no place in heaven.

"For not on downy plumes, or under shade
Of canopy reposing, heaven is won[1]."

O how pitiful, how dreary, how unutterably despicable will appear, when the end cometh, a life spent in doing nothing;—how dreary, when the end cometh, will appear the life of the worldling and the sluggard, the life of the unlit lamp, and the ungirded loin, the life of the buried talent and the neglected vine!

[1] Dante, *Inf.* c. xxiv.

"For they rest from their labours; and their works do follow them." What works? Not those, which, if you were to judge from men's lives alone, you might suppose; not for instance the gold and silver which they toil for, which shall be squandered perhaps when they are gone, on purposes which they hated, by hands which they despised; not the idle voice of praise and fame, to which the cold ear shall be as deaf as to the wind that whispers in the rank grasses of the grave; not the jewels they have worn, which shall flash on the brows of others, when the worm is on their own; not the costly robes which they shall exchange for the shroud, nor the stately houses which they shall abandon for the damp and narrow grave. One day, one hour, shall rob men of their pride, their pleasure, their influence, their wealth. They must do with these as the great king did who, when he received the message, "Prepare thyself, for now thou art going to the gods," laid aside his purple garments, and wrapped himself humbly in a linen sheet. It is not those works that will follow them, for they are valueless, perishing, and corruptible;—but their love, their truth, their purity, their generosity, the hearts they comforted, the souls they saved. And if you would know how these follow them, let the fancy of the Christian poet add meaning to the image of the inspired Apostle. "Thy works," he says, speaking of a Christian lady,

> "Thy works, and alms, and all thy good endeavour
>   Staid not behind, nor in the grave were trod;
> But as faith pointed with her golden rod,
> Followed thee up to joy and bliss for ever.
> Love led them on, and Faith who knew them best,
>   Thy handmaids, clad them o'er with purple beams
> And azure wings, that up they flew so drest,
>   And spake the truth of thee on glorious themes
> Before the Judge: who henceforth bid thee rest,
>   And drink thy fill of pure immortal streams."

"And their works do follow them," or rather, to render it literally, "follow with them[1];" as a living testimony, that is, that they by God's grace are not unworthy of their reward and rest. For here on earth their works very often have in no sense followed them. They have not been recognised, still less appreciated, still less recompensed; nay more, they have often met with obloquy for praise, and apparent failure instead of deserved success. They have worked honestly and honourably for the good of others, and all their reward here has been the indifference of the selfish, the contempt of the malicious,

---

[1] τὰ γὰρ ἔργα αὐτῶν ἀκολουθεῖ μετ' αὐτῶν.—Rev. xiv. 13.

and the sneer of fools. Not from men, or in his lifetime, does he reap the harvest he has sown. The hands of his contemporaries often murder the prophet before they build his tomb; the tongues that have blackened his living reputation, hypocritically gild his inanimate dust; the men he lived for often poison his happiness before they fling wreaths upon his grave. True fame belongs only to the dead: too often shame, and sorrow, and an aching heart, are the pay the world gives to her living benefactors. But life is short, and the end comes. What matters it? Their works do follow them, and Wisdom is justified of all her children. "Then," says the Wisdom of Solomon, "shall the righteous man stand in great boldness before the face of such as have afflicted him, and made no account of his labours. When they see it they shall be troubled, and amazed at the strangeness of his salvation, so far beyond all that they looked for. And they, repenting and groaning in anguish of spirit, shall say within themselves, This was he whom we had sometimes in derision, and a proverb of reproach: we fools accounted his life madness, and his end to be without honour: how is he numbered among the children of God, and his lot among the saints!"

"And their works do follow them;"—their true works, that is, not their schemes of ambition, or their dreams of hope. These are the dross that melts in the burning, when the pure gold remains. There is no deeper and more instructive lesson in history than this;—the manner in which all the deeds done by great men from self-interest or pride perish and rot, while their true works, their disinterested labours, their genuine beliefs, live and grow. Those are the house upon the sand; these the house upon the rock. Those are weak, evanescent, illusory: these are real, permanent, eternal. An English student, "toiling terribly," has it granted to him to discover the most general law which governs the universe. An English statesman, filled with generous indignation, wipes away from the page of a free country's history the infamy of the slave-trade. A private English gentleman ameliorates by his single efforts the condition of the prisoners of Europe. These are true works; these are the works which follow them when they have entered into their rest. But, on the other hand, compare with these the false works which in the world's eye look so much greater. A young obscure soldier becomes the lord of the destinies of a continent; he conquers, he reconquers kingdoms; he tramples on the flags and shatters the power of nations; he becomes the Emperor of a great people, and places on the heads of his brothers, his sisters, and his generals, many crowns. It was mere selfish, aggrandising, untrue work;—and even in his lifetime how does it end? In petty malicious squabblings on a lonely Atlantic rock! He had wrapped Europe in the whirl of triumphant war: but what came of it all even in his lifetime? Nothing. These are not the works that follow the blessed dead. This, it has been well said, is but "the blazing up of a dry heath." For an hour the whole universe seems wrapt in smoke and flame; but only for an hour. The fire goes out; the universe with its old mountains and streams remains unchanged. Far, far other—not rolling and blazing up only to die away, but glowing and brightening with the steady lustre of the sun and stars—is the work of the Sons of that beautiful Wisdom, who is "the breath of the power of God, and a pure influence flowing from the glory of the Almighty,—who, remaining in herself maketh all things new; and in all ages entering into holy souls maketh them friends of God, and prophets."

"Their works do follow them." Not necessarily works which the world calls great; not necessarily works that the world ever hears of at all. What is there in the letters of a man's name being handed down here on earth, if they be unforgotten by the Angel-witnesses? O my brethren, let us strive rather to be forgotten on earth if thereby we may be remembered in heaven. I stood once in a little church in Rome, dedicated to St Stephen, the earliest martyr, opened once a year only, on his day, and bearing on its frescoed walls the memory of that glorious Christian army who fell in the earliest persecutions. With but one or two exceptions their names are utterly unknown. Standing in such a place it was impossible not to think what work these men had done, and what reward they had received. What had they done? They had "through faith subdued kingdoms, wrought righteousness, obtained promises, stopped the mouths of lions, quenched the violence of fire, waxed valiant in fight, turned to flight the armies of the aliens;"—in a word they had Christianised the world. This is what they had done; and how had they been rewarded? By trial of cruel mockings and scourgings, by bonds and imprisonment, by being stoned, by being sawn asunder, by being tempted, by being slain with the sword,—by being destitute, afflicted, tormented,—in a word by being obscurely huddled into malefactors' graves. Yet,—standing in the very midst of those ghastly memorials of forgotten names,—was it not possible to see that their honoured blood had been the seed of the Church; that their monument was more perdurable than the very pyramids;—that their works had followed them? Against them were kings and emperors and armies,—the flame of the stake, and the wild beast of the arena, and the torture of the executioner: but God was for them, and His whole blue heaven was their shield, and though men obliterated their poor memories from every earthly record, and trampled out their lives with crushing scorn, all the powers of the banded universe were impotent against them whose names were written in the Book of Life.

Has all this nothing to do with ourselves? Is it those only who are great, or those only who are splendidly good, whose works do follow them? God forbid. What are among these works? are there not, as he himself has told us, such little things as the widow's mite, and the cup of cold water given for his sake? There is a greatness in unknown names, there is an immortality of quiet duties, attainable by the meanest of human kind; and when the Judge shall reverse the tables many of these last shall be the first. Do not be dazzled by the world's false judgments. The slave is often nobler than the sovereign, and the common soldier than the general. The general who is brave in the hour of danger does his duty, but then he knows that his shall be the glory of battle: is it not a greater thing when the common soldiers, poor and ignorant and often unconscious what the quarrel is about, still do their heroic duty because it is their duty, and charge unflinchingly on the cannon that vomit on them a storm of fiery death, though they know that their names will be forgotten, their fate unnoticed, and that where they fall they shall lie;—are these not greater, these "unnamed demigods[1]?" Yes, because they have done their obscure duty, their unknown, unnamed, unhonoured, unrewarded duty, because it is their duty, and done it well. Nor is it otherwise on the battle-field of life. There is, believe me, yet a higher and a harder heroism;—to live well in the quiet routine of life; to fill a little space because God wills it; to go on cheerfully with a petty round of little duties, little avocations; to

---

[1] This remarkable expression (and possibly others in the paragraph) occurred in one of M Kossuth's speeches.

accept unmurmuringly a low position; to be misunderstood, misrepresented, maligned, without complaint; to smile for the joys of others when the heart is aching;—to banish all ambition, all pride, and all restlessness, in a single regard to our Saviour's work. To do this for a lifetime is a greater effort, and he who does this is a greater hero, than he who for one hour stems a breach, or for one day rushes onward undaunted in the flaming front of shot and shell. His works will follow him. He may not be a hero to the world, but he is one of God's heroes, and though the builders of Nineveh and Babylon be forgotten and unknown, his memory shall live, and shall be blessed, and he shall sit down before earth's noblest and mightiest at the marriage supper of the Lamb.

Your life here, my brethren, will result and issue either in those good works which follow the blessed dead,—or in no works,—or in bad works. In one sense the second alternative is impossible, for "no works" are really and truly in their inmost character, and in their necessary nature—"bad works." But if any of you grow up without any noble purpose or steady aim in life, and yet do not fall (if this be possible) into flagrant and destructive sins,—if you spend your lives in killing your time, day after day, in the frivolous search after amusement,—if your life be like a barren tree yielding neither shade nor fruit,—then I suppose we may call this a life of "no works." But the chances are that a man who will do no good works does not stop short of the bad works. Sometimes while seeing some picture wherein a mighty artist has polluted the vestal fires of genius by kindling them on the altar of sin,—or when lighting on the songs of poets who have but too faithfully recalled the scornful image of St Jude that they are "raging waves of the sea, foaming out their own shame," or the language of Isaiah that "the wicked are like the troubled sea, when it cannot rest, whose waters cast up mire and dirt,"—and while I remember how many evil imaginations have lasted long long after they who originated them were dead, still pouring forth their corrupt streams, still poisoning the air like the carrion from which life has long departed,—I have thought that here too men's works do follow them; follow them, nay pursue them rather; pursue them as the clouds of smoke, and flakes of burning ashes, and long tongues of quivering flame pursued the man who rode out of the city he had fired; pursue them, as the furies of old mythology pursued the guilty with snaky tresses and shaken torch. But alas! it requires no genius to do bad works, the effects of which will live. The veriest fool can do them, and perish in them. The wisest of men stood amazed at this pernicious importance for evil of a fool; and we, who see much of varied life and character, may well stand amazed at the giant influence of wrong even in those of the feeblest intellect and the meanest heart. Of these too we say, and say with a terrible truthfulness, that "their works do follow them."

If you take home nothing else, take home with you this one question, Are your works good works, or no works, or bad works? If they are worthless, if they are pernicious, pray to God with all your heart and soul that for Christ's sake he do not make you eat of the fruit of such works, but enable you to do such good works which he that doeth shall even live in them. Whatever your work is—gold, silver, precious stones, wood, hay, stubble,—that work, and every man's work "shall be made manifest; for the day shall declare it, because it shall be revealed by fire; and the fire shall try every man's work of what sort it is."

XIV.

THE WAR IN WHICH THERE IS NO DISCHARGE.

(Preached before the 18th Middlesex Volunteers, in Harrow Church, May 7, 1865.)

ECCLES. viii. 8.—"And there is no discharge in that war."

DEATH is the immediate enemy spoken of in this verse; but the language of all Scripture, from Genesis to Revelation, warrants us in extending its meaning to every enemy who assaults the peace of man or the life of nations, and, above all, to Sin—to that spiritual wickedness of which the world's ruin was the immediate result, which gives to the grave its victory, and to death its sting.

The war, then, in which there is no discharge, is the war against Sin. It is this holy war of which Scripture is full. Not only were many of its saints actual warriors but, with a signal and startling frequency of recurrence, its very metaphors are chosen from the scenes and images of war. How is the Christian's life described? He is to stand fast in the conflict; he is to war a good warfare; Christ is to be the Captain of his salvation. Though the weapons of his warfare are not carnal, they are weapons still—the armour of God, the armour of light, the armour of righteousness; righteousness is to be his breastplate, and faith his shield, and salvation his helmet, and his sword is to be the sword of the Spirit, which is the Word of God. His hope in the present is to be victory, through God's grace, over the world, the flesh, and the devil; and in the future, victory over the thraldom of death, and the dust and darkness of the grave. Life, then, is of necessity a battle-field; and hence it is, that even the innocent and new-born babe is ushered into the militant Church with the watch-word of strife; over the smiling features and on the baby brow we sprinkle the baptismal dew, and "do sign him with the sign of the cross, in token that hereafter he shall not be ashamed to confess Christ crucified, and manfully to fight under his banner against sin, the world, and the devil; and to continue Christ's faithful soldier and servant unto his life's end."

And though this battle is secret in the heart, no less than open in the life, it is of the latter— of the public, the national life, the life of each of us as a citizen, that to-day I would speak; occupying this place simply as one under authority, bound to do so by the duty which calls me here; and, in spite of doubt and self-distrust, longing very earnestly, as in God's sight, that this may be no idle and empty occasion, but that each soul may find in the word spoken some thought to elevate and to improve.

For history, too, is a battle, and its greatest men have been fighters. Such, in Scripture, were Gideon, and Barak, and Samson, and Jephtha, and David; such were the great Maccabean princes; such were many of the Christian legions of Constantine, and the holy warriors of Christendom; such were many of the iron soldiers of the Commonwealth, and of the stout Covenanters of Cameron; and such, thank God, have been and are many and many of the gallant soldiers of England, both of those who are living now, and of those whose graves, like the graves of Vicars and Havelock, lie far away on the bleak shores of the Euxine or under the burning sun of Hindostan. Nor are soldiers the only heroes. In Scripture, Samuel and the Prophets are ranked with warriors and kings. St Paul, the gentlest-hearted of men, of an affection well nigh womanly in its tenderness, and with a voice which breaks with tears, fought with lions and with men fiercer than lions[1], and chose as the fit expression for the close of a long career, "I have fought a good fight." For, even in history, the fight against bigotry, and ignorance, and error—against evil customs, and favourite idols, and victorious lies—is a harder and a deadlier fight, and requires a more dauntless courage and a more unshaken faith, than the fight against armed hosts. And such warrior-heroes have been all the glorious army who came out of great tribulation, and washed their robes, and made them white in the blood of the Lamb. Such heroes were many of the fathers, and martyrs, and confessors of the Church in every age. Aye, and it is not too much to say that you will not find one great man, in our own or any history, who did not fight in the teeth of clenched antagonisms with the stern courage of a heart that could dare dauntlessly in the cause of God, or of freedom, or of truth.

Think not, my brethren, that that Divine teaching of Christ's Sermon on the Mount, which

[1] Εἰ κατὰ ἄνθρωπον ἐθηριομάχησα ἐν Ἐφέσῳ.—1 Cor. xv. 32.

you have heard this day, contradicts any one word of truths like these. "Blessed are the peacemakers;" yet he who loves peace most must fight for it, when the need has come ; and as for gentleness and love, would they even be possible without the warm spirit of scorn for that which is contemptible, and detestation for what is wrong? Many of our best and most resistless fighters have been men whose hearts could tremble with the tenderest pity at the wrongs done to a dumb animal, and blaze out with the fiercest wrath at him who should cause the tears of a woman, or the wailing of a child. As the spirit of the lightning lies in the dew-drop, so a power of righteous anger often slumbers in the noblest breasts, like a fire of God, side by side with meekness and compassion. Even in Him our Lord, our Teacher, our Saviour, our Divine Example, in dwelling on his forgiveness, his lowly-heartedness, his long-suffering, his love, his patience, forget not that there was another side to his character as well. He who wept at the grave of Lazarus also knotted a scourge of small cords, and overturned the tables of the money-changers, and drove forth those who had made the House of his Father a den of thieves. He whose love would.

have gathered the children of Jerusalem together as a hen gathereth her chickens under her wings, yet scathed and laid bare the seared consciences of Priest and Pharisee, and dropped the molten lead of his scorn and indignation upon the souls of the formalist and the hypocrite. He who, out of his great love for all mankind, never shrank from touching the white sores of the leper, and who suffered the penitent harlot to weep her hot tears upon his feet, and wipe them with the hairs of her head, yet faced unflinchingly the fury of an excited synagogue, and sent back a contemptuous message to a reckless and bloodstained king.

We have need, then, of the dauntless spirit and the tried nerve of the soldier, even in the Christian's course. Easy, indeed, it were to slink through life, lapped in silken effeminacies, never to strike a blow for hated truths, never to stand by a maligned man, or an unpopular opinion, never to face obloquy, never to defy ridicule, never to brave opposition, never to smite at folly, never to confront tyranny, never to denounce injustice, never to rebuke vice. It were easy to spend our lives in getting food and clothing, and in hoarding our little dues of money, or in using it for such paltry comforts and mean enjoyments as we are fit for—forgetting all but our petty selves, forgetting that we are Christians and citizens, forgetting that we are Englishmen, forgetting the blood and race of which we came. Yes, easy and common too, but for all that contemptible. Let us never dignify such wretched selfishness by the name of Christian quietude, or deck out our slavish pusillanimity in the guise of religion. He to whom the whole round of heaven and earth is shut up in his farm or his merchandise, is only fit to live as a traitor or a slave. But he who would be a good soldier of God, and the worthy citizen of a glorious and Christian land, if there be in his spirit one spark of what is noble, or generous, or manly, must, when occasion comes —whether it be for God, or for truth, or for pity, or for right, or for home and native land— must, I say, when the occasion comes, fight, and fight hard—strike, and strike home. Let no one dare to disintegrate Christianity from that manliness, that freeborn courage, which in the ancient languages is the very synonym of virtue, and which is the might and glory of a man. Timidity is no Christian virtue, but the fitting legacy left by sin and shame. Let the cheat, and the liar, and the drunkard, and the adulterer be haunted through a shivering life by the phantoms of remorse and fear; to the Christian soldier belong the high glance and the free carriage, and the fearless soul. The wicked flee when no man pursueth; but the righteous is bold as a lion. The meekness of the Christian must never bear the brand of the coward, nor should we suffer the servants of Satan to boast and swagger, as though all the daring and all the strength were theirs alone.

My brethren, these thoughts may be profitable or profitless, as we make them so for ourselves; but of this I am sure, that the better and braver we are as Englishmen, the better too shall we be as men. For sin ruins nations no less than men. The tradesman who uses false balances or dishonest ways, the farmer who robs the labourer of his hire, the rich man who grinds the faces of the poor, the poor man who squanders in drunkenness the wages of innocence and industry, and all who are indolent, and malicious, and sensual, are the curse of their native land. For it is that deep-lying selfishness, wrapping us round and round with the swaddling-bands of our own narrow, private, personal, individual interests, which is the source of half men's sins, and the worst enemy to all that is best and greatest both in our country and in ourselves. In this respect we are behind the very ancients and the Pagans. There may have been less purity and less high principle in their life than in ours; but there was less also of mere mammon-worship and mean contentment with the pettinesses of life, and there was more of magnanimity, more of patriotism, more of public spirit. It is well for us to be aroused from this absorption in the personal, this concentration in the selfish, which is a disease of modern society that we carry into our very religion. It was not for nothing that God planted us in nations; and if in the thick clay of our own private concerns we forget the gratitude and the duty which we owe to the State of which we are subjects, and the country in which we live, then "the glory of that country will be but the blazonry of our impeachment; and its name, for which we are often too proud, but never sufficiently thankful, will but heighten our fall and aggravate our condemnation."

And never, assuredly, in all our history had we more cause for this national gratitude than now. Never with more unspeakable wealth and freshness of beauty have the trees and flowers been bursting into green life from the tomb of winter than during these divine and vernal days, so rich with their memories of that other and greater resurrection, which breathes into man's heart the hope of immortality. And how many things have happened to make us thoughtful and thankful during these Easter days! How often has the lightning spark, wherewith God has taught us to flash our messages with the speed of thought along the electric wire, flashed to us such tidings of dread and heart-shaking significance that the reading of every newspaper became a solemn moment of instruction, and each passing event bore with it its own dread note of warning, or summons to heartfelt thanksgiving! Abroad we have seen the first-born of an emperor[1] smitten with some new and strange disease, removed to the balmy air of Southern France, and there lingering out the last days of his youth in the untold agony of a death-in-life —beckoned inexorably away from the splendour of an Imperial crown, and the heirdom to a sovereignty which would have wielded the destinies of a third of the human race—beckoned from youth, and life, and hope, and the affection of a family, and the reverence of an empire, and

---

[1] The late Czarowitch.

the sweet love of a youthful bride—beckoned into that dark Unknown where the prince and the beggar stand neither as beggar nor as prince, but only as naked and sinful souls before the eye of God. And in violent contrast to this still scene of death, we learnt, but the day after, of another ruler, the guardian of interests no less stupendous—not an untried youth, but a grey-haired man—not born to the purple, but rising from the ranks of common life—not fading away slowly in the perfumed chamber at death's repeated whisper, amid the tears of friends, but suddenly, in the box of a public theatre, in the flush of health, in the hour of hope and well-won triumph, dashed to the earth—murdered, bleeding, speechless for ever—the thread of life slit, as by a fury, in a moment, at the proudest and happiest culmination of his career. And rarely has history shown a life more significant or more rich in noble lessons than this man's, whose murder a world mourns. If Abraham Lincoln was not great by genius he was something more; he was great by exalted goodness. Never, perhaps did a simpler, a sweeter, a homelier nature, shape the decrees of a great people; never certainly did a leading ruler depend with so steady and entire a humility on God, or feel with deeper piety, and avow with manlier courage, that he was but a weak instrument for the purposes of the Almighty. Here was a truly good man;— a man who, encircled with temptations, yet lived without avarice and without ambition;—a man who, while others blustered, never uttered one boastful sentence, and while others raved, never penned one vindictive word;—a man whose very face, they say, in his last days was illuminated with the hopes of peace and the power of mercy;—a man whom misfortune did not depress, nor success unduly elate—

"A good man, struggling with the storm of fate,"

through good report and through ill report calmly, humbly, hopefully bearing up, and doing his manful duty to the bitter end. And God rewarded him: the swift death which sounds so horrible to us was an euthanasia to him. Though his death was sudden, he lived long enough to reap the pure triumph of proclaiming the principles of amnesty and forgiveness, exulting that his ear—so soon to be stopped with dust—had caught the notes that rang out the death-knell of slavery, and the pean of an emancipated race; that his eyes—so soon to be filmed with death— had yet gazed on the sunset of a great tyranny, and the flushing dawn of a mighty and enduring freedom. Have these tidings no significance to us, as men and citizens? Do they not teach us that, whether summoned to our fate down the lingering declivities of disease, or by the swift stroke of sudden death, our life is but as fleeting and uncertain as a mountain mist, or as the shadow of a bird's wing on the sunny sward? Do they not teach us to place our hopes and our interests higher than that which death can trample out in a single hour? And if, whenever it comes, death shall not fail to find us at our duty, and if, by God's grace, our souls be so calm and so familiar with the thoughts of eternity that they shudder not at the grim spectre of sudden destruction, let us at least learn, as the members of a nation, a deep lesson of gratitude. At home no public crime has sharpened the sword of tyranny, or riveted the fetters of oppression; the hopes of our rulers have not been cut off; we heard but a week since that our light burdens are to be further lightened, that our immense wealth has been yet increased, and that peace and plenty flourish over our fields. Long years ago did we wipe off the dark blot of slavery from the stainless shield of England, and for more than two hundred years the blood of Britons has not polluted the fair fields of English soil.

On the very day when the heart of America was numbed and paralysed by the horrid tidings of a triple assassination, we were keeping our Paschal Feast—we were joyously celebrating our great national holiday—our hearts were being pleasantly stirred by the strains of martial music, and by the grand sight of England's assembled army of soldier-citizens, her youth, and her manhood, and her chivalry, marching past side by side, and united in unbroken brotherhood for a common cause; while we knew that not one of those 20,000 had stirred under any stress of influence and compulsion, but simply from the sense of patriotism and the dictate of duty; that amid all the din, and smoke, and trampling of mimic war, the thoughts of every one of them were thoughts not of defiance but of defence, and the motive which stirred their hearts was not the criminal passion for an unhallowed glory, but the true-hearted love for pure and peaceful homes. And so, without one serious casualty, the day—so joyous to us, so heavy with sorrow to other nations—passed away, and the wind wafted the smoke-clouds from those green downs; and I doubt not that, as you marched homewards by the sea—which then so smiling, and oftentimes so stormy, was the fit emblem of an uncertain peace—you may have remembered that its narrow girdle was no longer adequate for our defence, and that, for that defence we must trust first to God, and next to that stern and noble gallantry in the temper even of peaceful men, which saves them from grovelling degradation and craven fear, and which should least of all be wanting in the breasts of a noble, a puissant, and a Christian nation. Truly it becomes us to take the cup of salvation and praise the name of the Lord. Marvellous indeed have been God's mercies to us; and of these mercies I say again, as we are the inheritors, so we too must be the willing, the permanent, and the righteous guardians.

We must be, and by God's help we will. My brethren, I should be the first to scorn myself were I to appear in the novel guise of a flatterer; yet I say but the simple truth in declaring that when I consider the names and the character of many in our ranks—what good Christian men they are, how upright, how calm, how wise, how true—and when I remember that in this respect we have no right or reason to suppose our corps to be superior to a hundred others—then I am full of pride, and full of hope for my native land. That charge of national degeneracy which has been openly brought against us by our enemies, and whispered doubtfully even among ourselves, seems to vanish when we consider facts like these. From freedom to glory, from glory to wealth, from wealth to vice, has been the career of many nations; but in our beloved England, though there may be meanness often, and mammon-worship, we do not yet see that insolence of impiety, that drunkenness of luxury, that decrepitude of effeminate self-indulgence, which has ever been as the hand pointing to ruin on the dial-plate of a nation's destiny. Let us cherish, every one of us, in our own hearts, that righteousness which exalteth a nation, and we shall not need to fear. This will be a breastplate of adamant, invulnerable by any foe. And, as I would urge on all, so let me urge especially on every Volunteer, to be herein a defender of his country. It may be that none of us will live to take part in any battle fought with an invader on our own shores; but in these great battles of history and of life, however low our station, however limited our sphere, we are and must be daily combatants. Let all of us, then, old and young, remember that we do not stand alone, and manfully acknowledge that the bond of union which binds us together as the members of a common corps, is a bond which also pledges us to the necessity, and aids us in the endeavour, to live upright, godly, and righteous lives.

My brethren, and you, above all, young men, who walk in the pride of your strength, hardly knowing as yet how many are the snares and pitfalls of life, believe me, this is no easy battle —believe me, it is a warfare in which there is no discharge. To live lives of heroic devotion to all that is brave, and honest, and true—to live in temperance, soberness, and chastity—to avoid those dark and slippery ways which are the ways of death, and that alluring banquet where the dead, and those who are hated of God, are guests—to be in such charity with all men as to scorn all petty malignities, whether of word or deed—to loathe every form and shape of impurity or falsehood—to love the Lord Jesus Christ with all our hearts, and never to grieve the Holy Spirit of God by sin wilfully indulged—this is the hardest of all tasks, the longest and the sternest of all toils. To this, as God's minister, I exhort you; to this, not God's ministers only, but your own consciences, which speak with the voice of God within you, and the words of Scripture, and the lessons of life, and the hopes of immortality. Oh shut not your ears to these voices of God. Resolve, if you have not done so hitherto, resolve this day to be true and pure, and to fight manfully under your Saviour's banner against the world, the flesh, and the devil. If in that warfare there be no discharge, nevertheless in that struggle there is no failure; and thus, more than by any service, will you be the living columns of your country's prosperity. Oh, if we all were thus, what a hope and glory of all lands would England be, and how would the very angels and spirits elect point gladly to her as to a home of God's chosen people, as they lean from the crystal battlements of heaven! May God grant it to our prayers! And so, when the last battle comes—when He, who is the Faithful and the True, whose eyes are as a flame of fire, and whose vesture is dipped in blood, rideth forth to tread the winepress of the wrath of Almighty God; when kings and their armies are gathered together to make war against Him, and the angel standing in the sun summons all the fowls that fly in the midst of heaven to the supper of the Great God, that they may eat the flesh of kings, and the flesh of captains, and the flesh of mighty men—then may we, having well fought the good fight of faith on earth, be found among those armies of heaven which follow the Lamb of God to final victory, "upon white horses, clothed in fine linen, white and clean."

XV.

THE LOCUST-EATEN PAST.

(Preached at All Saints', Huntingdon, January 6, 1866.)

Joel ii. 25.—" And I will restore to you the years which the locust hath eaten."

FOR a pastoral people, a people who lived under their own vines and their own fig-trees, amid the luxuriant herbage of rich valleys, or on the slope of hills whose terraces were beautiful with the white flowers of the almond, and the silver leaves of the olive,—it must have been a moment almost too terrible to conceive, when first, in the quiet noon, they saw here and there a locust dropping down upon their fields and vineyards. Eagerly, almost wildly, they strained their eyes towards the horizon to see if these few were the harbingers of more; and when, far off, on that horizon they marked a black speck ever spreading and spreading into a pitchy, rushing cloud, we can barely imagine what agitation seized them ; how, in the passionate language of the prophet Joel, whose book is suggested and occupied by this terrible visitation, the inhabitants of the land cried, and all faces did gather blackness. Well might they cry : for the advent of the locust was the advent of famine, of ruin, of despair ! Nearer, nearer, nearer, the dark cloud moved, until a noise broke from it like the noise of chariots leaping upon the hills ; and the very sun was hidden ; and the dense air shuddered with innumerable wings. Then indeed they knew that the locust was upon the land ; and that the noise and motion was the noise and motion of their flight, more dreadful to the terrified husbandman than the beating wings of the Angel of Death. The excited imagination of poet and prophet spoke of them as God's great army ;—an army irresistible as horsemen, and devouring as flame, that no sword could wound, that no walls could stay,— swift, and winged, and numberless,— before whose camp the Lord God uttered His great voice. But in truth it needed not the delirium of terror to exaggerate their ravages. Where they came, farewell to the pride of vintage and the hope of harvest, for the corn was wasted and the new wine dried up: the fields of the forest that had clapped their hands, and the valleys that had laughed and sung in the sunshine and the rain, were blackened and loathsome, so that the eye could see no green thing, and every footfall crunched on the griding scales of these crawling or dead invaders. The very branches of the palm, the pomegranate, and the apple-tree were bare; the seed was rotten under the clods, and the once-green fields were strewn with heaps of putrescent death; what their raging hunger spared, their touch and their foulness infected; their corrupting swarms bred plague and pestilence; their horrible fertility, passing through various stages of existence, cut off even the hopes of the future by the numberless multitude of their multitudes; the land was as the garden of Eden before them, and behind them it was a desolate wilderness.

Yes! the coming of the locusts was a day of the Lord; a day of darkness and of gloominess, a day of clouds and of thick darkness, a day of bitter and heart-rending calamity, of which fathers would tell their children, and children to the generations yet unborn. And, as all things are double one against another,—as the types of the physical have their antitypes in the spiritual world,—so, is there not something of which the locusts are an emblem, and which is yet more terrible than they? a mysterious something, at which in our healthy state we shudder, as though an evil spirit passed us in the darkness;—a something dimly imaged by the canker that blights all beauty, and the leprosy that eats away all life,—a curse that broods over the green fields of humanity like the shadow of a poisonous tree? Aye! so it is! To him whose conscience of sin is afraid;—to him whose eyes are opened to see the unseen realities of the moral world;—to him who tries to see as the Saviour saw, and who would judge not by the standard of man but of his Maker, —the fall of the first accursed locust on the smiling plain is not one-tenth part so awful as the first little cloud of evil that flung its shadow over the innocence of a still-youthful life,—of the life of each one here, while he was yet young. To those angels who behold the face of our heavenly Father, the first base word spoken without a blush,—the first oath that profaned unwonted lips, the first lie dictated by cowardice to screen delinquency, the first duty wilfully neglected,—the first wicked thought consciously harboured, and rolled like a sweet morsel under the tongue,—the first tear called on a mother's cheek,—the first pang caused to a father's heart,—the first lapse into drunkenness or dishonour,—the first desire to taste of the tree of the mystery of evil, and to be as gods, and to whisper to the soul, Thou shalt not surely die,—the first wilful act whereby the erring soul defies its knowledge of that which is true and right, and lifts as it were the banner in the armies of the enemies of God,—these, these are the deeds which the holy ones chronicle in their tablets of sorrow; and these,—far more than the storm, and deluge, and ruin of the groaning and travailing creation,—these far more than the ravage of the pestilence, or the carnage of the fight—force from them "such tears as angels weep." We may have forgotten it;— to us it may be hidden far back in the mists of memory, that first word, that first act of conscious wickedness;—as much as the first locust is forgotten, when the myriads have come down; —as much as the first spark on the dry leaf is forgotten, when it has wrapped the roaring prairie, and the primeval forest in the flame of its conflagration. But they forget not, and God forgets not. He, who foresees "in the green the mouldered tree," knows and marks what sin it was, that first settling on the fair promise of a young life, caused the root to be as bitterness, and the blossom to go up as dust; He sees the pregnant evil grow and multiply, and leave the seeds of its destruction to spring up into their deadly existence in future years, until the field has been blighted into a wilderness, and the soul, which is the garden of God, has become black and noisome as the valley of Hinnom, and of Death. O my brethren, be not deceived, God is not mocked. I know how lightly it is the fashion to think and speak of sin: I know how lightly the young will don and wear that gay robe, which shall cling to them hereafter and tear their flesh like the poisoned tunic of fable: I know how boldly and easily they will laugh away "the troubles of the envious, and the fears of the cowardly, the heaviness of the slothful, and the shame of the unclean:" yet I do not fear for a moment that any wise man will consider the analogy too terrible; if so, let him pause and think whether it may not be because the veil is upon his heart, and he has sunk into that stupor of worldly comfort, that living death of spiritual apathy, that easy acquiescence and tolerance of habitual sin, which is too often the curse and disease of middle life. Alas! I know that in many a man, who has gone on long undisturbed in guilt, the soul and the conscience "may die a natural death" amid the dull comforts and occupations of the world, until the very sense of guilt is gone, and sin to him has lost all its sinfulness and all its shame.

But if anybody here be thus indifferent now, if God have thus sealed his eyes in penal blindness, and suffered his conscience to be clogged with the stupefaction of an unpunished course, to him more than to any one is it our duty not to speak smooth words or to prophesy deceits. For when the day of the Lord has come upon him, when the torchlight of the world's dim theatre has been quenched for ever, and instead of delusive shadows, the awfulness of the eternal reality has burst upon his aching sight; then, when self-deception is possible no longer, and the deathful slumber of the seared conscience has been broken short for ever; then indeed will every sinner long that the voice of every one of God's ministers could have rung, not with feeble and conventional orthodoxies, but as with that voice of a trumpet sounding long and loud which once shook the burning cliffs of Sinai, or with the thrilling alarm of that "warning voice," which he who saw

> The Apocalyse heard cry, in heaven aloud,
> " Wo to the inhabitants on earth!"

Most of us, my brethren, are young no longer. Much of our destined term of life lies already behind us, and silently the chariot of the hours and days and weeks is rolling on, and bearing us to a dark river and an unknown land,—and bearing us by a path which we can never pass again. For better or for worse, for good or for evil, a large and memorable portion—and indeed for the moulding of no small extent of our destiny by far the most important portion—of our lives is over; over for ever; never to be obliterated, never to be recalled. No man bathes twice in the same wave; no man lives twice in the same time. The past has glided into the dim backward; for us it has vanished for ever, and is but a decaying memory; for God it hath been recorded for ever, and is an eternal, indestructible reality. Of the days of our years which a child might number; of the ever-passing, ever-renewed, moments which once only God grants (and to some here they may be very very few, ere the night cometh when no man can work), a large portion has been spent by us already; how has it been spent? Has it been composed of "years which the locust has eaten"?

It is a solemn question! For a few moments, on this first Sunday of a new year, let us turn our faces backwards, and gaze (a sad gaze even for the best of us!) on the time past of our lives. We have reached those distant hills which once looked so blue and bright, and now disenchanted, let us look back from these frosty and flinty steeps upon the region which we have traversed. Brethren, think, is it not a blank for many of us? In forecast those years were like the garden of Eden before us, is not their retrospect for many of us a desolate wilderness? A fire burned before them, behind them a flame devoureth. And is it not, is it not because the locust army of our sins has settled on those fair fields, which might still have been green and refulgent, had our many good resolutions been any better than the morning cloud or than the early dew? The locust army of our sins; singly contemptible, collectively irresistible; but whether singly or in multitudes, ruinous and abhorred. Why is it that, for so many men, sadness lies in looking back? Why is it that they would give anything, short of their very being, to recover those lost years? Is it not because their labour has been given to the locust, and their fruit to the grasshopper? How often have we prayed to be nobler, holier, better? How often have we determined to avoid this snare, and wrestle with that temptation! How often have we resolved to break off the bad habit, and cut short the selfish career! How often, with stifled warnings of conscience, with forgotten prayers, and violated resolutions, have we returned like the dog to his vomit again, like the sow that was washed to her wallowing in the mire! Must there not be at least some here, for whom thoughts of sin have ripened into wishes, and wishes been consummated in acts, and acts hardened into habits, which are those locks and bars of the gate of hell which no hand save the hand of God can burst? must there not be some for whom vice has become graver sin, and sin against God has become crime against man, and unknown it may be to all save his own soul and to God, vice, and sin, and crime have left all over the soul their darkening trails, obliterating all that was beautiful, weakening all that was vigorous, poisoning all that was pure, until it is as true of their wasted lives as ever it was of the fields of Israel, that "that which the palmerworm hath left hath the locust eaten, and that which the locust hath left hath the cankerworm eaten, and that which the cankerworm hath left hath the caterpillar eaten"?

Is not this the reason why there is so much of sad truth in the Arab proverb, that the remembrance of youth is a sigh? Very well: be it so. The sadness of such a thought is undeniable: to look back over the past years of life, and to be conscious that our deeds have come to nothing, or had better have remained undone; to be conscious that we have sown but evil seeds in a corrupted soil, and that now it only remaineth to reap the harvest; to be conscious that we have incurred a terrible debt and that nature is a pitilessly accurate accountant, that we have wasted our fair early years in storing up inevitable misery for those that are to come,—there is, and I may not deny it, in such thoughts a sorrow too deep for tears. Yet be it so: it is passed for ever; it cannot be helped; it is irrevocable even to Omnipotence. That which hath been shall be. It is God's not ours. The infinite air will thrill for ever with the words which we have spoken; the rays of light will carry for ever from universe to universe the picture of the deeds which we have done. All that is over, and we cannot alter it. We look back, and sigh to think how selfish, how foolish, how wicked we have been; it is a melancholy picture, but it cannot be blotted out. It cannot be blotted out, and therefore of all follies the greatest folly is to brood upon it continually. Nothing is vainer than vain regret. It may be well indeed sometimes to glance rapidly along the faultful past; but unless we deliberately wish to fill our souls with useless misery and dangerous despair, it is a mere paralysing madness to dwell on it too long. If I have pointed to any man the threatening clouds which gather over the past, it is only that we may gaze together on the unfading rainbow which by God's blessing shall span their gloom. Let us turn away bravely and wisely; let us turn to the hopeful future from the helpless past. And as the traveller who has lost his way by night, and startled suddenly to a sense of his danger by some lightning-flash which reveals the rocks and chasms around him, pauses terror-stricken to await the dawn; and, when the sun has dawned on his darkness, looking back to mark his error, shudders to see his own footsteps by the dizzy edge of the precipice, and the tottering pine-branch by which he stumbled over the torrent, and then rises with a deep sigh, and thanks God, and girding his loins presses forward humbler and holier, sadder and wiser, on the road which shall lead him right,—so let us too, brethren, resolutely close our eyes to all the wasted years which may lie behind us, and, praying God that the dayspring may arise in our hearts and lighten us into the path of repentance, press forward again with every surviving energy, towards the mark of the prize of our high calling. Thickly as the locust-swarms may lie over those years, utterly as they may have wasted a vain and misguided boyhood, or a passionate and foolish youth, yet the very worst of us need not despair. For what cause is it that God gives us the gift of time, if it be not that we may repent therein? For us, if we have been sinners, repentance is the work of life: O not that we may grow rich, not that we may grow famous, not that we may be at ease and live in pleasure upon the earth; not for such purposes is each new day allotted us, but only that our souls may be reconciled to God, and sheltered once more in his forsaken fold. Is the past dark? be it so! There at least lies the future before us; forward then, and onwards! it is as yet an innocent, it may be a happy future; it may be a noble future, a stainless future, a godlike future; take it with prayerful gratitude, and fling the withered past aside. Once more sow the seed, and plant the vineyard in the furrows of the contaminated soil. Poor may be the aftermath, scant the gleaning of grapes upon life's topmost branches that may be left for thee: yet do thou thy best to redeem these from the locust swarm. Do as Israel did when the locusts settled down. They remembered the God who had once swept away the locusts with a mighty wind, and drowned them by myriads in the Red Sea waves. "Rend your heart," said the prophet, "and not your garments, and turn unto the Lord your God; for he is gracious and merciful, slow to anger, and of great kindness, and repenteth him of the evil;" and they did turn and seek Him; and then mark God's gracious message to them,— "Fear not, O land; be glad and rejoice, for the Lord will do great things....And the floors shall be full of wheat, and the fats shall overflow with wine and oil. And I will restore to you the years that the locust hath eaten."

In one sense indeed they can never be restored; fresh years we can have, 'fresh fields, and pastures new;' but not the old ones, and not the lost riches they might have blossomed with. Never can we be again as though we had not sinned at all. Let us recognise this stern truth:—The remission of sins, as you may read amid the shattered ruins of many a life, is not the remission of their consequences, nor are the perfect freedom and unvexed fearlessness of the innocent attainable by the guilty even when they have been forgiven. In a day, in an hour, in a moment, we may destroy a character which on earth can never be rebuilt. For how many men has the sin of an instant proved the anguish of a life! And even if by God's grace the deadliness of the wounds be healed, yet the unsightly scars must remain for ever on our souls, and the malicious hand of merciless man will point to them. But, thanks be to God, God is more tender, more merciful, more long-suffering than miserable man. When our father and our mother forsake us, He will take us up. We cannot sink so low, but that He will stoop to us out of His shining heaven, if we look to Him: even if, after our riotous living, we hunger in vain for the very husks that the swine do eat, yet if we arise and go to Him, He will welcome us in His forgiving arms, and weep on the neck of His returning prodigals. For this

Christ died. He who lay at the table of the Publican, and shrank not from the sores of the leper, and turned not with loathing from the fierce and filthy Gadarene; He who touched the stained woman as she sobbed on the Temple pavement, and said to her in that unutterable gentleness "Neither do I condemn thee: go, and sin no more;" He who suffered the harlot, out of whom he had cast seven devils, 'to wet his feet with her tears, and wipe them with the hairs of her head;' He will receive us too, and love us graciously, and forgive us freely. Little need we reck of man, if God forgives us. And He does forgive us. The Holy One who inhabiteth eternity reaches to us out of His eternity the fingers of a man's hand, and touches into green life again the years that the locust hath eaten. Even the memory of guilt He will alleviate. Sometimes as we float down the river of life, memory flashes up from the hidden depths, and the dark wave is peopled with the innumerable faces of once forgotten sins, which (as in the nympholepsy of ancient fable) menace us from the waters, and prophesy of death. But God can enable us to gaze unshudderingly on those faces, and say with thankful emotion "Those sins are not mine; they were mine, but they are forgiven. They were my heavy burden once, but now they are nailed to my Saviour's cross. They were written against me, but He has obliterated the record with His own hand, pierced for me. Such things I did,—but I am washed, but I am cleansed, but I am sanctified, but I am purified. We may say, like the Queen in the splendid tragedy, that "all old ocean's waters" could not wash away the stain of our guiltiness; and that 'not poppy nor mandragora nor all the drowsy syrups in the world' could lull our diseased memories asleep;—aye, true!— but one drop of Christ's most precious blood can cleanse us for ever; one whisper of his 'Peace, be still' can silence the wrathful storms of an agitated conscience, and give us songs in the midnight of despair!

But remember, brethren, in conclusion, that we must not sit still. Let us not fall into the fatal error of fancying that we may die in our sins, and yet glide at once through the gates of heaven;—let us not imagine that the soul may pass from earth unforgiven, impenitent, leprous, degraded, and yet be clasped at once to the bosom of its God. It is a fearful delusion. When the locust came, the people lit huge fires and dug deep pits, and toiled night and day to exterminate them, and cried mightily to God. We too must awake 'with agonies and energies' to shake off the curse of sin which is upon us; we too must turn to the Lord our God. We must do it now; for even if we be not suddenly called away, still year by year, like a stream that hurries to join the sea, time is sweeping us on more and more rapidly, down its resistless wave; the hours are perishing and being imputed to us. Let us then waste no time in unavailing sorrow over the past; but rather, as that great chieftain of old, who, looking back in a dream, saw moving after him 'a huge and monstrous form thick set all over with serpents,' while wherever it moved everything fell crashing before it, and who, while he beheld, was bidden to go on his way straight forward and cast no look behind, and obedient to the mandate marched on to glory and victory:—so let us go onwards, faint it may be, yet certain of success. Is man against us? let us fly from his proud cruelty to the love of God. Are our consciences against us? let us fly from those things of which our consciences are afraid, to the mercy of God. Is the past against us? let us fly from it now to the yet innocent present which He still allows us; to the happy and holy future which He may yet enable us to attain; to the glorious eternity whereof the golden gates are as yet unbarred and are flung as widely open to penitents as to saints. So, when after a short span of fleeting years, the sea rolls, or the turf is green, over the mortal bodies of all who hear me this day, may many an immortal soul from this congregation meet and recognise in the light of heaven, and there in the white robes of redeemed innocence dwell, without sin and without sorrow, in the City which hath foundations whose builder and maker is God. There, if not fully upon earth, will God restore fully, restore finally to the humble, and to the penitent "The years which the locust hath eaten."

XVI.

SEEING THE FACE OF GOD.

(Preached before Harrow School, September 30, 1866.)

REV. xxii. 4.—"And they shall see His face, and His name shall be in their foreheads."

THIS verse is taken from the last chapter of the Bible, a chapter in some respects the most moving and beautiful of all. About it, as about the gates of Paradise, lingers a reflection from the hues of heaven, and a mysterious echo from angel songs. Its warnings fall with the solemnity of death and of judgment; its promises are unearthly in their images of peace. How unlike are all the promises of this book to anything which our own poor wishes could have framed. What should we have wished for, had we foreshadowed a heaven for ourselves? should we not have transplanted into it the passions and the selfishness of earth? Would not one have striven to realise his sensual vision of pleasure, and another his base ideal of comfort, and another his wild tumult of ambition, and well nigh all some deification of their own vanities,—till heaven were no heaven at all, but only, like earth, a struggle of selfish atoms, a tangle of ravelled hopes? Not such is the heaven of which we catch faint glimpses in the Apocalypse of St John. The vows and wishes of the world, the aims and hopes of common souls, are absent there. No shadow stains the crystal waters of that river of life: no step that defileth can pass upon that glassy floor. Man in all the base attributes of his individuality has disappeared; God alone remaineth. The crown of life, the leaves that heal the nations, the hidden manna, the new name, the song that endeth not day or night about the rainbow-circled throne,—these blessings,—and these not in differing degrees, not selfishly monopolised, not divided into lower or upper grades,—these are the blessings which the heart must recognise, which is calm enough and pure enough to enter upon that rest.

And of all the promises none is lovelier than this;—"There shall be no more curse, but the throne of God and of the Lamb shall be in it, and His servants shall serve Him. And they shall see His face, and His name shall be in their foreheads." Is it possible that such worms as we shall see the face of God? Even to imagine it, is to imagine ourselves lifted to infinite heights above our present degradation. For to see the face of God is to be in light. "Dark deeds are done in secret; drag them into the light, and they cannot stand it. A debased soul, brought into open daylight, and not rushing from it, is naturally purified; that which was darkness in the dark, becomes light in the daylight." Therefore to see God's face, is to be pure from every shame. And it is to be elevated above all earthliness. A Russian empress once built a palace of ice, and her guests danced and banqueted within its glimmering walls. But, when the sun shone, it vanished and melted into cold and dripping mud. Even so it is with the aims men toil for most. Death comes, and all they have longed for looks no better than a palace of icicles, which shone with opal colours under the moonbeam, but melts into hideous ruin before the light of God. Therefore to see God's face is to distinguish the real from the illusory, the true from the false. And it is to be at peace. For as the chaos became order and beauty under the wings of the Spirit of God, and as the troubled waves of Galilee sank into calm beneath the Saviour's feet, so there can be no disquietude in His presence, where the wicked cease from troubling and the weary are at rest. And it is to live in love; for it is to have our tears wiped away by His hand who made the soul, and who alone can understand it, and who gives to it—even laden with its infirmities, but washed, and cleansed, and forgiven for its Saviour's sake—that which man is too poor and too proud to give, a divine tenderness, a ceaseless love. To attain to these blessings is a height of which we might well despair. Yet never let the present "solicit us with its easy indulgence to despair of that sweetest and noblest hope." By aiming at it we shall at last attain. So have I stood deep in an Alpine valley, and still wrapped in the cold and darkness far below, have seen the first sunbeam smite with its fierce splendour the highest mountain-top, and thought that it must be impossible by any toil to reach, from our dim, low region, that encrimsoned height;—and yet, as the sunrise leapt from peak to peak, and flowed and broadened in its golden streams down the mountain side, have climbed on and on with long toil, and under the full daylight have mounted to that topmost crest of eternal snow, heaved high into the regions of blue air. So is it in the moral world. He who ever toils uphillward with his eye upon the summit,

> "Shall find the toppling crags of Duty scaled,
> Are close upon the shining table-lands
> To which our God himself is moon and sun."

But is this a promise for the future only? Is it only the peaceful, the happy, the victorious dead, whose work is over while we toil on;— who have gained the shore while we are heaved up and down upon the labouring sea;—is it they alone who see God's face? is it not suffered us to see it even through the vapours of mortal life? Not fully, my brethren; only in part; only as through the dim reflection of a silver mirror—$\delta\iota'$ $\dot{\epsilon}\sigma\acute{o}\pi\tau\rho o\upsilon$ $\dot{\epsilon}\nu$ $a\dot{\iota}\nu\acute{\iota}\gamma\mu a\tau\iota$; only as Moses saw some gleaming of His robe, hid under the hollow of His hand in a cleft of the burning hill. And yet even thus to see God is our only chance, our only hope of happiness here. In thinking of any man's present or future, I ask not, 'is he rich? is he noble? is he strong? is he wise? do men praise him? do his plans succeed? is he unharassed by mean cares?' Many of whom all this is true, are the miserablest of men, and all the more miserable because they know it not;—but I ask, 'does he now see, does it seem as if he would ever see, the face of God?' That alone can make and keep him,—I say not happy—for there is something infinitely higher and better than happiness at which every good man aims,—not perhaps happy, but at noble peace with God and man, enjoying trustfully all that the poor present can give him, enjoying with yet calmer certainty the glory of his future hopes.

Therefore what I would wish most earnestly for every one of you, what I would wish for you more than knowledge, more than health, more than many friends, more infinitely than the fool's paradise of success—is that you should see the face of God. And to see it you must seek it. He will see the face of God most brightly, who strives most earnestly to live the life of God on earth; and his life will be most like the life of God, whose prayer rises oftenest and most sincerely to his heavenly Father. Prayer and a holy life must be his who would see his Maker. In prayer you grasp the golden key of the gate of Eden; by a holy life, you may walk, in something more than fancy, among its seraph choirs. With these the path of life lies open to the very foot of the Tree of Life. It was for rebels only that the avenue to Paradise was closed. For him who approacheth it with prayer and holiness the cherubim vail their wrathful faces, and the waving blade of the flaming sword is sheathed.

But are there any other less obvious helps, by the use of which we may the sooner win this blessedness? Are there any other ways in which God reveals Himself to mortal man? My brethren, to the clear and open eye, to the pure and simple heart there are many ways; and of one or two I would speak to-day.

I. First, then, we may learn to see the face of God in nature. By nature I mean the sum total of God's works and laws. My brethren, I cannot tell you one tithe of what I feel on this subject. I know,—for I find it alike in Scripture and in experience,—that the love and study of the works of nature, the walking through the world with open and loving eyes, is one of the very best aids to faith, and one of the very simplest sources of happiness. Men of the world despise it; they call it enthusiasm and sentimentality, as they call most things which are good and true, so that to them the elevation of the soul and the innocent delight which God's works inspire is thrown away, and the suns rise and set before blind eyes, and the air rings with music to dull deaf ears. God never meant it so; it is the diabolism of sensual disbelief. When Job lay sick and stricken on his dunghill, sneered at and taunted by his little religious friends, how did God redeem him? what lessons did He teach him out of the whirlwind? Do not trust my answer, but take your Bibles, and read for yourselves and see. Was it some logical formula? was it some dull, dismal, Pharisaic theology;— or was it by pointing him to the birth of the dewdrops and the fountains of the dawn,—to Orion, and Mazzaroth, and Arcturus, and the ocean doors,—to the wild ass scouring the desert, and the wild goat leaping among the crags, —to the soaring of the eagle, and the plumes of the ostrich, and the glories of the peacock's wing,—to the pawing of the war-horse among the glittering spears, and the wallowing of the sea-monster in the foamy depths? Such teaching it was, and not the pedantry of scholasticism, that made Job say, "I abhor myself, and repent in dust and ashes." And when Christ sat on the green grass of the mountain-side, how did He soothe the troubles of that care-worn multitude? Was it not by pointing to the more than regal loveliness of the lilies of the field, and bidding them learn the tenderness of their Heavenly Father by His care for the falling sparrow, and for the raven's callow brood? Blessed be the "enthusiasm," hallowed the "sentimentality," which teaches lessons such as these. Try, my brethren, to learn them. Study and love the works of God;—they are better worth reading than the words of man;—they will give you simpler tastes and purer pleasures; they will dower the youngest son among you with a wealth not to be dreamt of in his father's home; in happy moments they will make you happier; in friendless moments they will give you companionship; in troubled moments they will breathe you peace. Nor is this all, you will see God in them. He will be everywhere. All things will be full of Him. The earth we tread, and the air we breathe, the Universe and the Conscience, "the starry heaven above and the moral law within," will all be witnesses of His presence. And the more you know about these works, the more will you feel it. Science does but read aloud the awful lessons of that great open Bible, the Universe of God, on which many of you forsooth look down from the whole height of your towering ignorance. In proportion to your knowledge of this Revelation will be your interest in it. He who loves and admires Creation, yet knows nothing of its plan, is like one who stands in a cavern of which the riches and beauty are but dimly seen;—but to him who enters it with the torch of knowledge its dim walls become illuminate with ten thousand glories. Exchange, while you can, a wise knowledge for a feeble and ignorant contempt. Enter it, while you can, with holy and humble hearts, and

> "Bid with lifted torch its starry walls
> Sparkle, as erst they sparkled to the glow
> Of odorous lamp tended by saint and sage."

II. In Nature then you may see God, and secondly you may learn to see Him in his revelation to the minds of other men. You may find that revelation in the books which they have left. Never was anything good, or true, or wise, written or spoken without the inspiration of God's Holy Spirit, and in reading such words you read a revelation of Him. Books, which are "the true reliquaries of the saints but without imposture,"—books, which with a potent yet innocent necromancy enable us to evoke from their dim tombs the spirits of the dead,—books, which are the best hearts' blood of great men "embalmed for a life beyond life"—my brethren, they are well-nigh the richest privilege, and quite the worthiest, the most unshaken and incorruptible friends we can possess. Few of us reverence and value them enough. Oh! when I remember how many good and great books there are,—books which a life-time could not exhaust, books every one of which would make the true reader wiser, better, nobler,—loftier in intellectual stature and in moral strength,—and which yet are left unread,—I stand amazed to think of that silent assembly of uncrowned kings which is beckoning to us in vain, while yet you will not ask the philosopher for the gathered treasures of his wisdom, or the orator for the thunder of his eloquence, or the poet for the magic of his song. And for whom will you forsake them? for the bald and disjointed inanities of personal talk. There, in our Library, are many great and precious volumes of wise men's words;—and for what will you abandon them? I forbear to characterise fully the literature of which some among you seem fondest, or which I see oftenest in their hands,—books which are no books,—the nameless outpourings of obscure vulgarity, the raw conceptions of unknown sensationists, the brainless buffoonery which turns even what is noblest into jest. And this prison-literature, this romance of the counter and the stable, this noisy and utterly ignoble trash, can interest and amuse many boys who, as I have long since discovered, barely know the names of their greatest poets, or have heard so much as the titles of the books of their wisest contemporaries. However we view it, such a taste is a calamity, and such a literature a nation's curse. Believe me, in such books you will never see the face of God.

But, thank God, there is one book at least, the Book of Books, which we all perforce hear, and in which day by day we read. In all great literature you may learn to see God, but best and clearest there; and we might be content to sacrifice the rest of human wisdom for all which that one sentence means, "Come unto me all ye that are weary and heavy laden, and I will give you rest." Oh! if you can read nothing else which is calm and good and true, read that book; its teachings may stay with you in lines of blessing when the world itself has begun to fade away. It is told of one of our sweetest poets that during his latter years he barely opened any book but this; it is told of another high intellect—one of heaven's great ones slandered by earth's little—that when all other reading had lost its charms he would ask for the Bible which he had once used among the cottages. Yes, the Bible is often degraded by superstitious usage;—the dogmatist gets out of it a "charlatan's philosophy,"—the ignorant quotes its words as though they were a material talisman,—the fanatic snatches from it the weapons wherewith he would stab his neighbour's hopes;—it has been made, times without number, the cloak of the Pharisee, and the shield of the tyrant, the faggot of the inquisitor, and the fetter of the slave,—but, however men may pervert, they cannot rob it of its glory, they can never make it less than that which it has been, and is, and must be still, the hope and anchor of the soul, sure and steadfast, the lighthouse lamp, that glows unwavering amid the hurricane, and beams in divine calm above the frothy uproar of impotent waves. Oh! if you would see the face of God, you must have learnt well its teaching—aye, and learnt in your lives to apply its truths.

III. And thirdly, we may see the face of God in the life of Christ's true servants and followers. They see his face, his name is on their foreheads now. It has been observed that, whereas in the heathen world there were barely one or two to whom we should venture to apply the epithet "holy," among Christians, on the other hand, there always have been and are many "whose mere presence has shamed the bad, and made the good better, and has been felt at times like the presence of God Himself." In the lives of such men, as you read them in Christian biography,—in the conduct of such men, if you have ever had the happiness to meet them in daily life, you may see reflected, as a planet reflects the sun, some faint image of the face of God. Such men are the salt of the earth; their mere being saves it from corruption. Their names shine out from the waste and dimness of common society, nobly exceptional, magnificently alone.

There are two kinds of life, my brethren,—one is the life we all live, the other the life of those who have left all and followed Christ, giving up for His sake father, and mother, and friends, and home. We live lives respecting which I should be a flatterer if I were to say that, as far as I can see, they differ in any perceptible excellence from the lives of the world;—lives which anyone can live. We get and grudge,—we spend and save—we surround ourselves with comforts,—we secure what luxuries we may;—we do what we can for ourselves, and shew but little care for the interests and feelings of others. But these men! these impractical enthusiasts, these derided sentimentalists, have been grandly simple, and nobly poor, and eccentrically good. I imagine them entering in among us here;—saints of God whom we should have patronised; martyrs to whom we should have condescended; confessors whom we should have thought we were honouring if we shook them by the hand,—these "faithful who were not famous," these rank and file who kept back the enemy in the battlefields of life. We should have smiled at their coarse dress, but their raiment is shining now; we should have called ourselves their "superiors," but now they are in the heaven of heavens; they were poor, but they made myriads rich; they were ignorant, but they taught the world more and infinitely worthier lessons than whole generations of little scholars. For they knew that

"The high desire that *others* may be blest
Savours of heaven;"

their eyes had been opened and disenchanted to see what alone is best, what is alone worth living for; their souls, conscious of their high dignity from God, brooked not the mean vulgarities of the worldly life. Read such lives as that of the Plymouth cobbler who was the founder of ragged schools, and the Yarmouth seamstress who was the reformer of prisons:—read them, and understand that though few noticed or cared for them in life, yet the Priest and the Pharisee might have sat very humbly at their feet.

In these three ways then,—in Nature; in the books of the great and wise; in the lives and conduct of the good,—and more than any book in the Bible, and more than any life in that life of Christ on earth which good men can but feebly imitate,—we may learn to see the face of God.

Alas! my brethren, had I rather spoken of how men lose sight of that face, and live in the darkness, would not many of you have felt that I was describing your own experience? For more rapidly than the clouds roll athwart the sun, do the exhalations from an erring heart blot out the face of the Sun of Righteousness. He who is growing up in forgetfulness of God, careless and prayerless from day to day,—he who is living in pleasure, dead while he liveth,—he to whom the world and its earthly hopes are all in all, and whose imagination, crowded with earthly images, never reaches to things beyond,—above all, and worse than all, he who suffers the lower passions of his nature to pass into such a tyrannous and fatal curse, that even his mind and conscience are corrupted and defiled,—alas for him the face of God is visible no longer, or visible only in gleams few and distant, and ever dimmer and more distant as life goes on. My brethren, above all my younger brethren, may you never know what this must be. In the gay bright days of youth, unvexed by care, when Pleasure has not yet stripped off her mask, a sinner may not feel the curse of living without God. But life is not always undisturbed. Men *do* live to lose all that they have gained; men do live to have their hearts eaten away into emptiness by bosom sins; men do live to be bereaved of all whom they had loved, and pass lonely to the grave; men do live to be wounded in their tenderest affections, and to see their children become their curse; men do live to lose health and to be racked by disease and anguish in every limb. Are you safe from these myriads of human misfortunes? not one of you is safe from one of them; most, if not all of you, will live to experience one or more of them:—and how will it be with you then? If you have seen God's face, you can be peaceful and hopeful, if not happy, still: but if that face be turned away how shall you bear such crushing burdens? How shall you pass that last dark river, beyond whose billows no fields for you will "stand dressed in living green"? O seek His face now; call ye upon Him while He yet is nigh. Earnestly would I entreat you young new comers amongst us to remember this,—that, if you turn but a little aside from the right path now, you may wander infinitely far;—if you embark now on the forbidden stream, before you know it the stream will be a river, and the river will have mingled with the sea, and then there will be "no springing back from the boat upon the shore."—In the course of 11 years I have seen many vacancies on those seats which you now occupy;—of those vacancies some,—not a few,— have been caused by death, and of those we can think with peace and hope, nay almost with gladness now:—but some, alas also not a few, have been caused not by death but by disgrace—and of those that have thus been banished from the midst of us some there are that have gone from bad to worse. These are the dead who point our saddest moral, these the dead over whom most we mourn. They sat there, and listened to our words, and laughed and sinned; and so, little by little, became bad boys, and disgraced their own lives, and brought dismay and misery into their parents' hearts. Yet they were once innocent, young, new boys; think you, that when first they listened to the solemn words from this pulpit, as you sit listening now,—think you, that they ever dreamt in what shame and failure their Harrow career after a year or two would end?—Dear brethren, the beginning of sin is as the letting out of water:—be warned in time!

One word more. Many of us kneeling side by side at yonder Holy Table will be striving there to pierce the mists that encompass with perplexity our mortal lives, and to see some dim gleaming of the face of God. Before this term has ended we hope that very many of you will join us there. Let us all be united there in our thoughts and prayers to-day. Pray for this great school; pray for us; pray for yourselves; pray for those young new comers of whom I spoke. Let us strive there, kneeling side by side, to attain if haply it be possible, more love, more sympathy, more nobleness, more happiness, more hope. "When thou saidst, Seek ye my face, my heart said unto thee, Thy face, Lord, will I seek."

XVII.

THE TEMPLE OF GOD.

(Preached before King's College School, at the Reopening of King's College Chapel, June 23, 1864.)

1 Cor. iii. 16.—"Know ye not that ye are the temple of God, and that the Spirit of God dwelleth in you?"

THE three different senses of this phrase "the temple of God," mark very distinctly three different eras of God's dealings with His Church. In the Old Testament it is applied without variation to that stately sanctuary of marble and gold and cedar-wood which Solomon built in the zenith of his power. In the Gospels, on the lips of our blessed Lord, we find it used in a new sense, which filled the unaccustomed Jews with amazement,—"He spake of the temple of His body." Lastly, in the Epistles, and especially in those of St Paul, the term Temple receives a significance yet more marvellous, for it is applied, as in the text, to the mortal body of every Christian man. Let us for a few moments glance at these three temples, which mark three mighty dispensations in religious history—the temple at Jerusalem, the temple of Christ's human body, the temple of every Christian's heart[1].

1. The Most High, my brethren, dwelleth not in temples made with hands. Lo, heaven, and the heaven of heavens cannot contain Him, how much less any house that man can build? If that mighty cathedral, whose dome is the body of heaven in its clearness, whose pillars are the mountain summits, and its cresset lamps the sun and moon and stars, be yet too mean for His dread magnificence, how shall any perishing structure of human toil be deemed sufficient for His abode? Yet, out of that mercy which knew and provided for the spiritual wants of man, He Himself directed the fashion of this earthly tabernacle, and deigned to place the symbol of His presence between the outstretched wings of the golden cherubim. Through dreary ages of darkness and error that Temple stood as the visible witness against all idolatry of God's creatures;—the witness that, though

---

[1] The history of the word is beautifully stated in Bishop Hind's little work *The Three Temples of the True God*.

the great heavens continued dumb, and the world rolled on in unbroken silence, and sin, and sorrow, and unbelief, and blasphemy, and lust, rioted unrestrained among the dark places of the earth,—yet God was sitting above the water-floods, a King for ever;—a King ruling in righteousness, although His way is in the sea, and His path in the great waters, and His footsteps are not known;—not, as the Epicurean imagined Him, indifferent to the sorrows and sins of men, but an infinite and merciful Father, yearning in love for the souls of His sinful children; who, though He be so high, yet hath respect unto the lowly of heart, and who willeth us to give of our best and richest to His earthly temples, as a proof alike of our love and reverence to Him, and of His everlasting presence in the midst of us to accept our thanksgivings and hear our prayers.

2. But after a thousand years our Lord spoke of the Temple of God in a manner unheard before. "Destroy this temple," He said, when asked for some sign of His mission, "Destroy this temple[1], and in three days I will raise it up." "Forty and six years was this temple in

---

[1] John ii. 19—21.

building," answered the indignant Jews, "and wilt Thou rear it up in three days?" But He spake of the "temple of His body." His use of the word made a deep impression: it was turned into the main charge against Him in the trial before Caiaphas; it was hurled as the bitterest taunt against Him as He hung upon the cross; it was remembered as the key to His most mysterious prophecy after He had risen from the dead[1]. It well might be remembered, for it was full of awful significance. Truly hereby the veil of the material temple was rent in twain, and access was given to God by a nearer and truer way. God Himself had reared His tabernacle in mortal flesh; the tent of His eternal Spirit had been made "like ours and of the same material[2]." And though that temple of Christ's body lasted on earth, not for many centuries, but only for a few short years, yet let us not forget that it *still* lasts eternal in the heavens. Earthquakes and storms may sweep over the world; the iron rocks may be shattered, and the everlasting mountains rent; the great gorgeous globe and all that is within it, and the universe, with all its suns and stars,

[1] Matt. xxvi. 61, xxvii. 40; John ii. 22.
[2] Archbishop Leighton.

may sink and perish hereafter in the surges of some fiery sea; but for ever in the heaven of heavens that living Temple shall endure; for ever and for ever shall the Godhead and the manhood be truly, perfectly[1], distinctly, indissolubly conjoined; for ever and for ever, through the thunder "shall come a human voice;" for ever and for ever a face like our own face look down upon us in pity from the throne of God; and He who loved His own on earth shall love them to the end, and fold them safe, amid the universal ruin, in the bosom of His everlasting love.

3. Nor must we forget that it was through the temple of Christ's body, as through some glorious vestibule, that the Spirit of God passed into the temple of every Christian heart. It was the promise wherewith our Lord had comforted His trembling disciples; and very soon after the temple of His mortal body had been taken up into heaven, was the new living temple filled with the Glory of the Presence, and the brows of the assembled apostles were mitred by the cloven tongues of Pentecostal flame. Since that time the mortal body of every one of us

[1] ἀληθῶς, τελέως, ἀδιαιρέτως, ἀσυγχύτως. Cf. Hooker, v. liv. 10.

has been a temple of God—a temple of the Holy Ghost; and the Spirit of God has loved

"Before all temples the upright heart and pure[1]."

There is no doctrine on which the Apostles dwell with more insistency than this, alluding to it repeatedly in their Epistles as to a mainspring of spiritual life. "Know ye not," St Paul asks twice over of his Corinthian converts, "know ye not that ye are the temple of God, and that the Spirit of God dwelleth in you?" "Quench not the Spirit," he teaches the Thessalonians. "Grieve not the Holy Spirit of God," he urges on the Ephesians; and again, "Ye are the temple of the living God." Even now imagine him to be addressing his old question to each one of you; "Know ye not that the Lord Jesus Christ dwelleth in you, except ye be reprobates?" *except*—oh, what a fearful alternative is there[2]!

Nor were the early Christians backward to realize the same high doctrine—a doctrine too mysterious for the heathen world to understand. When Ignatius, the poor and aged bishop, was

---

[1] Milton, *Paradise Lost*, I. 18.
[2] 1 Cor. iii. 16, 17; vi. 19; 2 Cor. vi. 16; 1 Thess. v. 15; Eph. iv. 30; 1 Pet. iv. 14, &c.

carried before Trajan, the haughty victorious emperor, the emperor comtemptuously called him a κακοδαίμων, "a poor devil." Ignatius took hold of the word, and said that one who bore God in him could not be called a devil, seeing that the demons depart from the servants of God. "Who is it," asked Trajan, "who carries God with him?" Ignatius answered "He that hath Christ in his heart." "Do you mean," said Trajan, "Him that was crucified?" "Him that hath crucified my sin," answered Ignatius, "with the inventor of it, and put down all demoniac error and wickedness under the feet of those who bear Him in their heart." "Dost thou then," sneered Trajan, "carry the Crucified One within thyself?" Ignatius said, "Yea; for it is written, I will dwell in them, and walk in them." Thereupon Trajan pronounced sentence, "We ordain that Ignatius, who says that he bears the crucified within him, be flung to the beasts for the amusement of the people." Happiest of martyrs! for though the Libyan lion might bathe his jaws crimson in the human blood, he could not touch the celestial habitation. And hence Ignatius was called Θεοφόρος, the God-bearer, because he spoke of his carrying Christ in him. But his quotation from Scrip-

THE TEMPLE OF GOD. 337

ture shows that he would not have claimed it for a special title, "but that he looked on every Christian man as one who bore God within him, whether he was mindful of his high and awful privilege or not[1]."

The true "Shechinah, then, is man[2]," and "there is but one temple in the universe, and that is the body of man. Nothing is holier than that high form." Truly, in the words of the Christian poet,

"We are greater than we know[3]."

Let us try to realize the thought. God within us!—not only ever with us, unseen; not only watching us in our secret moments, and reading the very thoughts of our hearts; not only covering us with the shadow of His wings and lighting us with the light of His countenance; but within us, our bodies His temples, our hearts His home! What a glorious dignity! What an imperial inheritance! We are the children of God, the heirs of immortality, but a little lower than the angels, crowned with glory and honour. This is

---

[1] See Maurice's *Ecclesiastical History*, p. 176. The conversation is given in the *Martyrium S. Ignatii*, and is here somewhat abridged.

[2] Novalis.   [3] Wordsworth.

the only thought that can give true "grandeur to the beatings of the heart;" this is the only thought which, however mean and narrow be the stage whereon our life is played, can yet make the drama "of stately and most regal argument." Oh, if we could but grasp the thought, we should live lives nobler and more beautiful; we should breathe a purer, a sweeter, and a calmer air; time would present to us a richer aspect, and its daily voices echo in our ears with a sweeter melody; for then, from the cradle to the grave, the dark waters of life would be illuminated, and its dense clouds would be pierced through and through with the splendour of heaven—with the unchangeable sunlight of that eternal life which is hid with Christ in God.

The great city of Ephesus was proud to call herself the Νεωκόρος, the temple-sweeper of the goddess Diana; and shall not we, if we realize this awful dignity, devote our whole energies to see that this spiritual temple be erected in a cleansed heart, a heart worthy that the fire of God should burn on its altar, and the light of God stream over its shrine? For if any man defile the temple of God, him shall God destroy. But can a man wilfully, willingly, lay waste and desecrate its inner sanctities who once has felt its awfulness? Can he ever suffer the walls of its very presence-chamber to be defaced with the guilty picturings of a foul imagination? Can he, truly honouring himself as a temple of God, be mean, or a liar, or a coward? Can he pervert the hand and the eye of Christ, and make them the instruments of sin and shame? Can he ever sink into the swinish self-indulgence of the drunkard, or take the members which are dedicated to his Redeemer, and stain them with a dark and all but ineffaceable stain by making them the members of a harlot? Verily no, he dare not! he will prize at too high a rate the precious jewel of his godlike faculties to wreathe them around the withered mask of pleasure, or place them as a crown round the foul brows of sensual death. He will feel that to devote his best and brightest years to vice and self-indulgence, is to hang a jewel of gold in a swine's snout, or a diamond on the forehead of a skull. Truly, in the words of our greatest poet, "he that holds himself in reverence and due esteem, both for the dignity of God's image upon him, and for the price of his redemption, which he thinks is visibly marked upon his forehead, accounts himself both a fit person to do the noblest and godliest deeds, and much better worth than to deject and to defile with such a debasement and pollution as sin is, himself, so highly ransomed and ennobled to a new friendship and filial relation with God. Nor can he fear so much the offence and reproach of others, as he dreads and would blush at the reflection of his own severe and modest eye upon himself, if it should see him doing or imagining that which is sinful, though in the deepest secresy[1]."

Think, my young brethren, of this mighty doctrine, from which flow naturally and immediately all the great duties of our life. For if, by God's grace, you can once attain to this high consciousness, it will fill you with so exalted and abiding a self-respect, as shall be the truest source of all virtuous and godlike action; it will cause in you a pious and just honouring of yourselves, which shall be a talisman against all meanness and all sensuality; a thrilling sense that all sin is to be loathed and hated as a weakness, a corruption, a degradation;—a realization of the holiness of your baptized bodies, which shall work within you like the perpetual presence of a king. Thus will you loathe to stain the festal robes of your youth by any pollution;

---

[1] Milton, *Reason of Church Government.*

thus will you shudder to lay on your white souls the stains of lust, or cruelty, or lies; thus will you shrink from the contact of all foulness, as the naked skin shrinks from a spark of fire; thus will you learn how terrible it is "to burn away in mad waste the divine aromas and plainly celestial elements from our existence; to change our holy of holies into a place of riot; to make the soul itself hard, impious, barren!" Thus will you recognize "what virtue is in purity, and continence of life; how divine is the blush of young human cheeks; how high, beneficent, sternly inexorable, if forgotten, is the duty laid on every Christian in regard to these particulars[1]."

There is no time to develop or say more on these awful truths; but, oh! if I have but impressed on one young heart a new sense of the sacredness of his mortal body, and the nearness of eternity as the shadow of God's wing under which we play out our little lives—I have said enough. And I will but add a few more words on the immediate occasion which has brought us together. All those who are interested in this great institution have been striving to make

---

[1] Carlyle, *Life of Frederick*, II. 36.

this chapel more worthy, by its beauty, of that God to whose honour it is dedicated. It is fit—both for our own reverence and for God's glory—that the Church which, as St Chrysostom says, is "the place of angels and archangels, the court of God, and the image of heaven," should receive our best and most willing gifts. It is true that He who interpenetrates the whole universe with His presence, even as the light of Heaven interpenetrates every atom of a crystal globe, no longer overshadows one spot only with the glory of His presence. It is true that in one sense the stateliest cathedral is less awfully His temple than the baptized body of the meanest Christian child. It is true that, in the words of an ancient father, "Moses in the midst of the sea, Job on the dunghill, Hezekiah on the bed of death, Jeremy in the mire, Daniel in the den, the Children in the furnace, St Peter and St Paul in prison, calling unto God, were heard," and that the floor of the simplest cottage may, by faith and by prayer, be made sacred as the splendour-bursting crags of Sinai, or the rounds of that ladder on which the angels trod. Nevertheless, every place of holy and Christian worship is more especially God's house, wherein it pleaseth Him to dwell; and you may thank God with all your heart, that here, alone with your own hearts, in quiet devotion, in heartfelt worship, you may meet Him day by day, and learn that the House of God is none other than the gate of heaven. Suffer not that service, my young brethren, suffer it not to become—as there is so often danger that it should become—a tedious waste, or a heartless form. Believe me, it is no light privilege to meet here for brief self-communion, for sincere thanksgiving, for earnest, uninterrupted supplication, day by day; no light privilege here to retire from the vain noises of the world, and to shut out its weary anxieties and passionate strifes, and to kneel in humble and heartfelt adoration, while we commune with our Heavenly Father as a man communes with his friend:— "Wherewithal shall a young man cleanse his way? Even by taking heed thereto according to Thy word." Oh, may that word be your safeguard and your delight! The day may come, nay, of certainty it will come to each one of us, when the very simplest lesson learnt in our childhood out of Sacred Writ shall be infinitely more to us than all the impassioned thunder of Attic eloquence, or the lyrical sweetness of Roman song; when, however dim they now may be to us, its messages shall gleam forth with a splendour more awful and oracular than the graven gems of Aaron's robe. An Arab was once passing over the desert, nearly dead with heat and thirst. He thought that his camel's furniture contained one more water-skin, and, as a last hope, he eagerly opened it. It was full of pearls, and, as he dashed it down to be scattered on the burning sands, he cried aloud in anguish, "Alas! it is only pearls!" Even so will it be, my brethren, with our thirsty souls, if we only supply ourselves with the treasures of earthly experience and earthly knowledge, and not with the pure waters from the living fountains of God's truth.

My brethren, be it otherwise with you. So shall God's grace give to each one of you a heart precious in God's sight, pure as the wing of a dove, or the aureole of a saint—a heart "bound up by the grace of God, and tied in golden bands, and watched by angels;" a heart which shall enjoy perpetually the Vision of God: so shall He preserve you uncorrupted in your youth, and lead you safely by the hand through the storms of life, and make you the children of God without rebuke: so shall the preacher, as he leans from this place, cast a look of pride and hope and thankfulness upon this youthful congregation, as he exclaims, in the full confidence of a fervent and an overflowing heart,

"THE TEMPLE OF THE LORD, THE TEMPLE OF THE LORD, THE TEMPLE OF THE LORD, ARE *THESE*."

Δόξα τῷ Θεῷ.

XVIII.

THE BLESSED TRINITY.

(Preached before Harrow School, on Trinity Sunday, May 26, 1861.)

REV. iv. 8.—"Holy, holy, holy, Lord God Almighty."

IT was the Trisagion, the repeated cry of the six-winged immortalities, which Isaiah once heard calling to one another through the incense smoke, which St John now heard as he gazed far upwards into the crystal depths. For, not to the Philosopher in his study or to the Emperor in his palace, but to him, once the Galilean fisherman, and now the convicted slave in the mine of a bleak Ægean isle, the golden gates of heaven were opened, and it was given to him to hear with mortal ears the celestial melodies of angel multitudes, and to see with human eyes the unimaginable glories of the Everlasting Throne. Never yet to human ecstasy had such unutterable visions been vouchsafed; visions such as poet never conceived, visions which dazzled into dross and darkness the pomp and prodigality of earthly kings. The spirit who in the heathen dream had led the mortal into the region of stars, reproved him for his glances downwards at the earth[1]; but there was no need of such an admonition to the disciple whom Jesus loved. His eagle soul bathed in the empyreal lustre, and he uttered all he saw in that grand poem which was read as the epistle of to-day,—a strain written as though his ears still rang with the harp-notes of seraphim, and as though one ray of the divine glory still illuminated with splendour unspeakable the dimness of his mountain cave.

O my brethren, if we had meditated on divine things as St John had meditated, who knows whether to us might not sometimes be permitted some glimpse of the excellent glory? But how shall we hope for it if our hearts and our thoughts are always on the earth; if we are always raking in the dead ashes of earth for the fires which are not there; if our thoughts are for ever of ourselves, of our own interests, of our food and our raiment and our reputation, rather than of our

---

[1] " Quæso, quousque humi defixa tua mens erit?"—Cic. *Somn. Scip.* 4.

Creator; if even when those thoughts are fixed on spiritual truths, they revert more to sin and to sorrow, to remorse and punishment, to some selfish dream of happiness, to some selfish dread of hell, than to God's glory and God's laws. Let us to-day at least humbly silence the importunities of self; let us in deep meekness and unfeigned humility bow ourselves in heart before the majesty of God.

My brethren we commemorate this day an awful mystery; a mystery which the very angels desire to look into, and before which they tremble and adore. Far be it from me on such a subject to darken counsel by the multitude of words without knowledge, or be one of those "Fools who rush in where angels fear to tread." The very heathen would reprove such rashness. Between the contending deities in the Hindoo legend, the Supreme shot down a pillar of light, and one of them winged his way upwards with the speed of thought for a thousand years, yet found not its summit, and the other sped downwards like lightning for a thousand years yet could not find its base. You know how when the great Father of the Christian Church was writing his discourse on the Trinity he wandered along the sea-shore lost in meditation, "when suddenly he beheld a child who having dug a hole in the sand, appeared to be bringing water in a shell to fill it, and told Augustine that he intended to empty into this little hole all the water of the great deep. Impossible, said the saint. Not more impossible, oh Augustine, replied the child, than for thee to explain the mystery on which thou art now meditating." True, brethren; but the logic of the intellect is transcended by the logic of the heart: " He that goes about to speak of and to understand the Trinity, and does it by words and names of man's invention,—he will talk he knows not what. But the good man that feels the power of the Father, and to whom the Son is become wisdom and righteousness, and in whose heart the love of the Spirit is spread; this man although he understands nothing of what is unintelligible, yet he alone understands the mystery of the Trinity. In this case experience is the best learning, and Christianity is the best institution, and the Spirit of God is the best teacher, and holiness is the greatest wisdom ; and he that sins most is the most ignorant, and the humble and obedient man is the best scholar." In this spirit, with God's blessing let us think of the Trinity to-day ; and may He who raised Abraham when the horror of great darkness fell upon him; He who covered Elijah from the earthquake and the storm in Horeb; He who strengthened Peter, when he cried, "Depart from me, for I am a sinful man, O Lord:"—may He be with us this day, and give us grace to speak of Him, even as He gave eloquence to the stammering lips of Moses, and sent His flying messenger to touch the mouth of Isaiah with a coal of living fire.

"Holy, Holy, Holy, Lord God Almighty." I would not ask those who dare in presumption to profane with light words of daily blasphemy this glorious and fearful name, but those who in moments of prayer or thought have felt something of His greatness,—I would ask them whether they have ever realized the blessing of that Revelation which has unveiled before us the Living God? Look at the nations of the world, and see what their unguided spirits taught them to worship. Thank God that we do not, like the Egyptians, enshrine some noxious reptile in our pictured temples; that we do not worship a material element like the magi, or a demon such as they adore in the far islands of the sea; or a brute force, or a dead soul of the world, or an irresistible vortex of conflicting laws; thank

God that we have not, like the Romans, reared our altars to Fear and Gluttony and Laughter and Despair, or even,—to take the most beautiful of wandering imaginations,—that we do not first idealise and then idolise our own weak manhood, so flinging a veil of romance over the deformity of vice and passion, and "painting the gates of hell with Paradise," like those who sang about

> "the azure heights
> Of beautiful Olympus, and the sound
> Of ever-young Apollo's minstrelsy."

Our God is "not a God of thunder and lightning, not a doll of gold and jewels, not an incarnation of lust and blood;" not "the fire, or the wind, or the swift air, or the circle of the skies, or the violent water, or the lights of heaven,"—not Nature, which is but God's art of governing the world; not Fortune, which is but His "unseen Providence, by men nicknamed chance;"—but the Lord, high and mighty, King of kings, Lord of lords, the only ruler of princes,—the God of gods, the very God; the God and there is none beside Him; the God and there is none before Him; the God and there is none like to Him; the God and there is none good but He;—the only God, who rides unchangeable upon the rolling waves of chance and change; the God whom heaven and the heaven of heavens cannot contain, yet who deigns to dwell in the humble heart of a little Child;—the Light, and the Father of Lights, and He whose shadow is the sunlight, and He who dwelleth in the light unapproachable;— Jehovah, the Alpha and Omega, the I am that I am, who is and was and shall be, Elohim the plurality in Unity, the God of Hosts, the infinite in power, the universal in presence, the Ancient of Days.

And this Awful and Supreme Majesty,—this invisible, unsearchable, incorruptible Spirit,— this immortal, immutable, Almighty God, is our Father. As a Father, Christ came to reveal Him. Times indeed there were when, standing in the pure and fragrant light amidst the gorgeous enchantments of the summer and the spring, even the poets of the world could see that "we are all his offspring." But if Christ had not so revealed him, if He had not spread abroad in our hearts the Spirit whereby we cry Abba Father,—this would have remained but a dim fancy or a splendid guess. And how deep, how unutterable, how crushing would have been the despair, which must then have settled on the heart of man. When we look up on some starlit evening and see the broad heavens bursting to disclose their light, and fading away into the intense void of systems and galaxies; when we know that this world is but a point, a speck, an atom in its own universe, and that its very universe is but a finer point, a smaller speck, a yet more delicate atom in that immensity which is sprinkled like the floor of a palace with the golden dust of innumerable worlds;—or when again we look into the mighty microcosm of a single waterdrop, and see how, invisible yet infinitely divisible, the realms of being stretch down fathomlessly beneath us, never to be sounded by the plummet of our philosophy, never to be measured by the coarse and feeble calculus of our imperfect minds,—would not such great realities as this,—shewing to us that we are but atoms, lost imperceptibly between two inconceivable infinities[1],—shewing us that we are nothing and less than nothing, with abysses stretching over us and abysses yawning beneath us, encircled by infinite contradictions, striking ourselves at every step we take against the adamantine wall of our own impotence,— would not, I say, such dread realities as these bewilder us into utter madness, or startle us

---

[1] Pascal.

into self-inflicted death? But what then? are we but waifs of wrack tossed aimlessly, accidentally, hopelessly on the shoreless immeasurable ocean of being? are we indeed but grains of dust evolved amid the mighty crashing wheelwork of revolving worlds—no better than "the sand which is blown about the sea-shore, or the motes that people the evening wind?" Ah! no, my brethren! to us, even to us, God is a Father;—out of these dark gulfs of nothing he stretches to us, in our struggles of agony, the fingers of a hand; amid these crashing wheels are the eyes of His Providence, the Spirit of His love, and the wheels move not but as the Spirit moves. Marvellous thought, full of all blessing! To us, even to us, God is a Father; a Father by creation, by redemption, by regeneration, by adoption; a Father taking us as the eagle taketh her young upon her wings; and though human love may be sometimes found divine in its pureness, and agonising in its intensity, loving us His frailest, His vilest creatures, with a tenderness yet more delicate, a love yet more divine. After meditating on such thoughts as these, who would not burst into the triumphant thanksgiving, borne to us so often on the wings of familiar music, O come let us worship, and fall down, and kneel before the Lord our Maker. For He is the Lord our God, and we are the people of His pasture, and the sheep of His hand!

"Holy, Holy, Holy, Lord God Almighty." But how shall we approach, how shall we worship this Spirit incomprehensible, before whom the wings of mortal imagination drop down as in a vacuum? How shall we paint before our souls a glory which is dark to us from its excess of brightness? Not as in some smoking furnace or a flaming lamp—not as in the burning bush of Horeb, or the stormy heights of Sinai, need we conceive the Being to whom we pray. Above the firmament of terrible crystal, above the dreadful rings, and the enfolding fire, and the likeness of a throne, the exile by the river of Chebar saw the appearance of a man; amid the ten thousand times ten thousand, in the midst of the throne that rose before the sea of fiery glass, the exile on the rock of Patmos saw a Lamb as it had been slain. Thanks be to God then, we need not "dazzle ourselves blind by star-gazing at Omnipotence and Infinitude," but we may approach God in the likeness of ourselves. The Son of God, the second person of the ever-blessed Trinity, stands at His right hand in the likeness of sinful flesh, in our image, in our likeness; through Him we have access unto the Father, and in His censer He offers up our prayers. A face like our own bends over us, tenderly listening, now; and, when we die, a hand like our own hand shall throw open to us the gates of Life.

> " So the All-great becomes the All-loving too;
> So through the thunder comes a human voice,
> Saying, 'O heart I made, a heart beats here;
> Face, my hands fashioned, see it in myself.
> Thou hast no power, nor may'st conceive of mine;
> But Love I gave thee, with myself to love,
> And thou must love me who have died for thee.'"

But here another thought will come upon us. It is this. Not only is God unspeakably awful, while we are infinitely frail—but He is our King, and we have rebelled against Him; He is our Creator, and we have broken His laws; He is our Father, and we have rejected His love; He is pure, and we have polluted His temple; He is holy, and we have profaned His name. Who shall roll away from us the mighty load of the sins we have committed? who shall bear the punishment for the duties we have left undone? Most true it is that the rocks cannot hide them, and that all the rivers cannot wash them clean,—but yet Christ's righteousness can cover, His blood can cleanse. Herein is Christ Jesus our Redeemer. To redeem us from this downcast horror of guilt He died. How this was, how it could be, I know not. All we need ask to know is this, that for the sin of man the Son of God was content to die. Most justly do we thank God above all for his inestimable love in the redemption of the world by our Lord Jesus Christ, for the means of grace, and for the hope of glory. For if indeed you cannot conceive this and find therein cause for gratitude, then try to conceive the reverse of it. Think, above all think in the moments of remorse and shame, what would be our case if there were a sin without a Saviour; a sorrow without an intercessor; an alienation without a mediator; a despair without a hope; a sickness without a balm in Gilead and with no physician there; how would it be with us, if, knowing that we had sinned many sins, we knew also that those sins could not be forgiven? It would be a burden intolerable, a remembrance grievous unto us; but it was from this horror of all horrors that Christ came to save us. But for His revelation, how should we have known the Father, from whose bosom He came? But for His death, how should we have been delivered from the snare of the devil? but for His intercession, how could we ever offer one acceptable prayer? but for His resurrection and ascension, how should we have known that anything lies beyond the dark river; how should we have known that it was not man's destiny to sink, after a few fretful years, into dust and nothingness, and to rot for ever amid the clods of the valley?

This revelation, this deliverance, this intercession, this leading of captivity captive, and robbing death of its sting, is the work of the Son of God. And one thing more, He not only taught us the truth, but He lived it, lived as men live, that we might see before our eyes a perfect example. "Be ye perfect even as your Father in Heaven is perfect," saith the Scripture. But how should we ever hope to imitate God, or attain unto these counsels of perfection, if Jesus Christ had not lived on this earth the life of a perfect man? if His footsteps had not illuminated the valleys of infancy, and the mountain heights of manhood? He left us an example of sanctity, not a theory of life. "Non elocutus est magna, sed vixit." He chose for our instruction a quiet, simple, ordinary course; not the gorgeous theatre of human magnificence, but the obscure village home; not the glory of a king, but the holier office of a slave; His greatness was not like earthly greatness, a fitful torch, " glaring with great emission and suddenly stepping into the thickness of smoke," but a life of constant and blameless piety, shining to all ages and generations of men for ever, like a serene and steady star.

Surely, my brethren, it is just this unostentatious nobility of demeanour, this silent chivalry, this ceaseless self-denial, this beautiful humility, which is or should be the object of our aim; and as he who would shoot his arrow high, curves his bow towards the clouds, so we set before ourselves no meaner example than the perfect Son of God. But have we not failed ten thousand times in these our endeavours after holiness? Even when we have conquered the grosser forms of sin, do we not find ourselves infinitely short of what we would be? Smaller vices flourish when the greater are subdued. We long to be holy, as Christ was holy;— whence then this meanness which we cannot conquer? this fretfulness under admonition? this base satisfaction at the failure of others? this malicious envying at their success? this ignoble desire to seem rather than to be? Oh! my brethren, in the best, the bravest, the manliest of us all there is more than enough to make us blush. How shall we become better? Only by lifting our eyes towards the hills, whence cometh our help; only by saying that it is our own infirmity, and remembering the years of the right hand of the Most Highest; only through the Third Person of the ever-blessed Trinity, whom the Son of God hath sent unto us from the Father; who sanctifieth, who is sanctifying, us and all the elect people of God. His work is not yet over; it commences at the cradle, it ends only at the grave. He is the Paraclete, ever willing and ready to help us to realise the great ideal. If we truly seek it, He will inspire our prayers to attain it; he will answer those prayers Himself; He will fill with the divine radiance of His own presence every corner of His Temple in our hearts; He will make us higher than the angels, and worthy through His own gift to claim our brotherhood with the Son of God.

On this Sunday, my brethren, culminate all the Sundays of the year. Through Advent, and Easter, and Whitsuntide we are led up to Trinity Sunday, and the remaining Sundays of the year are reckoned and named from it. It is well on such a day to ask ourselves if we indeed believe in this Triune God;—if we are loving the

Father with all our heart and soul and strength; if we are believing in and following the example of His blessed Son; if we feel the quickening and sanctifying influences of the Holy Spirit? Might not an altar be built in many and many a Christian city to the Unknown God? Are not many of us living without God in the world? If we truly loved God, how could "we be haughty for whom God became humble?" how could we be cruel for whom Christ died? how could we be impure and sinful for whose example the Son of Man lived a life tempted like as we are, yet without sin? Let us not be deceived. Not every one that saith Lord, Lord, shall inherit the kingdom of heaven, but he that doeth the will of the Father which is in Heaven. Lay your hand upon your heart, and ask yourselves whether you are indeed worshipping the Trinity of Heaven, or whether your lives shew rather that your devotion is given to the World, the Flesh, and the Devil—rightly named "the great Anti-Trinity of Hell."

Dissemble not with yourselves, brethren, or with God. Remember that His eye is upon you now;—that it shines full into the secret heart of every one of you, discerning all the thoughts that have been in your minds since you entered this chapel, discerning the sins to which at this moment your heart reverts. You see Him not indeed; you cannot imagine that He is here. But one day, sooner or later, we must all stand before His face,—we must stand before Him face to face, before the Father whom we have disobeyed, before the Son whom we have crucified, before the Spirit whom we have grieved. Loosen the frail silver cords, and draw the thin curtains of death—and lo! your soul has met its God! When last I spoke to you from this place, two months ago, I spoke of death, and I used these very words, "It is probable, it is almost certain, that one at least of you who hear me now, will be called from life before this year has run its course. Which shall it be? Who knows?" There were some who thought those words rash and improbable, as addressed to so young a congregation; and yet, my brethren, since then three among us have been down to the very gates of death; and there was then one sitting among your number in health and youth and strength, who heard those words,—and now his ears are stopped with dust. Little perhaps did he think that he was the one who should be taken. But God's hand beckoned to him, and he died, and his place knows him no more. One of you is now sitting in the very spot where he sat;—but now you are in the bloom of health, and the flush of life, and over him the grass of the churchyard is already green. To him is known the great unspeakable secret, which is not known to the best, the greatest, the wisest of living men. How do you know to whom among us God's hand shall beckon next; for whom next of us is the Shadow waiting, to whom next of us shall the secret be revealed? For one of us, I say again, it must be before long. Oh! my brethren, these thoughts are too solemn, too awful to dwell upon. This only will I add. Unhappy is he,—unhappy and miserable though he have rank, and wealth, and beauty, and though the earth twine her fairest and freshest garlands to wreathe round his diadem of youth—who knows not, and loves not, the living God. The madman, who is in his bare cell supposes himself to be a king; the starving wretch, who revels at the full banquet in his luxurious dream, is not more pitiable when his hour of waking comes. And on the other hand, happy alone is he—happy though poor, and ill-favoured, and ignorant, and despised,—happy alone is he who can say with fond yearning from his inmost heart, "This God is our God for ever and ever, He shall be our guide even unto Death."

XIX.

DELIVERANCE THROUGH CHRIST.

(Preached before Harrow School, 1864.)

1 SAM. xii. 20.—"Fear not: ye have done all this wickedness: yet turn not aside from following the Lord, but serve the Lord with all your heart."

AMONG the many words which our common conversation debases from its true significance, the word "friend" is perhaps the most lightly used. To hear men talking you might suppose that nothing was more plentiful than friends; every one appears to be surrounded by them. And there is in the world enough of courtesy and of easy goodnature, so far to lubricate the wheels of ordinary society, as to enable us to use the word without too transparent an irony. For indeed if the word be used in the truest and highest sense, there are but few men living—and they the noblest and the happiest—who have even one perfect friend. He who has a true friend—a friend, not in the hollow conventional sense, not a mere fair-weather acquaintance, not a mere agreeable associate, not even a familiar companion, but a friend, worthy of that high name—has a gift which is past all value. Even among you, in the warmer-hearted and more generous years of boyhood, there are but a few, I fear, who can own the possession of an entire and perfect friendship. How many of you have friends here to whom you could talk fearlessly and fully of the sunny memories, and tender associations of your home? to whom you could frankly confess your sins and failings? and from whom at any time you could look for sympathy and advice? before whom you would not be ashamed to weep in private, or to kneel down by his side and pray? How many of you have a friend, whom, even if you had committed some great fault, some great folly, some great crime, you might still meet, certain of unchanged sympathy, certain of free forgiveness? one whose great, holy, love should know your soul and hold communion with it;—whose affection is deep enough to outlive the dreams of youth, and the cares of manhood, and the accidents of rank, and health, and wealth, and fame—ay, even to survive the loss of innocence itself;

and who will take you into his noble heart not as you might be, but as you are, with all your egregious follies, with all your transparent faults, rebuking all that is mean in you with a faithfulness which cannot wound, evoking all that is best and truest with an alchemy which cannot be resisted? Thrice happy the man,—if indeed there be a man,—who has such a friend as this on earth.

But indeed on earth such a friendship is hardly possible; for although a friend may remain faithful in misfortune, yet none but the very best and loftiest will remain faithful to us after our errors or our sins. For the same nobleness which creates the possibility of an unselfish friendship is of necessity shocked and alienated by meanness or wickedness in the friend it chose and loved. Such a man loved us because he thought our hearts as grand and as noble as his own; but when in this he finds himself deceived and disappointed,—when the ideal of his imagination lies shattered before him in the dust,—in spite of himself his love grows cold, and he turns aside with a shudder or a sigh. And thus it is that the very faults and infirmities and sins which drag us down from our fixed height,—the very errors which bring our calamities or our disquietude upon us,—the very conditions which make us most need a friend, are the very ones which alienate from us those friendships which are truest and best worth having, and leave our souls alone in their hour of sadness, "like a dismantled ship upon the troubled waters, or like a desolate wreck upon the naked shore." You may remember such an instance, and that a touching one, in our own history. One of our greatest statesmen had but one dear and inseparable friend, and this friend after long years in which he had been loved and trusted, was impeached for high crimes and misdemeanours. "The blow fell heavy on Pitt. It gave him, as he said in Parliament, a deep pang; and as he uttered the word pang, his lip quivered; his voice shook; he paused; and his hearers thought he was about to burst into tears....He suppressed his emotion, and proceeded with his usual majestic self-possession,"—but the ravelled sleeve of that close friendship could never be knit up again!

Thus it is that all human friendship is of necessity a broken reed, on which when we need it most we lean in vain. Are we then alone in this world? are we terribly alone in the hour of sin, and shame, and failure, and ruin? Is there none on whose arm we can lean, no bosom where we may rest our weary heads? Ay, my brethren, blessed be God indeed there is; there is an arm that will encircle us when all human help has failed; there is a friend who will not be ashamed of us when all human love has perished, and all human countenance has been withdrawn; there is a hand which will tenderly remove the hands wherewith we hide our guilty faces, and will gently wipe away the burning tears: when human sympathy has been forfeited, there is yet an ear which will be open in the highest heaven to listen to our broken words; man,—cold, proud, sinful man—may despise and loathe us, but God the infinite,—God the Holy, God the All-pure,—He loves us, He pities, He will never spurn us away; He is our one, our only, inalienable, unshaken friend. When our father and our mother forsake us, then the Lord taketh us up. "Can a woman forget her sucking child, that she should not have compassion on the son of her womb? Yea, they may forget, yet will I not forget thee," saith the Lord. O happy indeed is the man that hath the God of Israel for his friend, and whose hope is in the Lord his God!

My brethren, it is the special and most perilous curse of sin that it obscures, or blots out altogether, or terribly distorts this vision of God in our hearts; it gradually reduces us to that most desolate of all conditions, "having no hope, and without God in the world." It makes us in one form or another forget God. It comes to the student of science and whispers to him, 'Look up into those illimitable spaces, sown thicker than dust with the light of unnumbered stars; the least of those twinkling points of light is a sun, vast as that which lights your own system, yet separated from every other and from you by eternities of time, by infinities of space, by untraversable immensities to which your whole universe with all its suns and moons and wandering stars is tinier than a mote in the sunbeam, or a grain blown from the desert sand;—what can this God care for an atom such as you, living out your little life on an atom such as this?' Or it comes to the historian and says, 'See with what awful silence, and in what awful darkness, the centuries have rolled and are rolling on,—centuries of ignorance, of error, and of sin,—of ignorance which no voice has dissipated, of error which no aurora has illuminated, of sin which no lightning-flashes have avenged. God is in some far-off heaven, and Providence is not, and we are

F. S. 24

but dust in the wheelwork of blind laws to which He has abdicated His power.' Or it comes to the open or secret rebel against God's laws, and says, "Tush, God careth not for it. Who seeth me? I am compassed about with darkness, the walls cover me, and nobody seeth me; what need I to fear? the Most High will not remember my sins.' Or once more, it comes to the remorseful, despairing sinner, and says to him, 'Do you think that such an one as God is will accept you? That the Holy, and pure, and true, will receive a soul mean and leprous as yours? No, God too hates wretches such as you. You have no chance. Go on in sin, until sin has exhausted you, and gives you up: for a time at least the wine-cup will drown the strugglings of conscience; the pursuit of sin will quench the last spark of reason or of remorse.'

All these are the accursed lies of the tempting spirit, which would hide from us that God is, and that He is love, and that He is not far from every one of us. The dread unimaginable darkness, the awful unbroken silence of which we spoke, are but the ghastly offspring of our own polluted fancy: there have been those, there are those now, in whose hearts on the contrary there is no darkness, for the light hath dawned upon them, and the perpetual day-spring hath arisen, and a gleam from God's own heaven lies like a sunbeam across their daily path;—there have been those, there are those now, who, so far from that silence, hold daily communion with their Maker, and hear His voice like a constant music, and talk with Him as a man talketh with his friend, and walk with Him as Adam walked of old under the palms of Paradise. No human friendship can bring a happiness like that friendship; no human soul but those who have experienced it can imagine the sweetness of that life. Suffer me to read you in his own words the reminiscence of a good and great man, about the first time that he ever heard that daily voice wherewith God speaks to us. "When I was a little boy," he says, "in my fourth year, one fine day in Spring my father led me by the hand to a distant part of the farm, but soon sent me home alone. On the way I had to pass a little pond, then spreading its waters wide; a rhodora in full bloom, a rare flower which grew only in that locality, attracted my attention, and drew me to the spot. I saw a little tortoise sunning himself in the shallow water at the root of the flaming shrub. I lifted the stick I had in my hand to strike the harmless reptile; for though

I had never killed any creature, yet I had seen other boys out of sport destroy birds and squirrels and the like, and I felt a disposition to follow their wicked example. But all at once something checked my little arm, and a voice within me said clear and loud, 'It is wrong!' I held my uplifted stick in wonder at the new emotion, the consciousness of an involuntary but inward check upon my actions, till the tortoise and the rhodora both vanished from my sight. I hastened home, and told the tale to my mother, and asked what it was that told me 'it was wrong?' She wiped a tear from her eye, and taking me in her arms, said, 'Some men call it conscience, but I prefer to call it the voice of God in the soul of man. If you listen and obey it, then it will speak clearer and clearer, and always guide you right; but if you turn a deaf ear or disobey, then it will fade out little by little, and leave you in the dark, and without a guide. Your life depends on heeding that little voice.'" "She went her way," he continues, "careful and troubled about many things, and doubtless pondered them in her motherly heart; while I went off to wonder and think it over in my poor childish way. But I am sure no event in my life has made so deep and lasting an impression on me"—an impression which brought its blessing to all his later days. For, my brethren, it is a thing of infinite blessedness to recognise the still small voice of God, our Friend and Father, described in this childish experience. He who has done so from his childhood upwards,—he who is not haunted by the threatening ghost of wasted years,—he who has never stained the festal robe of his youth by any pollution,—he on whose white soul rests no shadow of lust, or cruelty, or lies;—he is happier than if his head were crowned with the stars of heaven; he knows no fear, for perfect love has cast it out; misfortune itself is powerless against him, for he is the friend of God! The guilty Emperor of old[1], when the lightning flamed and the thunder roared across the heaven, was wont to fly in terror into the very recesses of his palace, and hide himself in the darkness under a bed,—but the crash of a shattered world can wake no terror in *his* breast, whom a pure conscience has armed invincibly against every foe. He can know no fear, because the God who holds all the elements of terror and wrath in the hollow of His hand is his Father and his Friend; he can know no

---

[1] Caligula.

loneliness, because even in the solitude of the desert

> "A still small voice comes o'er the wild,
> Like a Father consoling his fretful child,
> Which banishes bitterness, wrath, and fear—
> Saying 'Man is distant, but God is near.'"

But we have been speaking of the holy, of the pure, of the innocent; and my message is not to them only, but even more to the frail, the stained, the fallen, the unhappy. Which of us can say, "I have made my heart pure, I am clean from my sin?" "O Lord our God, other lords beside thee have had dominion over us." "We have gone astray, we and our fathers." "We have fed on ashes; a deceived heart hath turned us aside." We therefore are they who need friends most, because we have fallen most and are in the most sore condition; but, if even man despises and finds no forgiveness for our faults, is there any hope that He in whose sight the very heavens are not clean, that He will pity us, and take us to His breast, and suffer us to live in the glory of His Presence? Will He, who is the friend of the innocent, be a friend to the guilty too? Will He who loveth the good and gentle, love also the unthankful and the froward? You who have gone astray ever since your childhood—you whose whole thoughts are sick, like infected brass, with sin and vice, you who calling yourselves Christian boys, have yet neglected well-nigh every duty, and been tempted into many and many a sin, can He ever love you, can He ever be a friend to you?

Nay! He *does* love you; He *is* a friend to you! That is my message, my only message in the few plain words I speak to you to-day. He loathes your sins, but knowing that you are but dust, He loves your souls. He sent His Son to seek and save the lost; and when that Blessed Son had taken our nature upon Him, with whom did He live? Not with solemn priests and correct Pharisees, or even self-denying Essenes, but with outcasts and Samaritans, with publicans and sinners; not with the young and the beautiful, the noble and the rich—but with the aged and the withered, the homeless and the diseased, with the palsied and the demoniac, with the ignorant and the blind. He never shrunk away with loathing when His pure hand touched the foul skin of the leper. He never turned aside with disgust when the hot tears of the harlot plashed, and her long hair wiped His wayworn feet. He cast no look of scorn when the detected adulteress sobbed in her shame before Him on the Temple floor. He foresaw the penitent in the prodigal, and the awe-struck worshipper in the filthy Gadarene. Listen to Him as he weeps over undone Jerusalem in the day of His triumph: "O Jerusalem, Jerusalem, thou that killest the prophets, and stonest them that are sent unto thee,"—what follows? a call of flame from heaven, or the woe-fraught burden of some impassioned prophetic curse? Nay, but the music and the pathos of this tender image; "How often would I have gathered thy children together, even as a hen gathereth her chickens under her wings, and ye would not!"

O, my brethren, think of such love as this! a God, your God, the only God, the Lord of Heaven and Earth, yearning, dying in love for such mean, such guilty, such wayward souls as ours; calling to us, while we refuse, stretching out his hands, while no man regardeth? O think of it, especially when your heart is cowardly and bowed down with remorse and sin. Never despair; let the hope, nay the certainty of forgiveness bring back you, as it has brought back many a prodigal to his father's house. It may be that you feel and know that you are very guilty, corrupt and wicked and rotten to your very heart's core,—yet, let no amount of guilt or sin be a barrier between you and God. Let not sin or Satan ever rob you of that Unchangeable, Eternal Friend. Think of His great love, and do not grieve it; think of His cross of anguish, and crucify Him not afresh. Many a time, when all other pleas failed, I have seen the plea of affection move the stony heart; many a time, when some proud and wayward boy, whose whole life was a perpetual grief and anxiety to us, stood cool and hardened to every other appeal, I have in a moment learnt to forgive him and think better of him, when I have seen the large tears rush to his eyes, ay, and fall down his cheeks, at the simple question, "What will your father or your mother say to this?" And just as in extremes you would fly to your father or your mother first, because you would feel and know that even if all others gave you up, they at least would say to you, "Yes, we know all, and we forgive all, and take you back to our home and to our heart again, and will not love you less;"—so, even so, fly to God, who is our Father and our Mother for ever, who has seen all, and known all from the first,—ay, and far more than man can ever see or can ever know, and yet has forgiven all; so that under His pitying glance, the sin which was as crimson may become white as snow. For, though disobedient people, you have been and are His people; though lost and wandering sheep, you are yet the sheep of His pasture, the wounded lambs of His flock; though erring children, you are His children, His dear, His best-loved children still. This is the gracious message of my text and of many another text, "Fear not; ye have done all this wickedness, yet turn not aside from following the Lord, but serve the Lord with all your heart."

O then awake, and put on strength, ere you die and stand for judgment before the awful throne! As yet, each new day is to you a new chance. The past lies behind you, it may be wasted and withered, but, like the garden of Eden before you, lie sleeping in the sunshine, the golden fields of the present, the rich harvests of the future. Each day, each week, each month, each year is a new chance given you by God. A new chance, a new leaf, a new life—this is the golden, the unspeakable gift which each new day offers to you. O return to God, and use it rightly, letting the time past of your life suffice you to have walked in the hard ways of sin and shame, and turning at last sick and weary-hearted to the paths of virtue and of peace. The mistakes, the follies, the sins, the calamities of the past may, if you use them rightly, be the pitying angels to guide you through the future. Let them keep you in deep humility; never let them force you into wretchlessness or into despair. Are there, for instance, any of you here, who have wasted, and worse than wasted, your school life; who have alienated the love of those who loved you, and forfeited the confidence of those who trusted you? any whose time here has been profitless and ruinous to themselves, injurious and fatal to others? who have lived in daily disobedience, and daily idleness, and daily vice, until their character is forfeited, and they have gathered all that is meanest, losing all that is best and brightest in this great school—then to them, ay, to the very worst, to the most hardened boy in this chapel, God speaks—and would to God that this voice might come to you as the sweetest utterance that ever was breathed upon the evening wind—"Fear not; ye have done all this wickedness, yet turn not aside from following the Lord." Fear not but that God loves you still. You have one more, it may be one last chance. Even of your school-life six weeks still remain to you, redeem those six weeks; each of them is an opportunity for the peaceable fruits of repentance and righteousness; even those poor six weeks out of a whole school-life may make all the difference to your own souls, all the difference to the way in which during future years you will look back on your connection with Harrow School. For though God's mercy does not change, yet if you continue in wilful and willing sin, your capacity for receiving it changes, diminishes, evanesces daily. If you put off this present time for repentance, the convenient season may never come. As yet the door stands open before you: very soon it will be too late, and the door be shut.

O that in this spirit,—knowing, feeling, believing that God is our Friend and Father, and that He will not reject the very guiltiest of those who come to Him; O that in this spirit side by side every one of us might kneel before the Table of the Lord. Let the worst and the best kneel with equal humility to ask forgiveness, to implore for help.

"Let not conscience make you linger,
  Nor of fitness fondly dream;
All the fitness He requireth
  Is to feel your want of Him.
This He gives you;—
  'Tis the Spirit's rising beam!"

In perfect love and charity with one another, praying for one another, forgiving one another, helping one another, let us come before our offended but merciful Father, before the Son of God, whose dying love we to-day commemorate. To the worst prodigal of us all our Father will come with blessing and forgiveness when he returns to his abandoned home; oh! let no prodigal prefer to linger amid the gnawing famine of the land of sin. So shall he hear the Father's voice speaking to him as to apostate Israel of old, "Is Ephraim my dear son? is he a pleasant child? for since I spake against him, I do earnestly remember him still:...I will surely have mercy upon him, saith the Lord."

XX.

HOPE IN CHRIST.

(Preached after the First Communion of the Boys confirmed at Harrow on March 19, 1868.)

Is. lx. 1.—"Arise, shine; for thy light is come, and the glory of the Lord is risen upon thee."

WHEN any of the sweet and solemn events of life are about to happen to some member of an affectionate and united family, the thoughts of the rest are naturally concentrated on him. And in this our family, two events—two which are among the most solemn in life's history—have happened during a few days' space to many whom we love. They have received their youthful Confirmation; they have knelt at the Supper of the Lord. Thus they have stepped across that clearly-marked boundary which separates spiritual childhood from spiritual manhood. We all feel with them; we all hope in them; we have all prayed for them. Our thoughts are with them now: and though I hope that with God's blessing my words may not prove wholly profitless to any, yet these are they to whom I would mainly speak, earnestly desiring that what I say may chime in with all that is most holy and most beautiful in the present music of their thoughts. To them this day will be a memory to the close of life; may they also to the close of life remember that in this quiet chapel, which I trust they love, they heard on the Sunday after their Confirmation, on the evening of their first Communion, a few simple words of encouragement, of warning, and of hope.

That—with very rare exceptions—you are in earnest, that you desire to give your hearts to God, and to consecrate your lives to His service, and that the attitude of your souls is at the present moment an attitude of hope, I cannot doubt. It will be at once your duty and your happiness to cherish that hope; to keep it aglow by the breath of prayer; to suffer no evil influence (and all the powers of evil will in these days be doubly busy for your ruin) to dim or quench it. The loss of hope in a human soul is the gathering of the darkness; its increase is the brightening of the dawn. To be robbed of it even in our poor earthly life is a deep misfortune. For though energy may be possible without it, serenity is not; though duty may be faithfully continued, happiness is gone. But hope in our earthly prospects matters very little, if its eternal treasures be garnered up where man cannot rob us of them. It was an ancient fancy that if the hues of the rainbow fell on the aspalathus, the flower lost every harsher element, and gained an unwonted fragrancy. Let Hope, like that touch of the rainbow, transform and glorify the saddest and hardest heart of you who at His own Sacrament have felt your Saviour's gracious power. But let your hope not be the evanescent bow which overarches the thunder-cloud, but that steadier iris which gleams above the cataract. "It remained motionless," says one who had been watching such a rainbow, "while the gusts and clouds of spray swept furiously across its place, and were dashed against the rock. It looked like a spirit strong in faith, and steadfast in the midst of the storm of passions sweeping across it, and though it might fade and revive, it clung to the rock as in hope and giving hope. And the very drops which in the whirlwind of their fury seemed as if they would carry all away, were made to revive it and give it greater beauty." Even so, my young brethren, may the

[1] See Prof. Tyndall, *Faraday as a Discoverer*.

bow of Hope span the worst sorrow and tumult of your lives; and may it prove to you to be what Eastern fancy saw in it,—the bright and narrow pathway of just souls to heaven.

When some youth, in the happiest days of chivalry, was admitted into the noblest orders of knighthood, he spent his vigil with prayer and fasting in some lonely church beside his arms. And when morning came he was bathed and clad in white robes as a symbol of purity; he knelt humbly at the Supper of the Lord; the crosshilt of his consecrated sword was presented to him; and with priestly benedictions and solemn services, the Bishop bade him to be humble in all things, high in courage, strong in danger, patient under difficulties,—above all, to tell the truth always, to take Christ as his captain, and do his devoir to all the world. Then being clad in his armour, he received the accolade of knighthood,—he was bidden to be loyal, bold, and true,—and so, with high courage in his heart and holy vows upon his lips, he "rode forth in morning sunshine and faithful hope," ready at any moment in single encounter or on Syrian battlefield to yield his pure soul to his Saviour Christ.

It is even thus that I think of each of you, and

of the work both immediate and future which lies before you. The age of chivalry indeed is over; but that, thank God, was but a sunlit ripple on the abiding river. The accidents are gone, the substance continues: the circumstances are altered, the reality remains. For the vigil in the cathedral you have had the prayer and preparation of many weeks; for the sword-blow on the shoulder, the laying on of the Bishop's hand; for the vow of knighthood, the "I do" of the Christian boy. Purity, self-devotion, courage, as they were the knight's main duties, so are they yours; the chrismal fire of the seven-fold blessings is shed no less richly on you than upon him; his armour was but the symbol of your panoply of God; his foes but the embodied representatives of the powers which assault and hurt your soul. You too are following Christ to the gathering battle; you too are riding forth in the hope that He will make you more than conquerors. For the moment you have felt as if all things were possible to you. And all things *are* possible through Christ who loves you; and, to the faintest-hearted of you, victory is certain if you fight under your Captain's banner, and in the strength which Christ will give.

Now if any knight in legend or in reality,—if

any Christian hero in history or in life,—did great and worthy deeds, what influences have sustained him? what perpetual incense has kept the fire of God's love burning upon the altar of his heart? Whence did a Percivale or a Galahad,—whence did a Luther or a Milton,—whence did a Whitfield or a Martyn, win the mighty inspiration which made their lives so true, their swords so irresistible, their hearts so noble, their words so strong? Not assuredly in the Circean philosophy of the world; not in the foolishness of darkened imaginations which make a mock at sin; not in the haunts of the sensualist or at the tables of those who are full of meat,—nay, but in the stern school of youthful self-denial, under the hardy discipline of laborious duty, in the fiery truths of Prophets unglozed by the smooth self-complacency of Pharisees and priests. "Lift up your hearts," was the voice that ever sounded in their ears; "we lift them up unto the Lord," was always the fervent antiphon of their faithful hearts. "Whatsoever things are true, whatsoever things are honest, whatsoever things are just, whatsoever things are pure, whatsoever things are lovely, whatsoever things are of good report,"—they thought on those things. And you must think upon them too, and on the heavenly sunbeams of such thoughts must climb to the Father of Lights, who dwelleth in the Light unapproachable. With souls so inspired you may hope indeed; hope not only that you may ever shrink from the coarser and viler temptations of the world, as from the burning ashes that have been fed by the corpses of the slain,— hope not only that you may triumph over the subtler temptations of sloth, and cowardice, and spiritual pride,—but hope that you will by God's blessing be enabled to lead a life far higher and more heroical than the vulgar and sleepy standard of the so-called religious world,—that God's grace may inspire you with such a passion for integrity and truth, that you too may be hereafter among those saints of God who have inspired the souls of others by the conspicuous example of Christ-like lives.

Yes, my brethren, such thoughts, such hopes are as the unseen Seraphim who swing their holy incense in the spiritual temple; and such a temple your hearts should be. Greater are they that are with than they that are against you. Evil is not your nature, but its ruin; not the law of your life, but its apostasy; not the fulfilment of your destiny, but its frustration. All good angels lean over you with their glittering faces; the silent company of the immortal dead, the household and city of God above, are with you; the hearts of all God's true children among the living beat in unison with yours; the Son of God, and the Spirit of God, and the Lord God Almighty love the soul that they have created, sanctified, redeemed. There is nothing high, there is nothing noble, there is nothing godlike, to which you are not clearly summoned, for which you are not naturally fit. "Fear not, O Jacob, my servant, and thou, Jeshurun, whom I have chosen. Fear ye not, neither be afraid; ye are even my witnesses." Yet while you cherish to the utmost these high hopes, cherish them in humility, cherish them in trembling. "Let him that thinketh he standeth take heed lest he fall." You are buckling on your armour, not putting it off. If you do not learn the wisdom which is taught by fear—if you feel inclined to value yourselves and to say to others "Stand aside, for I am holier than thou"—God may teach you, by I know not what bitter ruin, that your trust must be in Him. You think, perhaps, that in trying for these six weeks to struggle with old temptations, and to abandon besetting sins,—and still more, in tasting to-day of the heavenly manna which Christ has offered to your souls,—that you have been disenchanted for ever from the sorcery of Satan. Yes, it may be so; it will be so if you struggle, and watch, and pray, and never turn your eyes from the face of God. But oh! it may be far different; a dangerous and deadly reaction may come over you; a great falling away, the terrible judgment of the backslider and the apostate. "Admitted to a holier sanctuary, you may be guilty of a more deadly sacrilege." I have stood, my brethren, on some mountain peak, some Cumbrian or Alpine hill, over which the dim mists rolled; and sometimes, through one mighty rent in that cloudy curtain, I have seen the blue heaven in all its beauty, and, far below my feet, the rivers, and cities, and cornfields of the plain sparkled in the heavenly sunlight; but soon, and almost imperceptibly as I gazed, the scene began to fade and waver as the thin edges of the mist crept together, and the grey atmosphere of the mountain was drawn around me, until for the vision and the glory there was nothing but chilly vapour and drizzling rain. Even so may it be with you. Now as it were through the sunlit vista of prayerful days you see heaven opened, and Jesus sitting at the right hand of

God; but subtly, invisibly, increasingly the dense vapours of sin and worldliness may arise, and blot out from your souls the light of heaven, and leave you disheartened and in danger, weary and alone. Many a young knight, in his over-confidence, has ridden forth in hope to return in humiliation; many a young Christian, in his unwatchfulness, has retired from life's battle, seamed, and scarred, and in shamefullest dishonour. David, the pure and gallant lad whom God took from the sheepfolds, to lead his people Israel, became, alas! a murderer and an adulterer. The same Peter who, when all were forsaking Christ, burst forth with the passionate confession of his Messiahship, yet afterwards denied him, with scorn and cursing, on that dark and terrible evening, by the firelight in the High Priest's hall. There is a life of one in the middle ages which has always seemed to me pregnant with instruction. It is the life of one whom God had splendidly endowed; he was beautiful, manly, eloquent, learned, subtle; he was wealthy and famous even from early youth; and not only as a philosopher and a divine, but from a natural abhorrence of all vulgar degradation, he lived till manhood an unsullied and upright life. Yet this man, in the full pride of his fame and intellect, fell into deliberate and most disgraceful sin,—met with sudden and most horrible retribution,—lived in unutterable anguish, died in a broken-hearted fall. Yes! the name of Abelard stands out like a Pharos upon some dangerous rock, to warn all those who are tempted in early life by intellectual eminence or spiritual pride. Oh! my brethren, hope indeed, but still work out your own salvation with holy fear. David in ruin and self-abasement received again the clean heart and the free spirit. The tender divine look of Jesus pierced into the very soul of Peter, and the cock crew, and he repented in agonies of tears. And in his old age, and anguish of body, and sickness of soul, God's grace reached the unhappy Abelard. His flesh came to him again, like the flesh of a little child; in the quiet abbey at Clugny he learnt to be meek and lowly of heart,—frequent in prayer, given to silence, a humble, simple, God-fearing, evil-shunning man[1]. But oh! through what rivers of shame and agony had each of these to win their way! May God in his mercy shield each one of you from such a fall; but oh! if you fall,

[1] Such is the testimony of Peter of Clugny in a 'letter describing Abelard's death-bed.'

may He grant to you also, even if it be through pain and ruin, a repentance as deeply-seated and as sincere.

But I should be guilty of a glozing foolish conventional optimism, which my soul abhors, if I were to imply that most of you felt this high confidence of being enabled hereafter to live a holy life: it is not so, and to any who may wish me to assume it, I would say as a friend of mine has said, "I would rather die than lie." Conversation with not a few of you has shewn me that though you may differ very widely from one another, and though all of you (except one or two who have not thought, or prayed, or striven at all) have felt *some* hope to-day, it has been to some of you like the last leaping of a flame among dying embers,— it has been often overshadowed by a gloom of distrustfulness, nay almost of despair. And to you, my young brethren, my heart yearns most; to you, most earnestly, do I desire to speak a few healing or helpful words. Your hope is the bruised reed which your Saviour will not break; the smoking flax he will not quench. You are deeply wounded; you have wandered far astray; you are sick with sin and a sense of weakness; you tremble not without reason for yourselves.

If we tell you that, now you are confirmed, you must not, you cannot have anything more to do with such common vices as swearing, as debt, as dishonesty in work, nay even as openly corrupt communication, you can but confess penitently that you have been guilty of these things, you can but make a humble promise "I will try to do them no more." But you hardly feel the strength to promise even these very easy things,—things from which not only Christianity, but even a certain inbred reserve, and 'honest haughtiness of nature,' has preserved many a heathen in his ignorance. Even of these you can but speak with a hesitating diffidence, born of bad habits and numberless transgressions. But oh! when we go farther, and bid you aim at the deeper, higher excellences of the Christian life,—when we urge upon you a strong manly diligence as an elementary duty immediately resulting from the very constitution of your nature,—when we tell you that it is now your positive duty to strengthen your brethren, and to the utmost of your power to save them from sin,—when we tell you that you must battle with the whole force of your souls against self-indulgence, against forgetfulness of God, against thoughts of wickedness, against the cherished idolatry and habitual tyranny of some base besetting sin,—then you, knowing your own deplorable weakness, knowing not as yet the strength and love of your Saviour,—knowing the severity of your bondage, not knowing the power of His deliverance, —can barely summon up the strength to promise. Your faint "I will try" becomes "I fear I cannot." "I have tried," such an one will say with confusion of face, "tried over and over again for years, and over and over again have failed. I know that I shall fail. The thing that I would, that I do not; the thing that I would not, that I do. To will is present with me, but how to perform that which is good I find not. There is a sinfulness and a degradation which I loathe, and into which I sink; there is a sweetness and a nobleness for which I yearn, and of which my soul despairs. There is nothing which can save me from myself, and from the sins which are engrained into my very being. Yes, I will make good resolutions if you bid me, but all my former good resolutions have come to nought; they have been as the morning cloud or as the early dew. God has hidden his face from me, and barely even in these days, burdened as I am and guilty, have I had the will or the ability to seek His face in prayer."

Ah! my brethren, when you say all this, my heart yearns for you, and I am certain that this is the message which God would bid me give. Whatever you do, hope on, try on. Hitherto your resolutions have been resolutions in name alone. Believe in God's love, and you, like many another wounded soldier, shall yet win the battle[1]. To say "I cannot" in matters of daily duty is weak and feeble; to say it of spiritual duties is blasphemy and death. It is blasphemy, for it charges God with sins which you pretend to be unavoidable; it is death, because it is the inevitable prelude to self-abandonment and to despair. And so God pleads with you to-night; He tells you that "bitter as you are with weariness and sick with sin," He still loves you tenderly as a Father. It was for you, and such as you, that Christ died; you are the lost whom He came to seek, the sick whom He came to heal; the prisoners for whom He has burst the brazen gates. Prodigals as you are, a place is still open to you in your Father's home. Come to Him just as you are; come to Him from the land of exile, and the trampled husks,

[1] Archbishop Leighton.

and the filthy swine; return to Him in all the shame of your desertion, in all the degradation of your sin, and even while you are a long way off, He will go forth to meet you, and fall upon your neck with tears. Yours, indeed, can be no prayer but the prayer of the publican, "Lord, have mercy upon me a sinner;" no cry but the cry of the Psalmist, "I am thine, oh save me!" No other prayers, my brethren,—but are not these enough? "Lord, I believe; help thou mine unbelief," the father cried, and lo! the spirit was cast out of his demoniac son. "Lord, save me, I perish," and lo! a strong hand is outstretched, and Peter is saved as he is sinking in the dark and stormy sea. Believe me, there is hope for you; if you have felt it, ever so faintly, cling to it for your life. You may yet live to say from your heart, as one has said who for long years suffered as you have suffered,

"I was a stricken deer that left the herd
Long since; with many an arrow deep infixed
My panting side was charged, when I withdrew
To seek a tranquil death in distant shades.
There was I found by One who had himself
Been hurt by archers. In His side He bore,
And in His hands and feet, the cruel scars.
With gentle force soliciting the darts,
He drew them forth, and healed, and bade me live[1]."

[1] Cowper.

To conclude then, my brethren.—Those of you who by God's grace have hitherto lived well, strive henceforth to live better, with holier purpose, with more courageous consistency, with self-devotion more entire:—and those of you who have lived imperfectly or ill, let the time past of your lives suffice you to have done the things whereof you are now ashamed. And alas! none of you must expect to be made perfect without long struggle. It is said that when the lightning has flashed full in men's faces, the electric flame passes in one second through every nerve and fibre, permeating and transfusing each atom of the sentient frame. It may be so sometimes in the spiritual world, but not often[1]. More frequently the grace of God works slowly, like the growing grass or the rising dawn,—the green and tender blade which ripens into the full corn in the ear,—the grey shuddering dawn, that broadens and brightens into the boundless day. Slowly, toilfully, not perhaps without many failures—by prayer, by watchfulness, by shunning idleness, by avoiding bad companions, by fleeing youthful lusts,—will you be made first penitent, then holy, then perfect as your Father

---

[1] South has finely called St Paul "a *fusile* Apostle."

in Heaven is perfect. If you have ever made good resolutions, oh! make them now afresh;—not in your own strength, say rather your own infirmity, but remembering Him who loveth you, and hath died to redeem you by His blood. Out of the crowd His hand has beckoned you; from your wanderings He has called you by your name. Go to Him, and say, "Lord, I know that I am stained, and sinful, and feeble, dead in trespasses and sins: but, O Lord, I repent, I long to return to Thee; hard and impenitent as it is, yet take Thou my heart, for Thou hast made it, and it is Thine; take Thou my life, and do with it as seemeth Thee best, so Thou wilt only employ it for Thy service." And believe that such a prayer will be answered. And what I said at the beginning, I say once more—Hope. "Hast thou not known, hast thou not heard, that the everlasting God,—the Lord,—the Creator of the ends of the earth,—fainteth not, neither is weary? He giveth power to the faint, and to them that have no might he increaseth strength. Even the youths shall faint and be weary, and the young men shall utterly fall. But they that wait upon the Lord shall renew their strength; they shall mount up with wings as eagles; they shall run and not be weary, they shall walk and not faint." So saith He; and

"Truly he cannot, after such assurance,
    Truly he cannot, and he shall not fail;
Nay, they are known, the hours of thy endurance,
    Daily thy tears are added to the tale.

Never a sigh of passion or of pity,
    Never a wail for weakness or for wrong,
Hath not its archive in the angels' city,
    Finds not its echo in the endless song.

Then, though our foul and limitless transgression
    Grew with our growing, with our breath began,
Lift thou the arms of endless intercession,
    Jesus, divinest when thou most art man."

www.ingramcontent.com/pod-product-compliance
Lightning Source LLC
Chambersburg PA
CBHW022112290426
44112CB00008B/647